Israel vs. Hitler's Scientists
Western Europe 1955–63

DENMARK

BALTIC SEA

NORTH SEA

Peenemünde

POLAND

Berlin ⊙

NETHERLANDS

Westphalia
9

EAST
GERMANY

7 Cologne
Bonn •

BELGIUM

LUX.

WEST
GERMANY

CZECH.

Stuttgart
1

FRANCE

Augsburg •
4

2
Munich •

AUSTRIA

Loerrach

3

5

6

Basel   Zurich

SWITZ.

N

— KEY —

1 Stuttgart Institute for the Physics of Jet Propulsion
2 Site of INTRA office and the disappearance of Heinz Krug
3 Dr. Kleinwachter's research office and site of attempted assassination
4 Messerschmitt aircraft factory
5 Site of Mossad operation against Heidi Goercke, 2 March 1963
6 Location of main INTRA office
7 Site of Dr. Pilz's research office and Mossad operation led by Peter Malkin c. 1959
8 Site of Hitler's rocket program
9 Location of the aircraft crash that killed Kamil's wife, 8 July 1962

0   50   100
Scale of Miles

W9-CEB-737

OPERATION DAMOCLES

ISRAEL'S SECRET WAR AGAINST
HITLER'S SCIENTISTS, 1951–1967

ROGER HOWARD

PEGASUS BOOKS
NEW YORK LONDON

OPERATION DAMOCLES

Pegasus Books LLC
80 Broad Street, 5th Floor
New York, NY 10004

First Pegasus Books edition May 2013

Interior design by Maria Fernandez

Library of Congress Cataloging-in-Publication Data is available.

ISBN: 978-1-60598-438-4

10 9 8 7 6 5 4 3 2 1

Printed in the United States of America
Distributed by W. W. Norton & Company

CONTENTS

CHAPTER ONE
Striking the Sword

During the bitterly cold night of February 12, 1963, three men sat huddled in their car, parked just off a main street, and waited patiently and silently for any sign of movement in the building opposite. They had started their vigil in the late afternoon, and each freezing minute of the long subsequent hours had been one of extreme discomfort as well as unrelenting tedium and considerable tension. But any minute now, they kept telling themselves, their elusive prey would finally break cover and they could spring into action.

All three men were specially trained to deal with such demanding situations, and highly experienced at doing so. For all were agents of the Israeli foreign intelligence service, Mossad, and each had been handpicked by the organization's European operations chief, Yitzhak Shamir, to undertake the most audacious and risky type of overseas operation—the assassination of a foreign national.

Their target was a forty-eight-year-old German scientist named Dr. Hans Kleinwachter. He had arrived back in West Germany from Egypt shortly before and was busy working at his laboratory in his hometown, Loerrach, close to the Swiss border.[1] He expected to return to Egypt just weeks later, though he was blissfully unaware that others, who had been monitoring his movements for some months from afar, had different plans.

His chief adversary was the Mossad chief, Isser Harel, who had by this stage become personally obsessed with eliminating the German scientist.[2] That night, though Harel was far away at his desk in Tel Aviv, he knew exactly what his agents were enduring as they waited for the precise moment to strike, and he was eagerly awaiting news of the operation. He had personally accompanied a team of assassins just a few nights earlier, also spending several hours in a stationary car, wrapped in a thick overcoat and a blanket alongside another of Shamir's trained killers, outside Kleinwachter's nearby home. That night had ended in disappointment when the German scientist had failed to appear; but now, at last, Harel thought Kleinwachter was finally in Mossad's sights.

Suddenly, around nine o'clock, there was a sign of movement as the building plunged into darkness and a figure headed toward the car. After hours of empty waiting, a carefully rehearsed action plan sprang into life.

Instead of following the car, the Mossad agents now headed off ahead of Kleinwachter, knowing exactly which route their prey would be taking to get home. They drove for a few miles and then, just a short distance from his house, they pulled up in a narrow lane and waited. In the distance they could see the front lights of the scientist's car, which was moving quite quickly, and just as he came around a corner, they pulled their vehicle in front and braked sharply, forcing him to make an emergency stop.

One of the agents coolly got out of the car and walked toward Kleinwachter, who was stunned and shocked by such drama. "Where is the home of Dr. Schenker?" the Israeli agent cried out. Without waiting for a response, he suddenly produced a gun with a silencer and opened fire. There was a crash as the bullet shattered the windshield and then got deflected and stuck in the scientist's thick woolen muffler. The assassin fired again but his weapon jammed, giving Kleinwachter time to reach for his own revolver, which he kept under the dashboard, as he tried to steady his shaking hands and return fire: a veteran of the Russian front during the Second World War, when he had served as a major in the German Army's Signal Corps, he had become well accustomed to difficult and stressful situations. But the would-be assassin was already running back to the waiting car, which sped off just seconds later. Kleinwachter had narrowly survived, even if from that moment on, he, like all the other scientists who were working on behalf of the Egyptians, could never relax again as long as they continued to involve themselves in a project that Mossad and the Israeli government so strongly disapproved of.

Back home, the shaken scientist was trying hard to calm his nerves when the phone rang. The caller, who spoke in French, did not give his name but had a simple and chilling message. "Those who feed on Jews," he stated curtly, "choke on them." The mysterious caller then hung up.

Kleinwachter immediately called the police, who later discovered the car abandoned just a few hundred yards from the scene of the attack. Inside, they discovered a passport in the name of the head of the Egyptian secret service, Ali Samir, which the assassins had left in a vain attempt to pin the blame on others. It was a quite unconvincing stratagem, though, because at the time of the attack Samir was in Cairo, where he was being interviewed by a West German journalist. No one who followed the case had any doubt about who was really behind it.

Months before, Harel had implemented a ruthless and daring plan to intimidate—or, if necessary, liquidate—a number of West German scientists who were deemed to have been instrumental in helping the Egyptian leader, Pres. Gamal Abdel Nasser, to develop long-range missiles that were capable of striking the Jewish state. If the missiles were fitted with ordinary explosives, then the repercussions for Israel's security would be serious enough, estimated some of the defense chiefs in Tel Aviv. But if the Egyptians used chemical, radiological, or even nuclear warheads, then the impact of the weapons of mass destruction (WMD) would of course be calamitous and conceivably even inflict a second Holocaust. By using brute force against Kleinwachter, the Mossad chief hoped to eliminate a key contributor to the missile program—the German scientist was a highly respected electronics expert—and also to deter some of the scientists who were either already in Egypt or else contemplating going there. This was the central motive of his campaign, code-named Operation Damocles, which he had initiated the previous summer. "There are people who are marked to die," as Harel had commented chillingly.[3]

But the use of such brutal methods was not just a breach of West German domestic law and of international law. It also raised a difficult conundrum for Israel's policy makers. For even if, in Israel's preferred scenario, the use or threat of violence did succeed in undermining Nasser's military program, how could that outcome be balanced against the obvious downside of such an approach? If Mossad was caught carrying out the assassination, or even if it simply got the blame, then wouldn't Israel's relations with West Germany, and perhaps much of the wider Western world, be gravely imperiled? Israel was notoriously indifferent to international law and to the United Nations, but could it risk acquiring a reputation as a country that dispatched assassination or murder squads to eliminate its perceived enemies? Did it risk becoming labeled a terrorist state, or were its actions just a legitimate form of self-defense? Such a label would be damaging enough for any country but was particularly awkward for Israel in 1963, when the leadership in Tel Aviv was working hard to establish full diplomatic relations with West Germany and desperately needed its military and economic support.

Over the weeks that followed, the Israeli dilemma became unmistakably apparent. On the one hand, Dr. Kleinwachter admitted in an interview with an American journalist that he was "fearful" of another assassination attempt and for that reason was reluctant to move back to Egypt, where he could have made a more powerful contribution to the missile program. But on the other hand, he emphasized that he would not be bullied out of doing what he wanted to do and would therefore continue to work for the Egyptians.[4] Just five weeks later, as relations between Bonn and Tel Aviv reached a new low point, Deputy Defense Minister Shimon Peres rushed back to Israel from Paris, urging his prime minister, David Ben-Gurion, not to do anything that could compromise an arms deal with the Germans that he had spent months brokering. Meanwhile, Peres's opposite number in Bonn, Franz Josef Strauss, was already hinting that a number of secret arms deals were at risk as a result of the events in Loerrach.[5] The Kleinwachter assassination bid was just one contributing factor in the sudden collapse of German-Israeli relations, but the diplomatic crisis illustrated how much Israel had to lose if it forfeited the goodwill of the Bonn government.

Ultimately, resolving this conundrum all depended on just how serious a threat the Egyptian missile program actually posed to Israel. If the acquisition of long-range rockets really did represent a grave and imminent danger to the Jewish state, and there was no other sure and effective way of stopping the scientists from contributing, then such a heavy response was arguably what any citizen of any country would want and expect their government to undertake. The use of lethal force, in other words, is a last resort that is employed when there are no alternative options.

But if, on the other hand, Nasser's project was just not sophisticated enough, or its completion date too far off in the future, then it was hard to see what Israel had to gain by using such a ruthless approach. The price would certainly be high—because Israel's reputation would be tarnished—and the benefits very limited or perhaps even nonexistent. Those who were more inclined to think in terms of the moral dilemmas involved, rather than realpolitik, would also have responded that, even if it had not lost its reputation, Israel would have "lost its soul" by taking innocent life when it was not strictly necessary.[6] "We hadn't come very far if we, as the chosen people, had to resort to assassination," mused one Israeli secret agent in his memoirs. "To do this was to align ourselves with Arab mentality."[7]

Yet, on this central question, Israeli chiefs were divided. Harel and Israel's foreign minister, Golda Meir, felt sure that the threat to Israeli security was very grave. This was not just because over the preceding summer the Egyptian missiles had been test-fired in full view of the world's media, leaving no doubt that the program existed and was bearing fruit. It was because they claimed there was clear evidence that Nasser wanted to mass-produce the rockets, which he would only do if he wanted to use them for some military purpose, rather than just to show off to the Arab masses. This evidence, claimed the hard-liners, was a letter written on March 24, 1962, by one of the leading German scientists, Dr. Wolfgang Pilz, to the Egyptian director of the missile program. In the correspondence, Pilz made a request for a large sum of money—3.7 million Swiss francs—to buy spare parts for nine hundred rockets, including five hundred Type-2 missiles and four hundred Type-5. Harel had shown this letter to his prime minister the previous summer, when lobbying him to authorize Operation Damocles, and David Ben-Gurion had reluctantly agreed.[8] Harel had already lost most of his family in one German holocaust and now, barely two decades later, it seemed to him that another could easily begin.

But, other Israeli intelligence and defense experts thought very differently. Meir Amit was the head of a rival organization, Military Intelligence, which was widely known by its Hebrew acronym, Aman, and held very different views from those of the Mossad chief. He felt that Pilz and anyone else in the program could write whatever they wanted, but the reality was that Egypt simply did not have the resources to develop a missile program on the scale Pilz's letter suggested. Even if it did, Amit continued, the rockets were militarily useless because they lacked the most fundamental asset—a reliable guidance and control system. A rocket could be launched into the skies, but it still had to land in exactly the right place if it was to have any value. Developing the guidance system was a hugely complex and demanding engineering task, and Israeli spies had overwhelming evidence that the Egyptians were nowhere near to accomplishing this feat.

"Perhaps we're being too complacent after all," commented Amit dryly as he read some of the more alarming reports about Nasser's plans. "Egypt doesn't only want to destroy Israel—it's about to take over the world."[9] Pilz, he speculated, had written the letter in a bid just to get as much funding as he could from his bosses, knowing full well that there was no likelihood of so many missiles being built.

Amit was equally cool about the prospect of the Egyptians developing WMD. Even if, in a worst-case scenario, they were pursuing such a program, he argued, the superpowers would not let them complete it or use such weapons. For the consequences of Egyptian WMD would be so destabilizing in an oil-producing region that Russia and the United States would exert overwhelming political or even military pressure to stop them.[10] Here was a huge difference of professional judgment as well as personal style. Harel was a great believer in the power of human instinct, intuition, and gut feeling, and saw the world in black-and-white terms of good and evil. Amit, on the other hand, was a top university graduate who had faith in hard rational analysis and raw facts, and who saw the world map as a much more complicated picture.[11]

Then there was a separate question. Even if the Egyptians had developed the missiles on the scale, and with the accuracy, that Harel feared, was the Cairo regime so untrustworthy that Israel could in good conscience employ almost any means it deemed necessary, such as Operation Damocles? Once again, opinions were sharply divided. Harel and many other Israeli chiefs pointed to the virulently anti-Israeli statements that Nasser had at times been known to make, and to his sponsorship of the Palestinian "fedayeen" insurgents, who used their Egyptian bases to launch pinprick cross-border raids against Israel.[12] They emphasized that, even if Nasser himself was not intent on destroying Israel, he could easily be swept along by the the Arab masses who were deeply inimical to the Jewish state: for example, in the event of another conflict or border clash between Israel and Egypt, could not Nasser easily be tempted to retaliate not by using land forces—any Arab army would have faced virtually certain destruction against Israeli forces—but missiles? And wasn't it the Arab countries, not Israel, that had started the 1948 war, when they had attacked the Jewish state just hours after it had won its independence from British rule?

But the Egyptians and the German scientists also had a counterargument, one that was perhaps shared by Israeli moderates like Moshe Sharett, the prime minister who opened dialogue with Nasser in 1955 and who argued against the use of force unless it was really necessary. There was no reason at all, as Kleinwachter told the American journalist, why Egypt could not pursue its own rocket program in the same way as any other country.[13] The Egyptian leader was also bewildered by the Israeli uproar about his missile program and the foreign assistance it received, and was recorded by his close friend and confidant, Mohamed Heikal, as telling the U.S. ambassador, John S. Badeau, that if the Russians and Americans could have their German scientists, then why couldn't Egypt have theirs?[14] In addition, continued his apologists, Nasser had never really shown any aggression toward Israel at all. They said he was only interested in defending his country against a state that, by its own admission, massively retaliated against tiny provocations and was intent on seizing more Arab territory to make room for its fast-growing immigrant population. It would simply not use such weapons unless it had to, because if it did, the retaliation by Israel, which possessed its own missiles and perhaps even nuclear warheads, would undoubtedly be so terrible.[15]

Over the months that followed the Kleinwachter assassination attempt, spokesmen pleaded their various cases before the one audience that, in the court of international opinion, mattered most—the United States. Eight weeks after the incident, Shimon Peres met Pres. John F. Kennedy in Washington and voiced Israel's concerns. While admitting that the missiles were of "doubtful value" without nuclear warheads, Peres argued that, in the Middle East, even conventional warheads could be "highly damaging." He added that the Egyptians would see them as their "salvation, for a missile was after all a bomb-carrying plane without a pilot." Kennedy was unconvinced and asked Peres if Israel's concern about the German scientists was genuine or just a propaganda bid to blacken the name of the Arabs and associate them with Hitler.[16]

Then, in the summer of 1963, Israel's deputy chief of staff, Gen. Yitzhak Rabin, made a presentation before a high-level audience in Washington, in which he argued that the development of the missiles would increase Egyptian confidence in launching a first strike against Israel. He was particularly concerned, he added, by the "operational advantage" of ballistic missile attacks in disrupting Israel's mobilization plans in the event of a conflict, and pointed out that the Egyptians would no longer need bomber pilots since "their work was done by the missiles."[17]

Two months after the incident in Loerrach, American officials had a chance to hear the other side of the story when they visited President Nasser at one of the presidential palaces in Cairo and heard him put forward his point of view. Egypt, he claimed, had "legitimate" security concerns, and Israel's own arms buildup had forced him to pursue an arms program of his own. If Israel had one biological-warfare research center, then Egypt had to have two, he said, and if Tel Aviv test-fired its own missiles, then his own country had to do the same. Nasser added that he knew something of Israel's ambitions to develop a nuclear bomb, being aware of "an unspecified Israeli nuclear installation," and for that reason he wanted to "research" this capability as well.[18] As Robert Komer, the American negotiator, summarized Nasser's argument, "[J]ust as we were developing a capability to strike back and destroy the U.S.S.R. even after it had launched the first attack on us, so he [Nasser] too was developing a capability which would permit him to strike back in revenge if attacked by Israel."[19]

Back in Tel Aviv, such claims did little to reassure Isser Harel, who preferred to work guided by his gut feeling and to assume worst-case scenarios. To his mind, using lethal force against Kleinwachter and any other foreign expert who was crucial to the Egyptian weapons program was wholly justified; and any cost to Israel's reputation, and to its relations with West Germany, was worth paying for the simple reason that there was no other alternative.

Harel and other Israeli intelligence chiefs had been arguing in favor of just such an aggressive and uncompromising approach against Egypt not only since the summer of 1962, when Nasser had first test-fired his missiles, but almost a decade earlier, when Cairo had first reached out to German experts, nearly all of whom had in various guises once served Hitler, and signed them up to help rebuild Egypt in its hour of need.

CHAPTER TWO
Building the Network

One morning in April 1951, a tall, swarthy young man stepped off a small passenger plane at Cairo International Airport and strode confidently toward customs. In his hand he held a British passport, which was stamped with a four-month visa issued by the Egyptian government's London consulate, and the officials who leafed through it saw nothing unusual about it or the visitor. He seemed little different from the thousands of other Western tourists who arrived there every year.

Nor, had they looked more closely at his documents or challenged him openly about the purpose of his visit, would they have had any reason to be suspicious. For John Darling was just a British businessman who was making a relatively brief visit to Egypt as a traveling salesman working on behalf of an electrical goods company. His employers simply wanted more information about the commercial possibilities of doing more business with Egypt, where they saw a lot of future prospects. True, he was unusually dark-skinned for an Englishman, but that was because, as his passport showed, he was born in Gibraltar. Perhaps, too, he looked more archetypally British than many of the British, dressed as he was in an immaculate sports blazer and smoking a pipe that seemed to be permanently lodged in his mouth. But then again, as the customs officials knew only too well, every visitor was different and they traveled in all sorts of guises.

It would have taken someone of outstanding qualities, specially trained in interrogation and highly knowledgeable about the aptitude of his adversaries, to find flaws in the story. For John Darling's real name was Avraham Dar and he was in fact a Jew, one who had been born not in Gibraltar, as he claimed, but in Jerusalem. And far from making any business trip to Egypt, he was instead working for Israel's secret intelligence services.

The nature of his spying mission was, at this stage, very basic. He was not there to carry out any daring operation, such as gathering sensitive information or killing some leading political figure, but rather to do something much simpler—just to touch base with a small number of local sympathizers, informers, and agents who were working for, or associated with, the Jewish state. He would be in the country only for a short time but just long enough, estimated his handlers, to do his work.

Dar's bosses in Tel Aviv knew that they had to be prepared for any eventuality because it was very possible that, at some unexpected moment, they might need to make full use of such a network. At this particular moment relations between the two neighboring countries were calm, but that could easily change: just one sudden clash along the tense and volatile border, for example, could rapidly spark a major confrontation engulfing the entire region.

Such a clash had been possible ever since the state of Israel had been officially born in May 1948. The border between Egypt and British-ruled Palestine had hitherto always been open and porous, and it had been cheap and easy for anyone, including a good number of Arabic-speaking Jews, to take the daily train that left the Palestinian towns of Lydda and Rehovot in the evening and arrived at Cairo's central station the following morning. But from the moment the declaration was made, the Egyptian leader, King Farouk, gave the order to mobilize an expeditionary force that was soon thrown into a full-scale attack on Israeli positions, fighting alongside other Arab armies in a joint campaign to either push back the borders of the Jewish state, as King Abdullah of Jordan wanted, or to destroy it altogether, as the other Arab leaders probably sought.[20] The Egyptians suffered badly during their attacks on Israel, but the hostility that they felt toward their new neighbor intensified even more in October when the Israelis broke a cease-fire and launched an attack in the south, seizing the vast Negev

11

Desert and continuing to advance until January, when a more permanent cease-fire, if not a formal peace, was struck.

More than three years on, the truce between the two countries had held; but there was, naturally, enormous mutual mistrust, suspicion, and ill feeling. Both needed to prepare for a worst-case scenario and, in Israel's case, that would mean establishing a spy ring of sleeper agents who could be activated at very short notice if the need arose.

For the spy chiefs, this mission was considered to be more important than any other equivalent operation taking place elsewhere in the Arab world. Although in 1949 Israel had not signed a formal peace with its Arab neighbors, it was really only Egypt that was seen to matter. This was because it was bigger in every sense—geographically, demographically, and economically—than any of the other warring countries. "Egypt is the only state among the Arab peoples that constitutes a real state and is forging a people inside it. It is a big state," mused Israeli prime minister David Ben-Gurion. "If we could arrive at the conclusion of peace with it, it would be a tremendous conquest for us."[21] But efforts, on both sides, to reach just such an agreement had come to nothing. Direct talks had been held between officials on both sides at Rhodes, Lausanne, and elsewhere but had come to nothing when the Egyptians made political demands—that Israel withdraw from the Negev Desert and allow the Palestinian refugees to return to their ancestral homelands—that were unacceptable to any mainstream politician in Tel Aviv.

As a result, Israeli chiefs were always keen to hear news, or even rumors, of any developments inside Egypt. The very least that an active network of spies could be expected to perform would be to feed back to Israel any talk of, for example, an impending coup—a very real prospect in any Arab state—that could bring an even more hard-line regime to power. Yet by the time "John Darling" arrived in Cairo, sources of information within the country had started to run dry. This was mainly because a great number of Egyptian Jews had emigrated to Israel in 1948, while those who remained had fallen under much greater scrutiny by the Egyptian security services.

It was true that Israeli intelligence had nonetheless scored a number of successes that had helped to fill the void. One highly successful agent was Yolande Gabai, a half-Jewish Egyptian woman who had been recruited into intelligence work in or around 1945, when she met Moshe Shertok, a director of the Jewish Agency Political Department, at a cocktail party. He quickly recognized her qualities, for she not only worked in Cairo as a journalist, and therefore had access to high-powered people, but was a petite, delicate, and very seductive blonde who could easily attract attention from men who were extremely influential within King Farouk's regime and elsewhere.

Soon Gabai had fulfilled all the highest hopes of her handlers in Tel Aviv. A senior official in the Arab League, who was privy to many top-level discussions, had become infatuated with her, and so too had the Swedish ambassador to Egypt. "Several months ago he was completely indifferent to our cause," another Israeli agent said about the ambassador, "but today he is an enthusiastic Zionist. Some of the information on the Egyptian army came from him."[22] These two men were just a tiny part of her very long list of lovers, nearly all drawn from Egypt's governing elite or from the foreign diplomatic services, who were a vital source of information.

But Gabai was captured in July 1948 and her handlers knew that she would be supremely difficult to replace. A number of Israeli agents did follow her path, although not providing nearly so much valuable information. Four months after her arrest, the Middle East Affairs Department in Tel Aviv sent one of its best informers, an Arab from Jerusalem, to Egypt to provide them with a more detailed picture of what was happening inside the country. Before he sailed to Egypt, his spy handlers made clear that they wanted to know "the approximate distance at which the ship was met on arrival by the Suez Canal authority pilot at Port Said"; whether there were any warships at Port Said, and which countries they belonged to; what the customs formalities at the docks and airports were like; whether the ex-Mufti of Jerusalem, Haj Amin, was in prison or under arrest; and what leading Palestinian exiles, who were based in Egypt, were doing in their private lives. The agent dutifully provided his handlers with limited information, all low-key and rather disappointing, before sailing home.[23]

The Israelis carried out a few other intelligence operations, all low-level, against the Egyptian regime at this time. Identifying King Farouk as one of the more intractable enemies of the Jewish state, agents of Military Intelligence's highly secretive Unit 132 briefly conducted a rather tasteless campaign against the Egyptian monarch. Responsible for conducting psychological warfare, its agents concocted photographs of the king in bed with prostitutes and distributed them in the Egyptian capital. Other leaflets and radio broadcasts also reminded the general public of the king's strong interest in pornography.[24]

Realizing that they knew virtually nothing of developments inside Egypt, Israel's intelligence services had turned to Avraham Dar at the end of 1950. Knowing that he could pass as an Englishman, he was sent to Britain six months later to establish a cover story and become fully acquainted with his supposed country of origin. Otherwise, if he was captured and questioned, any lack of firsthand knowledge might come to light almost at once.

Dar wondered what his role in Egypt would be. A few years before, he had taken a leading role in organizing illegal immigration into Palestine, helping European Jews to break the British-imposed blockade, and so he may have surmised that he would be playing a similar part in Egypt in the event of any sudden bout of persecution of the local Jewish population. Similar operations were also under way in Iraq, where Israeli agents were busy airlifting a great many of the 110,000-strong Jewish community out of the country. David Ben-Gurion had a policy of encouraging mass immigration into Israel, wanting to double or even treble Israel's population within a decade, and Egypt seemed a good place to look for new recruits. That was why one of Mossad's main functions at this time was helping to establish escape routes and arrange transportation for Jewish emigrants fleeing "countries of distress."[25]

He may have wondered, too, if he needed to keep a finger on the pulse of local politics, particularly the strength of feeling against the British. The story of British involvement in Egypt had started in the summer of 1882, when heavy rioting in the streets of Cairo had left around fifty Europeans dead and many others injured. Within days the British government had mounted a military expedition under Sir Garnet Wolseley, whose force landed at Ismaïlia and, after winning a lightning victory at Tel el-Kebir, suddenly had the whole of Egypt at its mercy. The British had never planned to occupy Egypt for very long and frequently promised to withdraw from the country as soon as they could. But getting out of the

Middle East, as ever, proved much more difficult than going in, and by 1951 the "temporary" occupation had lasted nearly seven decades, during which time Egypt became part of the British Empire in all but name. London was still exerting strong influence over the country and maintained a powerful military presence along the Suez Canal.

But after the Second World War, the mood among Egyptians had begun to change. Stirred up by the militant Islamist movement (the Muslim Brotherhood) and mindful that India had also won its independence just four years before, the Egyptian masses began to stage a series of riots and strikes in the summer of 1951. Political parties tried to capitalize on these sentiments, playing the nationalist card to hide their own flaws and whipping up anti-British sentiment even more, while insurgents loyal to the brotherhood and to the extremist Misr El-Fatah movement started attacking British military bases. The change in mood became evident in all sorts of ways: the traditional term for the outsider—*hawagat*—started to acquire contemptuous overtones, and a brand of strident nationalism began to surface: in the cinema, for example, the new national anthem was now always played first and anyone who refused to stand risked being physically attacked by members of the audience. Israeli planners needed to know more about the strength of this nationalist reaction, and about the possibility of any sudden political changes within the country.

Dar had been instructed to begin his mission by contacting a trusted sympathizer in the capital, who could put him in touch with a handful of prospective agents for the underground cell he had come to establish. Within a few days he had met all of them and had started to get the cell organized.

Eluding the watchful eye of the Egyptian security services did not promise to be an easy feat, but the Israeli spy had a plan that was well pre-pared and thought through. He placed an advertisement in Cairo's main English-language newspaper for a part-time secretary and then invited just one "applicant"—Marcelle Ninio, a member of his underground cell—to interview. When she started her new "job," her brief "working hours" during the week gave them both enough time to share and draw up plans and ideas about the cell. When he had returned to Israel, explained Dar, he would write her "business letters" containing carefully coded instructions that she would have to decipher and then hide in a cache that had been specially constructed inside her table lamp.

The Israeli agent also hit on a clever way for two other members of the spy cell, based in Alexandria, to avoid Egyptian counterespionage. Knowing that they could easily be recognized as Jews, at a time of growing suspicion and mistrust, and their conversations overheard, Dar suggested that the cell's two key members should meet not in cafés, hotels, or even street corners, but in a cottage on one of Alexandria's main tourist beaches. It was quite usual for the more prosperous families in Alexandria, or from farther afield, to rent cottages, and the cell members would be most unlikely to arouse any suspicion if they met there. Soon, a cottage on Sidi Bishr beach became the main meeting place for several Israeli operatives, all young Egyptian Jews who held a number of parties and dances there to help reinforce the impression of a holiday-season getaway.

In truth, the cottage was not just a meeting place but, for those brief weeks in the summer of 1951, a training school where a small number of young people were given a crash course in the arts of espionage. All were given a basic idea of how to decipher the codes that Marcelle Ninio would be forwarding them and how to evade capture and keep a low profile, and on the best ways of moving through customs without arousing suspicion. Such basic knowledge would keep them going, emphasized Dar, until they were invited to Israel for professional, specialized training. In the meantime, however, he judged them to be competent enough to undertake some initial reconnaissance work, and, on his instructions, two members of the cell began to survey points of military importance in the city, particularly around the port.

In the course of these few weeks, Dar's agents showed a lot of enthusiasm and a certain amount of ingenuity. They showed a sudden interest in rowing and yachting and on one occasion sailed—"by mistake"—into the military areas of the harbor. When a local newspaper reported that an American company would be shooting a movie at the harbor, they immediately applied for jobs as extras and, during breaks in the filming, were able to peer at the top-secret installations of the nearby naval base.

Exactly four months after he had first arrived, John Darling got ready to return home. In that time he had established two underground cells, one in

Cairo, the other in Alexandria, each of which was staffed by a small number of agents who were loyal and highly committed, if highly inexperienced and largely untrained. Each had its own secret meeting places, arms caches, and money supplies, and both were in direct contact with Marcelle Ninio, who was in a position to forward any instructions or messages from Tel Aviv.

Simple—even amateur—though they were, the underground cells would be ready when the order to move eventually came.

CHAPTER THREE
Sharpening the Sword

As he walked along a street in the center of Haifa one day in November 1952, a young Israeli man by the name of Avraham "Avri" Seidenwerg was surprised to hear a familiar voice call after him. Turning around, he was confronted by an old acquaintance whom he had not seen for seven years but whom he recognized immediately. Having fought alongside each other in the Middle East and Italy during the Second World War, the two men were naturally delighted to see each other again and catch up.

Over coffee, they swapped numerous stories and experiences. Seidenwerg, unlike his friend, had an unhappy story to tell. His marriage had fallen apart, he sighed, and his impressive army record in the Israel Defense Forces (IDF)—he had distinguished himself during the bitter Siege of Jerusalem in 1948—had been badly blemished by allegations of theft. After being charged with stealing a refrigerator he claimed was abandoned, he had been court-martialed and then demoted from the rank of major to reserve private. As a result, he had been stuck in a series of menial, dead-end jobs that had left him feeling depressed and even wondering if, at the age of just twenty-six, his best years were over. As the two men parted company, his old acquaintance promised that he would do everything he could to help, and would try using his various contacts to find Seidenwerg an opening.

A few days later, Seidenwerg received an unexpected message from the same friend. Would he make his way to a tiny café in a downscale part of Haifa, at a specific time and date, to meet up with someone who would be there, waiting for him? Intrigued, and knowing that he had nothing to lose, Seidenwerg decided to take the chance and see what would happen.

Within a matter of just weeks, during which he was interviewed several times, the young former soldier was recruited into the ranks of Aman, or Israeli Army Intelligence.[26] True, his military record had been a bad stain on his career; but his recruiters were prepared to overlook it, and Seidenwerg even wondered if the old adage "If you want to catch a thief, hire a thief" worked in his favor. But there was a very compelling reason his new bosses were willing to overlook any such blemishes in his past. For their new recruit also had some rare qualifications, and as a result was well suited to undertake a dangerous new mission.

The new recruit was unable to guess any details about the forthcoming mission from the numerous visits he made to the small, shabby, and cramped office in a nondescript street in the center of Jaffa. This was the home of Unit 131, another highly secretive unit within Military Intelligence that was responsible for specialized, high-risk operations abroad such as sabotage and the spreading of black propaganda.[27] Seidenwerg was introduced to its leader, Lt. Col. Mordechai "Motke" Ben-Tsur, a giant former basketball player, who asked him lots of questions about his past and present but disclosed nothing about what might lie ahead.

Initially, at least, Seidenwerg was not given any indication that he was such a rare and valuable agent. His pay and conditions did not differ from those of all the other operatives within the organization—$165 every month, which was the lowest on the civil service scale, as well as swift reimbursement of any reasonable expenses, such as rent and travel fares, he might incur during his stay. And like the other new recruits, he would initially be offered a one-year contract instead of a permanent job. This temporary contract would automatically renew itself for another three years unless his bosses decided to end it, which they could do, if they wished, without offering any reason or explanation.

Neither did his training differ in any way. At Army Intelligence School outside Jaffa, he was coached intensively in the methods of covert communication, using panchromatic paper, secret ink, and other chemical solutions to disguise messages. He was carefully taught the art of sabotage and shown how to manufacture homemade bombs and devices made up of chemical materials that could be bought almost anywhere. A condom filled with acid, for example, could act as a very effective delayed fuse, since the acid would slowly dissolve the rubber and then ignite anything that surrounded it.

The only thing that was different for Seidenwerg was the length of his training, which was reduced to four months instead of the usual eight or nine. He was told that this was because, as an experienced soldier, he did not need any longer. But another explanation was that he was particularly important, so much so that he was needed on active service as quickly as possible.

Intelligence chiefs had discovered that finding people suitable for any type of espionage work was difficult enough, but what made Seidenwerg so special to Army Intelligence was that he spoke German like a native.[28] This was because he had been born not in the Middle East nor, unlike so many of his fellow Israelis, in Russia or Poland, but in Austria. It was true that he had long lost any close familiarity with the land of his birth. He had left there in 1939, at the age of just thirteen, and headed for Palestine, fleeing the growing Nazi menace to which his parents, both interned in a concentration camp soon after the annexation by Germany of Austria in 1938, had already fallen victim. But his mother tongue was German, which he had put to good use in the Second World War during his days as a member of Shimon Koch's German Platoon, a special unit within the British Army that was created in 1943 and composed of Jews of German and Austrian origin. Speaking passable Arabic was also a help in the world of undercover operations, and as a divorcé, unrestricted by any commitments at home, he was considered to be suitable for long overseas postings. So too was his appearance, because Seidenwerg, a tall, powerful man, had blond hair and would not easily be taken for a Jew.

It was not long before his new bosses assigned him a new identity that he would have to quickly assume. "Learn the details by heart," urged Capt. Shlomo Millet of Army Intelligence as he passed his subordinate a long and detailed curriculum vitae of this fictional new personage. "Your life may depend on it." Paul Frank, as he would soon be known, was a thirty-two-year-old German who had been born near Oberfranken in Bavaria. Both his parents had been killed in the war, and his sister and her family had subsequently emigrated to the United States.

There was one aspect to the new identity, however, that deeply puzzled Seidenwerg, who searched hard to grasp the logic. For Paul Frank was supposed to be not a true Aryan German, as his name implied, but a German Jew, one who emigrated to Palestine in 1937. "What disturbed me most was the fact of his Jewishness," he wrote. "Passing me off as an Aryan German from a German-Jewish background seemed dangerous. Hell! It seemed downright stupid. Yet who was I to question Aman's decision? The personnel in Aman was thoroughly experienced and professional, I rationalised—highly professional."[29]

If Seidenwerg privately had a few doubts about the mission he was going on, then those doubts perhaps revealed something about the organization he had joined. Military Intelligence was run not by spies, highly skilled and trained at working undercover in foreign and hostile countries, but by soldiers, trained to assess an enemy fighting force and then defeat it. It was significant that the head of Aman, Gen. Binyamin Gibli, was essentially a frontline soldier, courageous and innovative on the battlefield but not by training or instinct an expert in espionage. During the War of Independence he had been responsible, it is true, for some intelligence work in Jerusalem, but otherwise had limited personal experience of what was involved. Yet in spite of this, Aman was still responsible for planning all special foreign operations, and in the course of 1951 it regained the right to carry out such operations without Mossad's prior approval.[30]

Seidenwerg agreed to continue with the training and carefully absorbed all the lessons he was taught. "Live, think, be a German. Avoid all contact with Jews, Israelis, and their friends—and the places they go," emphasized his chief trainer. "Above all, though, don't be overly security-minded. Nothing draws suspicion more than too much caution. Whatever the circumstances, act naturally, think logically. Cultivate yourself a habit: it may save your hide ten times over. Believe me, I know what I'm talking about."[31]

Gradually, in the course of these weeks of intense training, Seiden-werg got clues to where this new mission would be. When he was given an armload of books—*Islam, Ancient and New Egypt,* and *From Cairo to Damascus*—and told to write summaries as well as give his own interpreta-tions, he knew that he would be sent somewhere in the Middle East. And when an IDF officer who had closely supervised his training provided him with more detailed reading about the Egyptian army and its history, the new recruit knew exactly what his destination would be.

Egypt had suddenly become so important to Israeli chiefs for a number of reasons. The first was that a few months before, on July 23, King Farouk had been suddenly deposed in a bloodless coup that had been mounted by Free Officers, a group of senior army commanders led by Gen. Muhammad Naguib and Maj. Gamal Abdel Nasser. At first, Israeli strategists had cau-tiously welcomed the development, even if they were caught completely by surprise. Farouk had been viewed in Tel Aviv as an inflexible opponent of the Jewish state, and his departure, wrote Moshe Sharett, "removes at least one obstacle to peace."[32] The new regime leaders proclaimed themselves to be more interested in rebuilding their homeland than in fighting a self-destructive war against Israel, and their socialist values seemed to give them common ground with the government in Tel Aviv. Yet by October, Israeli hopes had been disappointed because the Free Officers were failing to show any interest in a peace settlement, or even active negotiations, and some analysts thought that Naguib was showing signs of real duplicity.[33]

At the very least, Israel would have to learn more about Egypt's new rulers and monitor events there more closely in case the regime adopted an even more hostile line. But what deeply concerned officials in Tel Aviv was that the new regime had vowed to adopt a more vehemently nationalist line than its predecessor. Almost immediately, the Free Officers vowed to end London's political influence within the country as well as force the British to surrender their military bases along the Suez Canal.

By this time, the British government was, in any case, actively consid-ering scaling down, or even ending altogether, its seventy-year military occupation of the country. This was partly because the strength of nation-alist sentiment had by this time already started to become overwhelming.

On January 26, 1952, "Black Friday," furious mobs had broken into Western-owned hotels, businesses, and consulates in the capital, killing, looting, and burning for much of the day. All the main Western European names were targeted—Thomas Cook, Shepheard Hotel, BOAC, Barclays, the British Council—and nine guests, including the Canadian trade representative, lost their lives at the exclusive Turf Club. For the first time in more than two decades, the Egyptian army had to be deployed to restore order while the police were forced to stand back powerlessly. "The horrible behaviour of the mob puts them lower than the most degraded savages now known," wrote Winston Churchill to the British foreign secretary, Anthony Eden. "They cannot be classed as a civilised power until they have purged themselves."

But the British still maintained a large military presence of eighty thousand men who were stationed along the banks of the Suez Canal. In London, a growing number of voices were calling for total withdrawal from the Canal Zone, arguing that Britain could not afford to maintain it at a time of postwar austerity and limited resources. In the days of imperial rule over India, everyone had agreed that the bases had been necessary, since they protected the canal, through which vital supplies to and from the Indian subcontinent had continually flowed. But India had won independence in 1947, they emphasized, and it was time to move out. As Eden argued in a cabinet memorandum in the summer of 1952, the bases were "placing a burden on the country's economy which it is beyond the resources of the country to meet."

But Israeli planners were becoming increasingly concerned by the prospect of a British pullout. As Seidenwerg's chief handler, Mordechai "Motke" Ben-Tsur, told him: "Israel is in grave trouble. Do you realise what will happen if the British pull out? They'll abandon to Nasser the mightiest military bases in the Middle East: thirty-seven military installations, including two fully equipped airfields, docks, dumps, hospitals, radar stations and some of the world's largest ordnance depots. It took the British thirty-eight years to build them."[34]

Not only that, but the presence of so many British troops was viewed in Tel Aviv as a form of safety valve, a neutral force that could help keep Israel and Egypt apart when their relations deteriorated.

By the time he joined Israeli Military Intelligence, Seidenwerg knew that the British might be pulling out. But what he was unaware of—and it was known only to a handful of very senior Israeli politicians and defense chiefs—was that, barely eighteen months before, a contingent of seventy-one German military experts, some of whom were veterans of both world wars, had arrived in Cairo. In the eyes of the Israeli defense chiefs, their presence changed the whole dynamic of the relationship between Israel and Egypt. In particular, they were concerned that, in the event of a clash over the canal bases, these German expatriates could be of real help to the Egyptian war effort. It was quite possible, for example, that the Israeli government might decide to launch a preemptive attack on Egypt just after the British pulled out, and if this did happen, the contribution of seasoned German military experts could make a huge difference to the strength of the Egyptian performance.

This was a concern that the Israelis shared with the British, who thought that, if negotiations failed and they decided to retain the bases, the Egyptians might be tempted to try and seize the bases from their grasp. With this in mind, Anthony Eden had complained to the German chancellor, Konrad Adenauer, that German mercenaries were aiding the Egyptian army at a very tense time when the British presence in the country was coming under heavy nationalist pressure. Officials in Bonn replied that they had no authority to stop these men from pursuing private work in Egypt if they so wished, even if their activities there could conceivably jeopardize their prospects in the new German army. There was nothing illegal under West German law about what they were doing, they countered, provided that no up-to-date hardware was sold to the Egyptians. The German veterans would simply be training their Egyptian counterparts in tactics and gunnery, as well as particular skills such as the disposal of explosive ordnance.

The Israelis and the British were particularly concerned, for the German training team included some impressive names, familiar to many who had served in the Wehrmacht during the Second World War. Sixty-two-year-old Gen. Wilhelm Fahrmbacher had more than thirty-five years' experience, having served in both wars and helped to organize the Reichswehr militia of the Weimar Republic. On his release from French custody in 1950, he had leaped at the chance to advise the Egyptians and help them build up their army. Capt. Theodor von Bechtolsheim was entrusted with the task of teaching the Egyptian navy new skills, and Maj. Gen. Oskar Munzel, who had years of experience as a German tank commander, was responsible for developing new armored units. Another leading figure was Gerhard Mertens, who was tasked with creating a parachute battalion.

Many of the German ex-soldiers who migrated to Egypt at this time were veterans of Rommel's Afrika Korps and had perhaps chosen to return to a country whose climate and conditions they had grown fond of. Others were simply looking for new professional openings, and would have taken almost any reasonably paid post, anywhere in the world, that was offered to them. Since the end of the Second World War, the demilitarization of West Germany meant that a good many professional soldiers and scientists had found themselves without any prospects in their chosen lines of work. Not only that, but many had to cope with the anguish and frustration of having once felt as though they were on top of the world—a situation in which they had had every chance of fulfilling their lifelong ambitions—before watching everything around them crumble into ruins.

There were others, however, who had a more compelling reason to move to Egypt. Among the first to appear in Cairo in the early 1950s were Leopold Gleim, a former Gestapo boss in Warsaw who had been responsible for Jewish affairs, and a senior SS man, Willi Brenner, who had helped set up and then run the concentration camp at Mauthausen in Austria, where perhaps as many as two hundred thousand "enemies of the Reich" had died. They had moved to Cairo simply because there was virtually no chance of being extradited either to Western Europe or to Israel: if even one German was extradited, then the new regime risked losing the trust of all the others.

Yet characters as unsavory as Gleim and Brenner were exceptions, and the majority of the recruits were simply military men whose expertise was hugely valuable to Cairo. If Egypt was ever going to be able to defend itself from foreign attack or even from insurrection within its own borders, King Farouk and his premier, Nahas Pasha, reasoned, then it had to find a helping hand from abroad. In particular, the dire state of Egypt's military machine had become painfully obvious during the 1948–49 war with

Israel, when its performance on the battlefield was considered to have been so inept, inefficient, and incompetent that senior commanders had urged the king to commission a thorough program of upgrading and improving almost every aspect of the armed forces.

Farouk and his commanders were at this time also approaching a number of German scientific experts whose skills and knowledge could help Egypt to develop its own arms industry. The central figure in this effort was not a scientist but an industrialist, Dr. Wilhelm Voss, who, during the war, had been general manager of two key Nazi factories, the Skoda production works in Czechoslovakia during the German occupation and the massive Hermann Goering Steel Mills. His seasoned project management skills, as well as his extensive contacts and knowledge of the arms industry, made him an ideal candidate to work for the Egyptians, and, soon after starting his contract in 1951, he quickly established close links with key figures in Cairo, where his strong influence earned him the title "the uncrowned ambassador."[35]

Within a few months of his arrival in Cairo, Voss was pressed by the regime to help develop a weapon that, in the light of its experiences two years before, it badly needed—a short- or medium-range battlefield rocket. Voss himself was not a scientist, but he was acquainted with German technicians who had the expertise to help the Egyptians, and he contacted a former colleague, Herr Fuellner, to help him. By the end of 1951, Fuellner had started work on the project and had signed up a number of other German experts to help him take it further forward.

These early efforts to recruit German experts to develop the Egyptian arms industry were not a great success. None of them were particularly well paid, and Munzel and von Bechtolsheim quickly became disillusioned with their work in Egypt. After blazing rows with their employers, they soon quit. And while Fuellner and his team made some progress in developing the "small-calibre rocket" that the Egyptians asked for, they lacked the core ingredients—particularly the specialized steel, propellants, and fuses—that were essential for the task. In 1952, just a year after work on the program had begun, Fuellner's bosses were badly disappointed by a test flight of the new rocket, prompting the German team, including Fuellner, to quit their posts and return home to Germany.[36]

But the Egyptian authorities were undeterred and in the spring of 1952 Farouk's commanders lured a mysterious French figure, Count de Lavison, into the program. Recognizing a business opportunity, de Lavison helped set up a new company, Compagnie des Engins à Réaction Pour Vol Accéléré, or CERVA for short. Based at a specially designed factory at Almaza Airport, just outside the Egyptian capital, its task was to develop jet engines that could be used for a fighter aircraft and a rocket, perhaps one with a considerably longer range than the Egyptians had originally envisaged.

The count's project had not been set up for long when his sponsors, the royal regime, were suddenly toppled by a political coup. But Nasser and his fellow members of the Revolutionary Command were well aware how vital German skills were to the Egyptian forces, and they quickly approached Lavison, Voss, and other members of the CERVA project to renew their contracts. Within just days of the 1952 coup, the new regime had offered Voss the role of director of the Central Planning Board and of primary consultant to the War Ministry. Under the new political order, the CERVA project was still hugely important, and Nasser and his fellow officers had no wish to let it fall apart.

Nasser regarded the contribution of these German experts as just one part of a much wider overhaul of the armed forces, and within months of the coup he had forced several hundred officers to retire, raised the salaries of those who remained, and improved the working conditions of the rank and file. New factories were also built, one to manufacture ammunition, the other to produce training aircraft, and new quays and harbors were constructed for the navy.

The new regime also sought German assistance to help them with this wider reorganization of Egypt's security infrastructure. It started by approaching the head of the West German intelligence service, Reinhard Gehlen, to ask him for his support in improving the quality of Egypt's own service. Gehlen's support would be a huge asset: widely considered by contemporaries to be perhaps the most gifted and formidable spy chief of his age, he had years of experience behind him. The commander of Hitler's intelligence service on the Eastern Front during the war, he had made daily assessments of Russian resources that were typically the basis for Hitler's next moves. Subsequently, he had fought out the Cold War, conducting fierce intelligence battles with his counterparts in the East German and Soviet intelligence services. Such a man was ideal for President Nasser, who knew that he badly needed a top-class spy service not only to keep tabs on the Israelis but also on his enemies at home, notably the militants of the Muslim Brotherhood movement.

Although the American government approved and encouraged Gehlen to support Nasser, whom at this stage they regarded as a real asset in the fight against communist influence in the region, the West German spy chief was too immersed in his own struggle against the East German spy ministry to be able to spare any resources of his own: there had just been an outbreak of very heavy rioting—close to civil war—in East Berlin, and as a result, nearly all of his officers were tied down, closely monitoring the tense situation to see what the East Germans and their Soviet partners were doing. But he was, however, willing to point Nasser in the right direction and put him in touch with an old Nazi acquaintance, Otto Skorzeny, whom he felt was well qualified to take the task on board.

During the war, Skorzeny had been a commando of legendary repute who had earned great fame, or notoriety, as the man who had rescued Mussolini and undertaken a great many other audacious and highly successful operations. Eight years later, he was living in Spain, where he was running a number of small businesses, including a successful engineering firm. He was not impressed, however, by the relatively meager salary that Nasser was offering, and immediately turned down the proposal. But, desperate to keep Nasser in power and Egypt out of the grip of communist control, the CIA at this stage stepped in and offered to up his pay if he accepted the role.

The CIA knew that Skorzeny had a vehement dislike of both Russia and communism, characteristic of almost every former ardent Nazi. His presence in Egypt, the agency's officers argued, would help steer Nasser away from Soviet control. It was for the same reason that Averell Harriman, a senior official in Washington, argued that "the departure of German scientists from Egypt would lead to their replacement by teams of Soviet scientists able to accomplish the same tasks and would not alter in any way the situation in the Mideast, other than increase Egypt's dependence on the U.S.S.R.."[37] Tempted by a CIA check, Skorzeny agreed to accept the Egyptian offer, on condition that his work there would be temporary and no more. He went on to spend the next year in Cairo, helping to train the Egyptian security services, before he returned to his home in Spain.

It was at Skorzeny's invitation, during this twelve-month period in 1953–4, that more Nazi veterans arrived in Cairo. Many of his invitees, however, were not former soldiers but ex-SS and Gestapo officers whose expertise lay in intelligence matters. Most of the two hundred or so who arrived in Egypt at this time had blood on their hands and came from parts of the world—notably Argentina, Brazil, Paraguay, and Spain—where they had taken refuge from postwar justice. Perhaps the major name was Franz Buensch, who had been a big shot in Heinrich Himmler's RSHA department and Goebbels's propaganda ministry, on behalf of which he had written some highly pornographic books and articles with unsavory titles such as *The Sexual Habits of the Jews*.

Meanwhile, Dr. Voss was pressing ahead with the battlefield rocket program and, within a few weeks of the Free Officers' coup, he had approached and signed up a brilliant young German scientist by the name of Rolf Engel. Just forty years old, Engel already had a hugely impressive curriculum vitae. Recruiting him into the CERVA program was something of a coup for Voss and his Egyptian bosses.[38]

Engel's involvement in the world of rockets and jet engines had started in his mid-twenties, when he joined the main forum for the great scientific minds of his time, the German Society for Space Travel in Berlin, and rubbed shoulders with figures, notably Wernher von Braun, who were later to become household names in Germany and beyond. Unlike nearly all of his acquaintances in these circles, Engel was largely self-taught, having spent only a year at a university before leaving and pursuing an amateur interest in rocketry. But with his natural aptitude in a field that the Germans were particularly keen to develop—the use of solid-propellant rockets—Engel caught the attention of the Nazi chiefs. Setting up his own firm in Danzig in 1943, he soon established himself as an expert in his field and was commissioned by the SS to help develop solid-propellant, fin-stabilized rockets that were three inches and six inches in diameter, as well as an antiaircraft missile. In the summer of 1944, he was appointed a departmental head of Waffen-Union Skoda-Brunn, an SS-run firm, based at Pibrans in Czechoslovakia, which played an important role in German arms production, and after the war he was recruited by the French to work on the Veronique rocket program.

When Engel joined the CERVA program in Egypt in the summer of 1953, he quickly got to work with other German expatriates on developing a five-foot rocket that was probably based on his particular specialty—the solid-propellants motor. Like Fuellner before him, he encountered a series of technical faults and problems that, in the circumstances, were too difficult to resolve. But the team did succeed in carrying out some flight tests, as well as developing a nationwide radar network.

Yet while Engel and his fellow scientists had been working hard to upgrade Egypt's defenses, Israeli spy chiefs in Aman's newly formed Unit 131 had been busily drawing up plans to try to stop them. After long months of preparation, they summoned Seidenwerg and explained to him the various aims of his mission, which would be—for the extra daily pay of just one dollar—an extremely crucial and dangerous one. He was, they instructed, to travel to Egypt and establish a new life as a German businessman. When he had done that, he would then have to provide an infiltration route for other Israeli operatives and set up a sleeper network that could be activated in the event of any national emergency. In particular, he had to be prepared for the eventuality of a sudden Israeli attack, launched as a desperate bid to dissuade the British from leaving the Suez Canal Zone.

But there was another more important goal that he would have to pursue, one that concerned the German expatriates and their work, as well as senior members of the Egyptian military such as Admiral Azzarat, Zakaria Mohieddin, and Gen. Ibrahim Abboud.

Here the order from Tel Aviv was simple: "Cripple by sabotage, maim by death."

CHAPTER FOUR
Israel Prepares to Strike

In late December 1953, just a few days before Christmas, "Paul Frank" boarded a passenger ship, the SS *Enotria*, and left Naples for Alexandria. It was not an easy passage, since in the midst of the Mediterranean the ship ran into a violent storm that left nearly all the passengers, and a good many of the crew, violently sick; but within a few days the Egyptian port of Alexandria loomed on the horizon. Never one to waste an opportunity, Frank managed to get snapshots of every naval vessel and military installation he saw before the ship docked and the gangplank was lowered onto the quay, where a mass of local Arabs were waiting, waving their arms in the air and shouting to attract the attention and business of the wealthy newcomers. Hordes of porters, dressed only in rags, prepared to rush aboard as soon as the first ropes were thrown across and the gangplank lowered. Standing behind them were clearing agents, who earned a daily living by taking the passengers through customs much more quickly than the process would otherwise demand. Then there were taxi drivers, hotel porters, hawkers, photographers, travel agents, and stevedores, all waiting in the background for new business to arrive.

The young Israeli had not previously visited Egypt, and he may well have been surprised by his first sight of Alexandria. Far from being the typical Arab setting, like Cairo or Luxor, it was a city that revealed a much stronger European influence, having been almost completely rebuilt at the beginning of the nineteenth century and designed with broad, straight streets; tall buildings similar to those of Paris and other French cities; and a wide avenue, known as the Corniche, stretching along the beach. Situated right on the Mediterranean, Alexandria also had an unusually strong European population and cultural influence, and a good many of the local people wore Western-style dress.

The secret agent who made his way through its streets was no longer Avri Seidenwerg, who was now an individual Frank had left behind in Israel. He had to live and breathe his new identity. When he had left Tel Aviv some days before, he had reassured his handlers that he had absorbed this new personage. As instructed, he correctly failed to show even a flicker of any acknowledgment of the most familiar faces as he went, even cursing not in Hebrew but in German—*Verflucht noch einmal!*—when something went wrong. His bosses smiled as they saw him leave. Their judgment had been the right one. Paul Frank was ready to start his assignment.

Soon after embarking at Alexandria, the young Israeli spy was on his way southward toward Cairo along the main road that was flanked on one side by a huge expanse of desert that stretched for four hundred miles all the way to the Libyan border, and on the other by the Nile Valley, which surrounded the great river and led south toward Luxor and Aswan. Finally, after a long and quite demanding journey, he reached the capital, a city he found to be "a spectrum of startling contrasts," where he would begin his espionage work.

Paul Frank had a first-class cover story with which to hide his true purposes. His orders from Tel Aviv some months before had been to obtain a job as a mechanical engineer with a German company trading in Egypt and then secure, by any means he could, a transfer to Egypt. He had answered a good many advertisements in local and national newspapers and used a number of forged documents to persuade his prospective employers of an educational and professional background that was really just the stuff of fiction.

Unknown to his handlers, he had also developed a cover story of his own, one that made him feel far more secure now that he was in enemy territory. Instead of posing as a German Jew—a story he had never felt comfortable with—he had thought of what was, in his view, a much better idea, or at least one that was no worse than the one he had been given. This idea was based on a true story he had heard during his days in the Middle East with the British Army, when he had learned of a group of eight German agents who had parachuted into Palestine, alongside some sympathetic Arabs, in order to stir up insurrection. The idea was a good one because Palestine was at that time British-controlled territory, and a rebellion there could have potentially diverted a good number of Allied soldiers away from the frontline, but its execution appears to have gone very wrong. The group had subsequently disappeared, and this meant that Frank could plausibly claim to have been a survivor, one who had managed to escape British capture and subsequently lived under the cover given to him by his Nazi handlers—that of an Austrian Jew who had volunteered to join the Jewish brigades that were then forming in Palestine. Feeling much more confident with this new cover story, the Israeli secret agent got to work.

Frank did not know precisely at what point he was going to receive orders to activate the network that he was tasked with setting up. Nor was he quite sure what his mission would involve. Like Avraham Dar, he knew he might be ordered not only to attack infrastructure or assassinate key personnel but perhaps also to help Egyptian Jews flee.

Since first arriving in the course of the second half of the nineteenth century, when a great many Jews had fled persecution in the Ottoman Empire, Egypt's Jewish community had never had good reason to leave the country. The native Egyptians had always referred to them with their traditional term of respect for foreigners—*hawagat* or "gentlemen"—and though most of the Jews were denied citizenship, they were nonetheless granted considerable freedom, and were allowed to have their own schools, to use their own language, and to run their own hospitals and other services. A member of the wealthy Kattawi family, for example, had been appointed as a senator and his wife had served as one of the ladies-in-waiting to the wife of King Fouad, during his five-year rule of Egypt during and after the First World War.

But this long-standing harmony was rocked badly in 1948, upon the outbreak of war between Israel and Egypt. Concerned that some members of the sixty-five-thousand-strong Jewish community might act as a fifth column on behalf of the Jewish state, the Egyptian police suddenly swooped in, arresting hundreds of people "suspected of Zionist activity." In the universities, in particular, radical activists of the Muslim Brotherhood movement started to recruit volunteers to fight against the Israeli army and then began to harass Jews, physically assaulting a number of them and sponsoring a resolution that called for a boycott against the presence of Jewish students in lecture halls. Jewish leaders received confidential information that Islamist militants were planning pogroms against them, prompting Cairo's Harat al Yahud—its Jewish quarter—to arm itself in self-defense. From around this time, the Egyptian Jews were no longer referred to as hawagat but rather as Saynonin, a contemptuous term for Zionists.

Although this sudden wave of persecution had faded by 1950, it caused deep alarm within the Jewish community in Egypt and in Israel. In 1949, anxious to restore the good relations with Egypt, the chief rabbi of Cairo, Chaim Naham Effendi, met a representative of the Jewish state who promised him that Israel would not do anything that could make the Egyptian government mistrustful of its local Jewish population. Effendi was intent on preserving these harmonious relations and didn't want his fellow Egyptian Jews to become involved in any way with the state of Israel, fearing that any such association could prove deeply harmful. This was one reason the Israelis were now so short of informers inside the Jewish community.

Frank's first aim was to gather as much information as he could about what the German expatriates were doing and how much they had achieved. Once he had established that and fed the information back to Israel, he would be in a position to get an accurate idea of their daily movements and the weak points in their armory. Only then would he be in a position, when instructed, to arrange their elimination.

An affable man with a good sense of humor, and posing as a businessman with excellent connections in West Germany, Frank had little trouble ingratiating himself with the German expatriate community. Almost as soon as he arrived, he was invited to social functions at the German embassy in Cairo and, using some of the introductions he had made along the way, was rubbing shoulders with some of the names that Israeli chiefs feared most.

Within just a few weeks, he had built up a working knowledge of the role the Germans were playing in Egypt, and in some ways his worst fears were fulfilled. "The recently established Staff Security Cadre seemed to be structured like Hitler's SS: shock troops and secret police," he noted, while "the Economic Department was a true replica of the SS Wirtschaftsamt, with a special Jewish section that had worked at full speed to register all Jewish property." Such similarities chilled him, for "as a child in Austria I had grown up during the beginnings of a nightmare: now history was repeating itself."[39]

But he also quickly became aware of the deficiencies of the Egyptian armed forces, which were desperately lacking in spare parts, organization, and efficiency. This quickly became apparent from his first meeting with Maj. Gen. Oskar Munzel, a veteran panzer commander on the Russian front who was now training Egyptian tank units. Sitting under a canopy beside a swimming pool, Munzel cursed the atrocious performance of the tanks he was now responsible for. "The worst problem we have is maintenance," he fumed; "they don't seem to learn." Munzel recounted the true story of Independence Day that year, on July 23, 1953, when the new regime had commemorated the fall of the Farouk regime by staging an impressive procession by forty tanks. "Would you care to know how many passed the tribune, Herr Frank? Twelve! Can you believe twelve out of forty? And one lost a track and almost ran down the saluting stand." The general shot forward in his chair as he recounted the story. "A thousand times I've tried to beat into their dead heads that pretty paint and big identification numbers do not a fighting panzer force make!"[40] The general concluded by remarking, "It is my opinion, Herr Frank, that the Egyptians will never have an army."

Frank heard similar stories of Egyptian ineptitude elsewhere. Another acquaintance he soon made in Alexandria was a former naval captain, Baron Theodor von Bechtolsheim, who was also working as an adviser to the Egyptian armed forces. As they talked together after dinner one evening, Frank remarked that, en route to Egypt from Italy, he had noticed three warships performing battle maneuvers and commented, "I thought they might be Italian or Egyptian until I saw the blue-and-white flag of the Israelis." But the baron seemed taken aback by the suggestion. "Oh yes, the

Israelis. They are bloody efficient. You would never encounter the Egyptian navy so far out to sea. They are afraid to steam beyond sight of land."[41]

General Fahrmbacher, whom Frank met for the first time in February 1954, also reiterated just how much work the Egyptians needed to do to raise their game. Although now in his mid-sixties, with fading blue eyes, thinning white hair, and rosy cheeks, the veteran German general still spoke with plenty of fire and passion as he described what was required. In his office at an army general headquarters near Heliopolis, which was filled with "maps, filing cabinets, documents and an air of seriousness," he told his young visitor of his plans for creating an Egyptian strike force of fifteen divisions, based on the old Reichswehr structure of 1933.[42] But he cautioned that this was a hard task, since "Egypt needs another seven to eight years before they can sustain the logistics of large fighting groups. Until then, I think that small groups, not more than company strength, should be built to expertly man their few modern weapons."[43]

But by far Frank's most important contact was the head of the CERVA rocket program, Rolf Engel. In the spring of 1954 he was invited to lunch at Engel's closely guarded villa, situated on a quiet street in Heliopolis. Frank immediately found the German scientist to be a charming man, as well as an enlightening, if naturally guarded, source of information about his secret work for the Egyptians. It was not long before Engel revealed the shortcomings of his project. He was struggling to maintain the program's independence from government bureaucrats, he told Frank, and strongly mistrusted his staff, even his fellow Germans like engineer Kurt Hainisch. But the program had clearly progressed beyond the stage of research and development because, more than anything, it badly needed special propellants that were vital for rocket production, as well as special types of steel sheets and heavy machine tools required to mass-produce the rockets. Engel hoped to acquire these from overseas sources but had no idea when this would happen. Astonishingly, he then took Frank on a tour of a plant where the rockets were being developed.[44]

But Frank's greatest coup came from a German acquaintance who was working full-time on the CERVA program. This contact was Dr. Count Willi von Kubie, an artistic, bespectacled academic in his late twenties who had come to Egypt from West Germany after finishing his advanced degrees in chemistry and nuclear physics. After a long bout of severe illness in the country, he had taken a job as a scientific photographer, making accurate records of the work that was being undertaken in the research establishment where he was employed. This was a job that was well beneath his abilities but one that suited him at the time: badly worn down after weeks of illness, he found it much easier to cope with than the more strenuous engineering work he had expected to pursue.

It was through von Kubie that Frank was able to meet some of the key figures in the CERVA project, such as engineer Kurt Hainisch, who proved to be a fruitful source of information about the program. The two men met at Cairo's Semiramis Hotel, overlooking the Nile, which was where "half the deals, shady or otherwise, [were] made in Egypt." Hainisch revealed that the program was desperately short of specialty steels that were vital for the construction of rocket airframes and warheads. He gave Frank a shopping list, composed mainly of rocket fuses and a mechanism for exploding rocket warheads, and Frank promised that he would use his European network to try and plug the gap. In actuality all he did was relay the information back to Tel Aviv as quickly as possible.[45]

There was another key reason, besides the access he enjoyed to the rocket program, von Kubie was an ideal person for Frank to get to know. Because he had been too ill to work for several weeks, the young German scientist was also in dire financial straits, struggling to recoup his travel costs to Egypt and sustain his living expenses. Like every trained spy, Frank searched instinctively for the vulnerabilities of the people he was dealing with, and in this particular case it was not difficult to find one.

In the course of 1954, Willi von Kubie started to become so financially destitute that he began to entertain some desperate ideas. If some German company was interested in buying the newly developed Egyptian technology, he suggested quietly to the Israeli spy, then he could get copies of the negatives of the blueprint plans. And if Frank was willing to pitch the idea to his professional network back home, then they could share the proceeds. "Those blueprints can be reproduced to the size of your thumbnail," whispered von Kubie; "nobody will ever know."[46] Frank knew from his spy training that the worst thing at this point would be to appear too keen about a plan that, if he succeeded in carrying it out, would be a huge spying coup for Israel, and he cautioned von Kubie about his idea. But within weeks, as he embarked on one of his periodic trips to Germany, Frank had with him eighty-five square negatives, all on thumbnail-size microfilm, that he slipped surreptitiously into the trunk of his car as he boarded the passenger ship at Alexandria and headed first for Brindisi.

On making contact with his spy handlers in Germany, Frank learned that Israeli intelligence already had some first-class information about the Egyptian rocket program. This was derived from the son of a large share-holder in the program who had sold a detailed plan of the layout of the CERVA factory for a fee of several thousand dollars. But Frank's blueprints of the rockets themselves were nonetheless "outstanding material." In fact, they were of such high quality that the spy chiefs wanted to know more about how they had been acquired.[47]

Having obtained enough information about the identities and roles of the German expatriate advisers and how far their plans had proceeded, Frank felt ready to proceed with the next step—to prepare to "cripple by sabotage, maim by death" those who were involved in these projects. From this moment on, he would be in Egypt as "a plunderer, a destroyer of life, a made-to-order killer."[48] He would have to get into position and be prepared to strike as soon as the order from Tel Aviv arrived.

By the time he felt ready to start the assassination plan, some of the German experts signed up by the Egyptian authorities had already packed up and returned home. Munzel, for example, had left the country on bad terms with his former employers, after a confrontation with Colonel Nasser and General Abboud during which he slammed his fist hard down on the desk in front of them before storming out of the office. A number of other less distinguished names also left to take up posts in the new West German army. Others, however, remained and were now in the Israelis' sights.

Assassination was just one part of a much wider operation. For Israeli Military Intelligence, the most pressing task was to firebomb a number of key Egyptian installations, making local insurgent groups look responsible and Nasser seem untrustworthy. If only the British would recognize this essential, underlying untrustworthiness, figured the Israeli spy chiefs, then they might just decide to stay put instead of pulling out of their prized canal zone military bases. This would be the essential aim of this hugely risky new project, code-named Operation Susannah.

But for Frank in particular, carrying out an assassination order promised to be challenging, particularly when some of those on the Israeli hit list—notably Fahrmbacher and Bechtolsheim—were individuals who, over the preceding months, he had come to know well and taken a liking to.[49] "To capsize the aims of my German and Arab 'friends' was one thing," he felt, but "to extinguish a human life was quite another."[50] Nor did he privately agree with such methods: "[W]e hadn't come very far if we, as the chosen people, had to resort to assassination," he later wrote. "To do this was to align ourselves with the Arab mentality. I lived a silent plea that those at home who had conceived and ordered the plan knew what they were doing."[51]

Like every trained intelligence operative, however, Frank knew that he had to try to put his feelings aside, and to proceed instead with the assassination plan. As instructed, he got in contact with the Israeli underground, set up by Avraham Dar, who was by now a major.

Yet before he touched base with its members, Frank had serious doubts about the quality of this network, knowing that only a handful had had formal training for intelligence work, and even the lucky few had done so some years before. Meeting the network's members confirmed his worst fears: "Organization was chaotic in both the Alexandria and Cairo cells; morale was low; communication with headquarters had been abandoned; leadership was non-existent; so was experience in either conspiracy or sabotage." But despite his doubts and reservations, he convinced himself that he could mold the group into a viable spy network, and so he proceeded with the mission.

Crucial to the whole operation was communication with Military Intelligence headquarters in Israel. According to the plan that had been worked out between the agents on the ground and the spymasters in Tel Aviv, each target would be identified by a code name. Instructions to eliminate each of those targets would then be transmitted to the Egyptian spy ring either by invisible ink, wireless message, or one of the two Voice of Israel programs—"The Program of the Housewife" and "The Program of Your Choice"—which could be picked up and listened to in Egypt. But for Frank this was a terrifyingly ambiguous situation to be in: "[K]nowing that at any moment I could receive the dreaded directive from one of these sources hounded me, to say the least," he wrote.[52]

Frank knew that the transmitter was vital to the success of the operation, since it was the only way he could send and receive instant messages to and from Tel Aviv. A location had to be carefully chosen where it could be safely located, and the network soon identified Apartment 107, Rue Hospital 18 in Alexandria as a suitable place. Ostensibly a studio for painting classes held by a member of the spying group, it had an unobtrusive entrance that led onto a busy street, allowing the spies to blend into the crowd and therefore come and go relatively unnoticed. Seven stories high, and outsizing all the nearby buildings, it was ideal for transmitting messages on the wireless kit—composed of a radio, transmitter, Morse key, earphones, tubes, crystals, and a smattering of spare parts—that was hidden inside. Messages were sent out with impressive speed because the spies knew that the more quickly they went out, the more difficult it was for their enemies to detect them. A direct link with Tel Aviv had now been established.

As the plan rolled into action, Frank renewed his acquaintance with those who, against his wishes, were on the hit list. But as he drove to meet General Fahrmbacher, with whom he had shared a good number of evenings and day trips, he was astounded by what he saw. For on either side of the general were two armed soldiers, both with fingers on the triggers of their automatic weapons. Frank had never once seen Fahrmbacher escorted anywhere before.

"It's good to see you again, Paul," the general greeted him. He paused as he saw Frank looking in amazement at the escorts. "For my protection," he said, trying to laugh. "The Egyptians claim they received information that the Jews want to kill me."[53]

Frank felt a bolt of cold fear run down his spine. "Kill you?" he stammered. "Why would they want to kill you?"

"Because I am training the Egyptians, I imagine."

"Are you sure, Herr General, the Egyptians aren't exaggerating?"

Fahrmbacher sighed. "Not this time, I'm afraid. They have definite information."

Within days, the Egyptian security service started to close in on the Israeli spying network. Its commanders captured one of the Israeli spies and wasted little time in acting on the information they prized out of him. Hearing that several members of the network had already been seized and that more arrests were pending, Frank acted fast, booking the first flight out of Cairo—due to the holiday season, he would have to wait another three days—and hoping that he could get past the ring of police and spies who would inevitably be monitoring the passengers at the airport as they prepared to board their flights. If he could do so before any of the captured Israeli spies revealed his identity, then he would probably make it home.

With three days before he could try to make his escape, Frank thought he had nothing to lose by trying to find out more about the CERVA rocket program while he still had the chance. Some weeks had passed since Willi von Kubie had given him more negatives of the blueprint plans of the rocket program, and in that time Frank had worked hard to keep his hopes alive with lies about interested parties who might be willing to buy the material. Now, just seventy-two hours before he hoped to leave the country, Frank tried to extract yet more information from his source.

"I've received word from my friend in Europe," he told von Kubie. "We may have a buyer for your material. Can you get more of it in case he's interested?"

"It's no problem," said von Kubie. "Let me know and I will have it ready in a few hours."

The next day von Kubie appeared at the bus station in Cairo city center with more negatives of the blueprint plans of the Egyptian rocket guidance system and, as an added and unexpected bonus, detailed copies of the secret radar scheme designed by one of the world's leading authorities, a German by the name of Dr. Paul Goercke. Frank gave him some cash as an advance payment, knowing how impoverished his acquaintance was, and the two men parted with a handshake.

On August 6, 1954, Frank arrived at Cairo International Airport along with a German family—a husband, his wife, and their children—whom he had become friendly with, and who happened to be heading for the airport that same day. Frank slipped the blueprints into the coat pocket of the young German woman at his side, knowing that she was the least likely of anyone in the group to be searched. Sure enough, she passed through customs unchallenged, allowing him, unencumbered by any suspicious packages, to follow.

With his "guts on fire" and "head ballooning" with trepidation, Frank now only had passport control to get past. The armed official took Frank's passport, leafed slowly through the pages, and checked to see if his name was on the blacklist the official carried in his other hand. After a few moments, he stamped the passport and handed it back.

He had made it through. Avri Seidenwerg would soon be back in Israel.

CHAPTER FIVE
Tensions Grow

In the early hours of January 31, 1955, two middle-aged men were suddenly woken in their jail cells, put into shackles, and led away into the dark silence of the night. For several months, both had been prisoners of Bab El Halek jail in central Cairo, but their time behind bars had now come to an end. For they were being taken to be hanged.

Their trial had ended three weeks before, and in the intervening period a number of people had made passionate pleas for clemency on behalf of the two convicted men, Moussa Marzouk and Shmuel Azar. The Egyptian leader, Gamal Nasser, had personally assured two of these advocates for mercy—Roger Baldwin, the president of an international pressure group for human rights, and a British member of Parliament, Maurice Orbach—that he would consider their request for leniency. But such assurances had amounted to nothing, for both men had been judged by a military tribunal to be guilty of espionage, working on behalf of a dangerous foreign enemy. As Nasser explained to various intermediaries, it would have been politically disastrous for him to show more leniency toward convicted Israeli spies than toward a number of Egyptian political fanatics, all members of the Muslim Brotherhood, who had been hanged shortly before.

Eyewitnesses later said that Marzouk had calmly mounted the gallows and gone to his death bravely and stoically, requesting only that he should be buried at the family grave, but Azar had died badly, shaking and crying out for mercy in his last moments.

They were not the first serious casualties of the failed Israeli espionage operation that Paul Frank and John Darling had organized and help to lead. On December 21, one of the leading defendants, Max Benet, had killed himself to avoid testifying in court, slashing his wrists with a knife that, despite close and constant surveillance of his cell, had somehow been smuggled into the prison. Another defendant, Moshe Cremona, may have personally witnessed the skills and experience brought to Egypt by former Gestapo and SS personnel who had arrived in Cairo over the preceding two years or so. For he died under torture just weeks after capture.

The other members of the ring were sentenced to long periods of imprisonment in the Sigan Harbi—"the military prison"—in Abbasiya, just outside Cairo. In Egypt, the name was deeply evocative and the threat of incarceration within its walls was enough to strike fear in any prisoner. As a military prison it was not subject to civilian law, and this meant that anyone confined within was deprived of any rights and instead dependent for his or her survival not on Egyptian law but on the goodwill of the guards. But because it was used as a political prison, where enemies of the regime were sent, guards were instructed to ill-treat their prisoners, using brutality, or the mere threat of it, to break their prisoners psychologically. During the day and at night, the corridors were said to echo with the screams of tortured prisoners.

Operation Susannah, the top-secret operation by Israel's Military Intelligence, had plainly been a rather bloody and messy affair. Its critics in Israel's intelligence services were not surprised, because they had always maintained that it was too risky and audacious to succeed, while experts in the Foreign Ministry would have maintained, if they had known of the operation in advance, that it was never necessary in the first place: once the British pulled out of Egypt, they would have said, the Cairo regime would be more amenable to a deal with Israel.[54] But its advocates within Military Intelligence had pushed ahead, keeping their plan secret. By planting bombs in Egypt that would be blamed on domestic dissidents and extremists, went the idea, the network of Israeli agents, first established by Avraham Dar, could sow mistrust between the Egyptian government and the West. This would mean that the British would not withdraw their military presence in the region—they planned to pull out their soldiers from the banks of the Suez Canal in the course of 1954—and the Americans would be far more wary of showing any support or interest in a regime that could not even keep order in its own back yard.

But the operation had backfired almost at once, in a way that hardly befitted the hugely impressive reputation that Israeli intelligence had already acquired. First of all, the agents manufactured some homemade bombs, putting them inside hollowed-out books that were then placed on library shelves just before closing time. But within a few hours the acid from the bombs had started to dissolve their containers and leak through the book covers, causing them to explode with a deafening roar that, fortunately, killed and injured no one. Then one of the other agents, Philip Nathanson, was nervously making his way to a target when a bomb, intended for a Cairo cinema, exploded in his pocket. Within a short period of time, almost the entire Israeli spy network in Egypt had been rounded up and put on trial, and only Avri Seidenwerg had escaped. Not surprisingly, the head of Aman, Binyamin Gibli, had resigned soon afterward. "I would never have imagined," mused a horrified Moshe Sharett, "that we could reach such a horrible state of poisoned relations, the unleashing of the basest instincts of hate and revenge and mutual deceit."[55]

During the trial, those who followed the fate of the defendants more closely than anyone, with the exception of their families and relatives, were, of course, the Israelis. All the defendants were Jews and all had been trained in either Israel or France. This meant that, more than anything else at the time, the fate of the prisoners would probably give a good indication of Nasser's true sentiments toward the Jews in general and Israel in particular. If the Egyptian leader had any interest in compromise with the Jewish state, the Israeli chiefs must have wondered, or any compassion as a person, surely he would revoke the death penalty? No one had been killed or even injured during Operation Susannah, they argued, and the agents' actions could even be described as harmless or, worse, farcical.

After Marzouk and Azar fell through the trapdoors that January night, they were widely mourned in Israel, even though, ironically, neither had citizenship of the Jewish state. Streets and other public places would be named after them, and the Knesset held a short silence in their honor. But the real importance of the affair was the rethinking it prompted in the minds of Israeli planners. Far from being an unknown quantity, as he had been over the preceding three years, and perhaps even Israel's least bad enemy, Nasser was now regarded as someone who simply could not be trusted. Premier Moshe Sharett, a true dove toward the Arab world, canceled a secret deal to hold high-level talks with the Egyptians: "[W]e will not negotiate in the shadow of the gallows," he sighed.[56]

Since seizing power in 1952, alongside Muhammad Naguib and several other senior Egyptian officers, Nasser had not immediately appeared to be an obvious or particular threat to Israel's interests. The Free Officers junta that seized power in the summer of 1952 appeared to have a very modest interest in foreign affairs, and its leaders, Nasser included, barely even raised the question of Palestine at all. Since the coup, Nasser and his associates had seemed more preoccupied with building Egypt up, pursuing an agenda of modernization and nationalization, than with fighting unwinnable and perhaps suicidal wars against foreign enemies. Right from the start, the junta had embarked on a radical reform program that included the reorganization of the country's political parties, a purging of the civil service, and extensive land reform.

This early mood of relative insularity and moderation did not change after February 1954, when army units loyal to Nasser forced Naguib to stand aside as president and proclaimed the thirty-six-year-old colonel Egypt's new leader instead.[57] Almost immediately, Nasser moved to reduce the defense budget and to demilitarize his side of the long border with Israel. Although he dared not admit to it in public, given the strength of popular feeling the announcement could have ignited, he secretly opened negotiations with his Israeli counterparts, notably the prime minister, Moshe Sharett, and even the much more hawkish David Ben-Gurion, with whom he corresponded through a number of intermediaries.[58] The Egyptian leader also met a good many American and UN envoys, who were tasked with brokering a peace deal between the two neighbors.

Nasser's moderate position was quickly noticed by a number of high-profile visitors, some of whom wanted to gauge just how much of a menace he posed to the Jewish state. In 1953 a young British member of Parliament, Richard Crossman, a committed Zionist, traveled to Cairo to meet with the Egyptian leader. Nasser, wrote Crossman, "at that time judged that Israel ought not to distract him from the problems of Egypt, those of the social revolution. He was neither anti-semitic nor even really pro-Arab."[59] When, at the same time, in May 1953, the U.S. secretary of state John Foster Dulles met with the Egyptian leader in Cairo, the international media reported that "Israel was not even mentioned during the interviews."[60] Some of his more radical enemies, notably in Syria, even angrily denounced Nasser because of his alleged "moderation" toward the Jewish state: Akram El-Hourani, leader of the Ba'ath Party, the socialist party of insurrection, described Nasser as an "ally of Zionism," claiming that he had always been opposed to more radical measures against Israel, such as a plan to prevent the diversion of the Jordan River.[61]

Under such strong pressure at home, Nasser had opened a diplomatic dialogue with Israel in early 1953 under strict secrecy. Using an official working at Egypt's Paris embassy as an intermediary, Nasser informed the Israelis that he was willing to negotiate and strike a lasting deal but would have to break off talks if they were made public. Early hopes for a compromise soon faded, though, when the Israelis asked for a secret meeting at a higher level but received no reply from Cairo.[62]

On a personal if not a political level, Nasser had even shown a certain amount of warmth toward some of the individual Jews he had encountered. He thought highly of the Israeli premier, Moshe Sharett, whom he considered an honest and moderate man.[63] In the summer of 1948, while serving as a commanding officer in the Egyptian military during Israel's War of Independence, he fought the Jewish army with great bravery but also established an unusually close rapport with an officer in the enemy ranks. For in October 1948, as he commanded Egypt's Sixth Battalion in a desperate situation along the front line at Fallouga, Nasser had met the Israeli officer Capt. Yeruham Cohen, who had been sent by his own senior officer, Gen. Yigal Allon, to discuss a cease-fire. The two men appear to have had long and close discussions, which they continued a year later when Nasser attended the formal burial of the war dead and met Captain Cohen once again. The two men got on well enough to exchange gifts—an exchange initiated by the Israeli officer—and years later Captain Cohen wrote a favorable description of the man he had met: "I found in him a personal charm, a frankness, an obstinate patriotism . . . he was interested in the social problems of his country. It was manifestly clear that he understood and approved of our struggle against the British. He was well acquainted with the combats of the Haganah and, on the basis of the Zionist struggle against the English, was making an effort at understanding the possibilities offered by a mobilisation of the masses in a resistance movement."[64]

This was hardly the description of an anti-Semite but was instead much more characteristic of someone who, in March 1953, was seen, along with Muhammad Naguib, leaving a Cairo synagogue, where he had been mixing with the local Jewish population.[65] Such personal tolerance was entirely in keeping with a man who, as a teenager, had grown up next to a synagogue and lived in a house that was owned by a local Jewish family, with whom he often dined.[66]

But Operation Susannah had now sowed the seeds of mistrust between Egypt's Jewish community and the Egyptian Arabs. Several of those who were implicated in the plot were Egyptian Jews, including a professor of engineering, a wealthy businessman, and a doctor at a Jewish hospital. For both Egyptians—Jews and Arabs—as well as for the Israeli authorities, the atmosphere from 1955 onward was suddenly one full of suspicion and mistrust. A great many Jews had already left Egypt by this time—the number had fallen from around sixty-five thousand in 1948 to about thirty thousand four years later—but now the community seemed set to diminish even more.

After the hanging of two of the alleged spies in January 1955, this mistrust sank to new depths, but it was not the only thing to make it do so. For a few weeks before, in September 1954, an incident had taken place in the Suez Canal that aggravated Israel's sense of injustice and persecution even more. That month, the authorities in Tel Aviv had deliberately sent a small cargo ship, the *Bat Galim*, through the Suez Canal, wanting to test the strength of Egypt's resolve to enforce its embargo on Israeli shipping.

When, on September 28, the ship was stopped at the southern entrance of the canal and its crew imprisoned, the Israelis hoped to put Egypt in the international dock.

The embargo itself was nothing new, since it had first been instigated by King Farouk's regime during the war with Israel in 1948. If they could stop crude oil shipments moving along the canal from Middle East exporters to Israel, reasoned the Egyptians, then the vast oil refinery at Haifa would be effectively redundant and would not generate the large revenues that the Jewish state desperately needed. The embargo had never subsequently been revoked, despite the signing of an armistice agreement in February 1949 and Israel's referral of the matter to the United Nations, which then passed a Security Council Resolution condemning the Egyptians' actions.[67]

Cairo had tried to hurt Israel's maritime trade in another way, because at the same time, in 1949, the royalist regime had seized control from Saudi Arabia of two small and deserted islands in the Straits of Tiran, which guard the entrance to the Gulf of Aqaba in the Red Sea. Because these straits are remarkably shallow, and shipping can only pass through one narrow channel that flows between the Egyptian shore and the island of Tiran, the Cairo regime's control over the waterway threatened to ruin Israel's declared ambition of building a port at Eilat, overlooking the Gulf of Aqaba.

So although, by 1954, Egypt's threat to Israeli shipping was a long-standing one, the Israeli authorities regarded its behavior toward the *Bat Galim* as just another sign of a growing and unmistakable sense of menace. A foreign regime that was prepared to ignore a UN resolution by stopping an Israeli ship, and arresting and detaining its crew for four months, was a regime that, in the eyes of the authorities in Tel Aviv, simply could not be trusted. An Egyptian government representative, Dr. Mahmoud Fawzi, tried to justify his government's actions, explaining to the British ambassador that ships flying the flag of a country that planned acts of sabotage against Egypt had to take the consequences of their actions. Yet such justifications hardly reassured anyone in Tel Aviv. Not only was Egypt deadly serious about enforcing the threats it had made over the previous few years, but it had done so at the most sensitive time, just as death sentences were being passed and carried out against the alleged conspirators.

Some officials in Tel Aviv felt sure that the Egyptian threat was now growing fast. David Ben-Gurion particularly feared Nasser's pan-Arab rhetoric, knowing that Israel would stand little chance of surviving a concerted Arab attack. "The spectre of a united Arab world haunted David Ben-Gurion," one leading historian of the time wrote, "who also saw Nasser as the equivalent of the modern Turkish leader Mustafa Kemal Ataturk, a man capable of moving his people from backwardness to a position of towering strength that would endanger Israel's future."[68]

As the Israeli prime minister told one of his aides around this time, "I could not sleep at night, not even one second. I had one fear in my heart: a combined attack by all the Arab armies."[69]

Developments on several other fronts were helping to reinforce Israeli fears. Particularly important was the violent and deeply unstable border between the Gaza Strip and Egypt on the one hand and Israel on the other. Palestinian irregulars—fedayeen or "sacrificers"—often tried to cross the border to attack Israel, and the Egyptian authorities tried, with varying degrees of success, to control them.

Much of this cross-border movement was a result of the displacement and dispossession of around seven hundred thousand Palestinians in the course of the 1948 war. Many of these refugees were simply searching for relatives, returning to their homes, searching for possessions, or harvesting crops. Some were also nomadic bedouin and others were involved in smuggling hashish, but a few wanted to carry out revenge attacks and strike Israeli civilians, even if the best estimates of the day put this number in a small minority.[70]

By 1954, there was a vicious circle of perpetual violence—attacks and retaliation by one side provoking yet more attacks and retaliation by the other. Unarmed Palestinian infiltrators were confronted by trigger-happy Israeli soldiers and therefore returned in organized, armed bands. Israeli soldiers sometimes responded to provocations with what one historian has called "barbaric acts that can only be described as war crimes," such as the dumping of 120 innocent Arab civilians in the Arava Desert without water.[71] Ill feeling and mistrust between Arab and Jew were growing fast, particularly when Israel's leader, David Ben-Gurion, and his defense chiefs drew up a policy of responding to pinprick fedayeen raids with "massive retaliation" against the neighboring countries the attackers had come from. Only such a hard-hitting response, argued hawks like Gen. Moshe Dayan, would deter would-be attackers.

On the night of October 14, commandos of Unit 101, led by Maj. Ariel Sharon, attacked the Jordanian village of Qibya in revenge for a fedayeen assault, a few days before, on the Israeli village of Yehud, in which a Jewish woman and her two children had been killed. Sharon's men made a well-planned and coordinated attack, using bazookas and Bangalore torpedoes to blow up forty-five buildings, including the village school, and destroyed the water supply, but killed sixty-nine civilians, mainly women and children, in the process.

Sharon later tried to excuse his actions by claiming that "some Arab families must have stayed in their homes rather than running away" and that in the dark his men had been unable to search the large houses and cellars before placing explosives in them.[72] The UN observer who inspected the scene disagreed, arguing that "the inhabitants had been forced by heavy fire to stay inside until their homes were blown up over them."[73] But while the UN Security Council fiercely condemned the raid, which also horrified Israeli doves like Moshe Sharett, Ben-Gurion pointed to the provocation by Arab irregulars, claiming that at least 421 Israeli citizens had been killed by fedayeen over the preceding four years.

Similar raids were conducted by both fedayeen and Israeli soldiers throughout 1954 and beyond, leaving the civilians on the front line who were caught up in the attacks, as well as the leaders and the general public on both sides, feeling shocked, traumatized, and humiliated. The worst was still to come. A general election in Israel was looming and, wanting to look tough in front of Israel's general public after the hanging of two Israeli agents, the leaders in Tel Aviv decided to retaliate by conducting a brutal raid on Gaza.[74] On February 28, an Israeli force that was led, once again, by Ariel Sharon left thirty-six Egyptian soldiers dead and dozens more wounded as the result of an attack that Sharon claimed had been provoked by the death of an Israeli orange-grove worker but which Palestinian militants said had really been a bloodless assault on an Israeli water-storage facility.

Most of the Israeli attacks were directed at Jordan—even though nearly all of the fedayeen raids were launched from Egyptian territory—and Nasser thought it was only a matter of time before Egypt felt the full force of Israeli might. He also knew that Egypt was painfully vulnerable to any such attack. According to its senior commanders, Egypt at this time only had six serviceable warplanes because the air force was too short of spare parts to maintain the remaining thirty. To make matters worse, its army only had enough tank ammunition to sustain one hour of combat and nearly two-thirds of its armor was in desperate need of repair.[75] Munzel's outburst to Avri Seidenwerg, some months before, had not been full of exaggeration and hyperbole after all.[76]

It was at this point, according to those who knew him closely, that Nasser's priorities completely changed. Although he was still deeply committed to modernizing Egypt and its economy, he now decided to make Egypt's ability to defend itself a priority. His close confidant, adviser, and speechwriter, Mohamed Heikal, wrote that the 1955 Gaza raid was seen "as a message from Ben-Gurion to Nasser that building hospitals and schools and steel mills was not going to protect Egypt from a ruthless neighbour."[77] As Egypt was rocked by mass demonstrations against Israel, Nasser was also stung by accusations that he was not doing enough to protect his country and knew that he risked losing face in front of the Arab masses. He now ordered a huge increase in the military budget, deployed a large contingent to the Gaza Strip, and broke off his ongoing secret communication with Moshe Sharett.[78]

This humiliating raid also prompted the Egyptians to ratchet up their support for the fedayeen. Up until this point, the Egyptians had had a consistent and firm policy of curbing Palestinian infiltration into Israel.[79] But on March 15, Gen. Abdul Hakim Amer, Nasser's chief of staff, arrived in Gaza to establish a new fedayeen force, under the command of Col. Mustafa Hafez of the Egyptian army, which would be specially trained in hit-and-run raids inside Israel. The 141 Battalion had just fifty volunteers to begin with, most of whom had been recruited from the local jail, where they were being held for illegal immigration. By the end of the year, the number of recruits had swelled to over seven hundred. Palestinian leaders were invited from Gaza to Cairo, where they were offered not the cheap accommodations they were used to but the luxury of the Shepheard Hotel, a favored venue of rich Westerners. Feted by ministers and the Egyptian press, they were then given the honor of being introduced to the president himself. The Gaza raid had infuriated the Egyptians as much as it alarmed them. Now Cairo had done all it could to provoke Tel Aviv.

The relationship between Israel and Egypt was degenerating into a series of never-ending and fast-escalating tit-for-tat reprisals. Besides building up his armed forces, Nasser had also made a number of statements supporting Syria and Jordan against Israeli expansion, and in Israeli eyes was responsible for encouraging fedayeen attacks against the Jewish state, or at the very least not doing more to stop them. "The seizure of the SS *Bat Galim* is but the latest expression of the Egyptian government's scorn for the Security Council and its resolutions," wrote Abba Eban, Tel Aviv's ambassador to the UN, which "must be viewed against the background of the mounting number of murderous Egyptian attacks in Israeli territory in recent weeks."[80]

There were other ways in which Nasser's actions reinforced Israel's growing sense of fear about the man who was at the Egyptian helm. Just a few weeks before he sent two Israeli agents to the gallows, members of the militant Muslim Brotherhood organization had carried out an unsuccessful attempt to kill him, firing eight shots at a distance of twenty-five feet. Nasser somehow survived and immediately instigated a crackdown on the group's members that was brutal even by Egyptian standards. Around seven hundred members were rounded up during the first two days of the repression and one hundred and forty officers dismissed, while a People's Court was set up shortly afterward in which some suspects were not even represented. The crackdown continued well into 1955 and the total number of those arrested and sent to wretched prisons may have exceeded twenty thousand. The final tally of those who may have been killed is impossible to guess. If Nasser could use such brutality against his own people, wondered planners in Tel Aviv, what was he capable of doing to his enemies abroad?

Though in the eyes of Israeli chiefs Nasser was undoubtedly a growing danger, it was less easy to see exactly how this threat might materialize. The idea of the Egyptian leader making an outright, premeditated attack on the Jewish state seemed most unlikely: every time his forces, or those of any Arab state, clashed with the Israeli Defense Forces, the result was the same. In the 1948–9 war, as well as during the Gaza raid in February 1955, the Arab forces had, with a few notable exceptions, been immediately overwhelmed by the vastly superior fighting power of their enemy. Having served, with distinction, in the 1948 war and seen firsthand the capabilities of the army that confronted him, Nasser was wise enough to know how heavy the human—and political—price of another such conflict would be. In the course of a war in which he had personally witnessed "the fires of hell" and endured "the saddest day of my life," he had vowed to "reflect a thousand times before sending our soldiers to war."[81] Like every Arab leader worth his salt, Nasser did of course pay lip service to the "duty" of "liberating" Palestine: in his work *The Philosophy of the Revolution*, he wrote that "when the Palestinian crisis arose, I had the firm conviction that the combat in Palestine was not a combat on foreign soil, and that it was not at all a question of sentiment but of the duty of legitimate self-defence." But in practice he knew only too well that any such actions on the battlefield would be an act of self-destructive folly.

Israeli planners feared that the threat to peace and security in the region was a subtle one. It was, for example, possible to envisage a situation in which Nasser ordered his soldiers not to make an outright attack on Israel, as in 1948, but instead to launch a retaliatory border raid that would pro-voke further Israeli retribution, and then to escalate with dramatic speed.

It was also possible that, instead of unleashing a premeditated attack, the Egyptian leader could be pushed into it by sheer force of popular pressure, for there could be circumstances in which, without taking some hard-hitting measures against Israel, Nasser could have lost face with the Arab masses, who otherwise might have seen him as weak and lacking resolve. Such an attack on Israel might have been close to military and political suicide, but Nasser could conceivably have calculated that he had more to gain from taking such dire risks than from doing nothing.

Israeli strategists may have felt that such a reaction would have been entirely in keeping with an individual who prided himself on being "one of the people" and totally in touch with the feelings of the Egyptian masses. To call Nasser a populist is an exaggeration, because no political leader can ever be ruled by the mob. But he did enjoy meeting his fellow nationals face-to-face, loved popular and traditional food and music, and in the same way may have supported the Algerian rebels because he felt that their cause, one of true pan-Arabism, was one that chimed with the sentiments and loyalties of the Egyptian people.

Anyone who had personally witnessed Nasser, or any other Middle East leader, addressing large groups of local people would have been aware of the dangers of his being swept along by the crowd: the French journalist Jean Lacouture, for example, personally witnessed a stormy visit to the University of Cairo in early 1954 by Nasser and Naguib, who were met by loud jeering and demands to "give us arms for the canal and for Palestine."[82] An occupational hazard when confronting mobs, perhaps, but could Nasser be relied upon to resist it?

Judging from some of his behavior, the Israelis had reason to think that he could not be trusted at all. For Nasser's populist streak had become plain to see in the summer of 1956, when he announced the nationalization of the Suez Canal Company. No one in Egypt had demanded this, but Nasser may well have come up with the idea and pursued it because he knew that, if he portrayed it as a genuinely patriotic measure, it would be a hugely popular move. By nationalizing the Suez Canal Company and seizing its assets, he could claim that he was giving his country and its people some reparation for the damage that the canal had once caused them—a large number of Egyptian lives had been lost during the long years of construction—as well as the revenues that it had lost in the intervening years. "The canal is Egyptian and should stay Egyptian," he argued, and the company should be put "in the name of the people" at the expense of the British who were "exploiters," "arrogant," and "colonialists" who lived off the "blood and sacrifices" of others. Yet this wish to make the West "go choke on its fury"—a phrase that was broadcast repeatedly on Egyptian radio throughout the summer of 1956—was an emotional rather than a rational one: almost certainly, Nasser hugely underestimated the massive Western reaction to his act of nationalization and did so because he was too easily blinded by a desire to please the Egyptian masses.

There were other occasions when Nasser seemed dangerously torn between the reasoning statesman and the man of the mob, heightening fears that he could not be trusted. When speaking on Egyptian radio and broadcasting on Voice of the Arabs, for example, he often used popular words and expressions—the Iraqi leader was a "traitor," King Hussein of Jordan "a midget," and, to use a humiliating Arab term, "the son of a woman"—which were totally undignified and hardly fitting of an international statesman. Yet hours later he would be meeting world leaders and envoys such as Selwyn Lloyd, Guy Mollet, Robert Anderson, and Eugene Black, addressing them with a calm and wholly sensible demeanor. The danger, in Israeli eyes, was that Nasser himself, or his people as a whole, would at some point be emboldened to challenge the Jewish state in the same way he had the British over Suez and the French over North Africa. And there were circumstances in which that might happen.

One would be if Nasser found a strong following not just in his own country or even within the Arab world but on the international stage. If this happened, then it was possible he might calculate that he could attack Israel, or other countries, with virtual impunity, assuming that other countries would come to his assistance. It was exactly such a status that he seemed to have acquired by the summer of 1955, as a result of the Bandung Conference held in April that year. For Nasser had made a huge impression on representatives of the twenty-nine countries that attended this international summit: speaking before a large and distinguished audience, the young thirty-seven-year-old leader had given a remarkable and compelling performance that had made a considerable impact on those listening.

Suddenly Egypt seemed to have found friends and admirers in countries the world over—notably Yugoslavia, India, Ghana, China, and Indonesia—and his new international status deeply impressed the Egyptian masses: "[O]n 27 April 1955," wrote a journalist who watched the president's return, "a warm breeze seemed to pass between the man and the crowd . . . a jeep emerged bearing a Nasser who stood tall, his bronze face relaxed into a broad laugh, carrying after him the unrestrained crowd."[83] And suddenly Israel had reason to fear the power of the man who was standing at the Egyptian helm, particularly if he succeeded in exploiting this new prestige and stardom to unify some of the Arab states and become a ringleader of a new anti-Israeli alliance.

There was another scenario that Israeli planners dreaded. If Nasser succeeded in obtaining the world's best weapons—weapons that were on par with those that Israel already possessed but which might even have a technological edge—then he, his people, and his fellow Arabs might feel emboldened. Again, the danger was not that he would actively use them to make any kind of first strike against the Jewish state—something that would of course provoke massive retaliation—but that he would act in a more assertive and audacious manner than ever before. He might send more fedayeen into Israel, perhaps provoke its army into making retaliatory raids that could then lead them into a trap, or perhaps step up diplomatic pressure on Tel Aviv—for example, by using such weapons as a political bargaining chip. What would happen if he publicly promised to surrender those weapons if, in return, Israel returned to its 1948 borders? Such a move would hugely embarrass both Tel Aviv and Washington, which had so much financial leverage over Israel and was in a position to exert immense political pressure on its leadership.

It was hardly surprising, then, that in the course of 1954 and 1955 Israel's spy service was searching hard for any signs that the Egyptian leader was managing to find a supply of the arms he so much wanted to acquire.

CHAPTER SIX
Killing Mustafa

In the early evening of July 12, 1956, a young Egyptian colonel by the name of Mustafa Hafez was at his home in Gaza, overlooking the Mediterranean Sea, and enjoying a quiet drink in the company of two other officers with whom he spent a good deal of time off duty. Unexpectedly, a messenger suddenly appeared from a nearby base with some dramatic news. A Palestinian Arab called Mahmoud El Talwouka had just crossed the border from Israel, the messenger informed him, and was now in custody. Because El Talwouka claimed to have an important message to relay to the Egyptian authorities, the junior officers at the barracks had decided that their colonel needed to be kept closely informed.

Colonel Hafez decided that it would be worth his while meeting the agent, despite the inconvenience of interrupting such a pleasant evening. After all, El Talwouka was well known to the Egyptian intelligence services and had previously acted on their behalf as an informer for several years, gathering information about what was happening on the Israeli side of the border in return for cash payments. Given the tension between Israeli and Egypt over the past year or so, Hafez wasted no time in joining the messenger and driving a short distance to the interrogation block where the prisoner was being held.

When the contingent of officers reached his cell, El Talwouka handed over a package that he had kept hidden inside his baggy trousers. It was, he said, an instruction manual for a radio transmitter and it contained details of a secret code that Israeli agents, operating within Egyptian territory, might use. Hafez was intrigued and slowly prized the package open, unable to stop something from falling out and onto the floor.

At precisely this moment, a deafening explosion tore through the building. Soldiers scrambled to the scene, rummaging through the debris of broken glass, brick, and wood to find the bodies of Hafez, another officer, and El Talwouka, all soaked in blood and very badly wounded but still alive. They were rushed to the nearest hospital, on the outskirts of Gaza, but within hours all three men were dead.

Just days later, a package arrived at a post office in the Jordanian capital, Amman, that was addressed to another colonel in the Egyptian army, Salah Mustafa. The colonel was driven to the post office by his chauffeur and picked up the parcel, which was sealed with the official stamp of the UN headquarters in Jerusalem and wrapped in its unmistakable colors and logos. He didn't hesitate in tearing the parcel open almost as soon as he got into his car and his chauffeur drove off. Inside he was surprised to find a copy of *The Commander and the Man*, the memoirs of Hitler's field marshal, Gerd von Rundstedt, which he probably assumed had been sent by one of his many friends at the UN offices who knew of his deep interest in military history. He failed, however, to spot the cleverly concealed bomb that was hidden inside, and when he opened the book, an explosion tore his car in half. Within hours he too was dead.

The state-run Egyptian press knew that it could not ignore the deaths of the two soldiers, because word always got around fast when someone important had died. But it did its best to disguise what had happened. On July 13, a short column in one Cairo newspaper announced simply, "Colonel [Mustafa] Hafez, who was stationed in the Gaza Strip, was killed when his vehicle ran across a mine. His body was transferred to El Hafish and from there flown to Cairo." Salah Mustafa's death, meanwhile, was blamed on the actions of a lone assassin who had allegedly thrown a hand grenade at his car as it drove past. The Egyptian propagandists may have been wondering how to portray this fictional assassin, who could perhaps have been fictionalized as a disgruntled Arab, a criminal, or an Israeli agent. But they never had to reach a decision because the news was overshadowed by an event that was vastly more dramatic—President Nasser's decision to nationalize the Suez Canal Company.

For the Israelis, the assassination of the two Egyptian officers was a crucial part of their strategy to curb the infiltration into their country of Arab fedayeen, whom they regarded as a serious menace. Colonel Hafez was viewed in Tel Aviv as a vital link in the militia's chain of command because he acted as chief of intelligence in the Gaza Strip and had also been personally entrusted by President Nasser with the task of training the fedayeen and organizing their forays across the border. Not only that, but the Israeli chiefs were well aware of his outstanding talents as a commander in an army they regarded as largely talentless. He had been highly experienced in combat, having served in the war against Israel in 1948, during which he had fought bravely and subsequently endured not just captivity but also a heroic escape from his enemy, undertaking an extremely long and arduous trek back to Egyptian lines. And his excellent tactical sense had propelled him to a high rank in the Egyptian army at the relatively tender age of thirty-six.

As Egypt's military attaché in Amman, Salah Mustafa was preparing to take a similar role for the fedayeen units that were based in Jordan. The Arab irregulars had launched their first raids the previous summer, and though these were largely ineffectual, the more hawkish authorities in Tel Aviv argued that drastic action would be required if they were to prevent the fedayeen from making much more daring, serious, and deadly attacks as they gradually became more experienced.

The Israeli chiefs also knew that, more than anything else, their ability to deter the Arab insurgents depended not just on their arms and soldiers, or tactics and planning, but on something much more important—fear. Everything, in their eyes, was psychological, for as long as the Arabs feared Israel and its retaliation, then the Israelis felt confident they could deter the fedayeen. But if, for whatever reason, that psychological shield was seen to fall, if it ceased to speak in a "language of force," then Israel would become vulnerable.[84] If, for example, the Egyptians did manage to acquire the battlefield rockets that the

German scientists had been trying so hard to develop, then it seemed only too likely that the fedayeen would regard them as defensive air cover under which they could launch much more ambitious and daring assaults against the Jewish state.

For President Nasser, the killing of the two colonels was a stark and brutal reminder of the danger that Israel posed to him personally and to his country. He had, of course, needed little reminding, for his intelligence chiefs had previously claimed to have unearthed sophisticated and determined bids—"too many to count," according to one Nasser crony—by foreign spy agencies to depose or assassinate the Egyptian premier from the time of the Suez Crisis.[85]

It was at this time, as a historian of the British secret service has written, that Prime Minister Anthony Eden instructed MI6 to put "thuggery" back on the agenda and to draw up plans—known within the service as "the horrors"—to eliminate Nasser once and for all. "I want Nasser murdered," one minister later remembered Eden saying.[86] The chief MI6 representative who covered the region allegedly admitted to his American counterpart that the British government was interested in assassinating Nasser and said that his agents had been in close touch with dissident elements in Egypt, prompting an alarmed U.S. representative, James Eichelberger, to leak much of what he heard back to Cairo.[87] And in the summer of 1956, the Egyptians reportedly discovered two separate British spy rings, one led by the business manager of the British-owned Arab News Agency, the other by two British diplomats. Both were said to be helping student organizations stir up popular protests that would then give London an excuse to get involved.[88]

Other plans by MI6 included using execution squads, exploding electric razors, and, as part of a project that scientist Peter Wright regarded as too difficult to implement, poison gas.[89] The French government reportedly planned to use rubber dinghies to send a commando team from its Cairo embassy, which was very close to the west bank of the Nile, and bomb the building where Nasser was then staying.[90] A number of Western-hired mercenaries also allegedly arrived in Cairo, only to promptly disappear, while Mossad hired a Greek waiter working in Groppi's restaurant—which arranged much of the presidential catering—to poison Nasser's coffee. The plan fell apart when the waiter lost his nerve at the last minute and gave himself up.[91]

Various secret services appear to have tried other dirty tricks. In particular, Mohamed Heikal claimed that an enemy intelligence service had cleverly forged a number of tape recordings, using a series of well-edited extracts, to compile several fictional speeches and conversations. In one such recording, speakers on Cairo's state-run official radio were heard arguing that Middle Eastern oil belonged only to the Arabs, not to the West, and that the profits of its sale should be shared among all the Arab peoples. In another tape, which supposedly contained a monitored conversation between Nasser and the Egyptian military attaché in Amman, the Egyptian leader could be heard discussing plans to overthrow King Hussein of Jordan. In both cases, the Egyptians hotly denied that any such conversations or broadcasts had ever been made and held a series of press conferences as part of a determined effort to discredit them.[92]

One of the main reasons Britain and France wanted regime change in Cairo was that each was concerned about its supply of oil. The Suez Crisis represented all of the British government's worst fears about the threat that Nasser seemed to pose. Anthony Eden argued that when Nasser nationalized the British- and French-owned Suez Canal Company on July 26, 1956, the Egyptian leader appeared to have Britain, and much of the Western world, with "his hand on our windpipe." Huge amounts of oil constantly moved through the canal from Iran, Saudi Arabia, Kuwait, and other Middle Eastern exporters to Western markets, and the nationalization of the company would—in theory, at least—allow Nasser to open and close the canal at will. This would give him huge economic and political leverage over Britain, whose economy was heavily dependent upon oil imports.

To the British, it seemed that the extraordinary charisma of the Egyptian leader would enable him to galvanize much of the Arab world and conceivably bestow upon him huge influence, or even outright control, over its flow of oil. In early 1958 Syria had already merged with Egypt to create a United Arab Republic, and it soon seemed possible that Iraq—a leading oil producer—would follow and fall directly into

Nasser's orbit. The Egyptian leader also had many loyalists in Saudi Arabia and Kuwait, and it was not inconceivable that, at some stage, they could seize power in the usual, customary way—by armed insurrection or a high-level coup.

The British and the Americans were also concerned about the Soviet threat to the flow of Middle Eastern oil, and were desperately seeking to win friends and influence in the Arab world in order to keep the Soviets out. In 1954 London had made moves to build a new defensive treaty, the Baghdad Pact, that would help maintain regional security: under the terms of this deal, each of the signatory countries—Britain, Iraq, Turkey, Iran, and Pakistan—would defend one another in the event of any attack.[93] But Nasser saw this agreement as just another clever British ploy to meddle in the Middle East and to bolster the regional influence of his main Arab rival, Iraq, at the expense of his own. In his eyes it was, quite simply, well-disguised neocolonialism. In the days that followed, the state-controlled press ran an intense propaganda campaign, revealing the full extent of the president's anger against the "lackeys of imperialism" whom he felt had succumbed to British pressure by signing up.

Nasser had another reason, quite apart from the hostility of the Eden administration, to fear the British. For Egypt had been ruled by Great Britain for seventy years, and this experience as the imperial underdog had inevitably left an indelible mark on the Egyptian mind-set. Through the eyes of Gamal Nasser and his fellow nationals, Britain was still essentially an imperial power, one that had not quite come to terms with the much more modest role it had found itself playing since 1945. The Suez attack of 1956 was seen to have been perpetrated by a deeply untrustworthy country that still had strongly imperial instincts toward the land it once ruled. As one ambassador wrote, "'[T]he British' had long been the bogeyman of Egyptian folklore, the 'hidden hand' behind Egyptian politics and policies, the puppeteers pulling the strings of Egyptian financial, economic, educational, agricultural and all other aspects of policy and development."[94]

Such sentiments helped to engender a love of national independence, or fear of foreign control, that defined Nasserism. Outside influences of any sort, but particularly British influences, were for him out of the question, except, perhaps, in moments of absolute desperation and emergency. "The Arab countries are for the Arabs" (*Bilad al-Arab lil Arab*) was one of his favorite and most frequently uttered sayings. "We don't need custodians," he told *Life* magazine in an article he penned in August 1959, and he often told his close friend Mohamed Heikal the same thing.[95]

Contemporaries noticed the intense mistrust, even hatred, of the British that many Egyptians harbored. In a letter written at Cairo's Grand Continental Hotel in February 1915, T. E. Lawrence described how "the Egyptian townsmen do hate us so. I thought it was only a coldness . . . but it is a most burning dislike." Children were sometimes brought up to admire Napoleon for defying the British, not just on the battlefield but even in exile on St. Helena. Ordinary Cairo civilians spoke openly of how they despised the British because, they felt, the British had always despised the Egyptians.[96] Such sentiments were often difficult for travelers to understand, because on a personal level many of the local people were enormously warm and welcoming to all of their Western visitors, from Britain or elsewhere: "[T]here was no hostility," wrote London's chief representative just four years after Suez, "even when I revealed myself as a British diplomat, toward the representative of a nation with which Egypt had so recently been at war."[97]

In the light of their historical experiences, the Egyptians could hardly be blamed for fearing foreign attack and subjugation, not just by Britain but by any foreign—particularly Western—power. Nasser also deeply mistrusted the French, for example, partly because he felt they were so closely allied with the British, as the events at Suez were to reveal. But there was also tension between Cairo and Paris because Nasser actively created it: if he regarded the French as a threat to Egypt's national security, it was not because Paris had aggressive imperial instincts, in the way he thought the British did, but because he provoked just such a reaction.

While the French did, of course, have just as much reason as the British to fear for their oil, their primary concern was for the security of their North African colonies. For while Morocco and Tunisia had won independence in March 1956, Algeria still fell under direct French control. Algeria was a big piece of a fast-diminishing empire, one that Paris had no wish at all to surrender. Home to a million and a half Frenchmen, and with three northern *départements* (Algiers, Oran, and Constantine) falling under the authority of French law, Algeria was legally and culturally an extension of the French mainland that no mainstream Parisian politician was willing to give up. In addition, France wanted to retain its influence in Syria and Lebanon, which had both won independence in 1943, and to stop Nasser from undermining it.

Soon after he had seized power in 1952, Nasser's ability to galvanize Arab nationalist sentiment against the established order had been noted in Paris, where he was quickly identified as a primary threat to French national interests. But fears for the security of Algeria, and of the malign influence of Nasser, had been fully aroused in the winter of 1954, when heavy rioting broke out among the local population. Led by the nationalist Front de Libération Nationale, the protesters had a simple and powerful message: they wanted the end of French rule.

The French authorities felt sure that the Egyptians had helped to stir up the trouble. The Egyptian military, they alleged, had secretly moved large quantities of arms from its main base at Sollum, in the Western Desert, into the hands of the FLN. Not only that, but they thought Gen. Francisco Franco—keen to embarrass the French—had allowed the Egyptian military attaché, Col. Abdul Mun'im al-Nagar, to organize a supply line running through Morocco and a training mission for Algerian fighters. In March 1956 the French intelligence service published a report claiming that Algerian commandos were being trained in Egypt, despite personal assurances by Nasser to the foreign minister Christian Pineau that there were no such links. Yet while the Egyptians appear to have supplied some arms to the FLN, and Cairo radio broadcast a constant stream of inflammatory propaganda, the French probably much exaggerated the influence and involvement of Cairo in a rebellion that ultimately had its own internal causes.[98]

This subversive influence, through French eyes, was the radical, dangerous side to Nasserism that the president had revealed in his booklet *The Philosophy of the Revolution*, published in 1954. In this publication he had argued that the world is composed of three separate, if interrelated, circles of political and cultural power and influence—the Arab, the Islamic, and the African. Although he claimed that Egypt had a central, pivotal role in shaping and leading the Arabs' destiny, he did not appear to envisage a separate Egyptian identity: Egypt's future, in other words, was ultimately inseparable from the future of the rest of the Arab world. These were the words of the same leader who in 1956 had drawn up a new constitution describing Egypt as "part of the Arab nation," and whose speeches were invariably full of references to "Arabs from the Atlantic to the [Persian] Gulf." For the French authorities, this viewpoint was a recipe for trouble in its North African colonies, and was wholly consistent with the leader they felt sure was actively stirring up nationalist unrest there.

Seeking regional allies against Nasser, the French government looked to Israel. The Jewish state offered the French what intelligence it had on Egypt's support for the Algerian rebels but exaggerated the extent of that support.[99] Israel also had strong supporters in Paris, partly because it was represented by a brilliant lobbyist, Josef Nachmias, but also because some of the top French diplomats were veterans of the Resistance movement and had worked closely with French Jews to fight Nazi rule in Europe. This was true of Pierre-Eugène Gilbert, France's flamboyant ambassador to Israel, who had strong pro-Jewish sympathies and now worked hard to build closer ties between the two countries. It was through his influence that, in the summer of 1954, at a time when unrest in Algeria was beginning to stir, the Israeli Defense Ministry succeeded in winning its first arms contracts with France. By the time Shimon Peres, the Israeli deputy defense minister, arrived in Paris for talks, the French authorities had already decided to deliver jets, tanks, guns, and radar to the Israelis, who soon received their first delivery of Dassault Ouragan jet fighters together with a commitment to send a squadron of the very latest model, the Mystère II. These deliveries undoubtedly breached a secret agreement that France had struck with Britain and the U.S.A. not to export arms to any other parties, but the Parisian authorities hardly seemed bothered.

There was another reason, besides the defense of his homeland, Nasser and his senior generals were so keen to sponsor a new arms program. For even the possibility of a heavy raid by Israel, an incursion by Britain, or an attack by France was a threat not just to his regime's stability but also to its prestige. By being able to defend Egypt from attack, Nasser avoided losing face before the Arab masses he loved. By possessing an impressive and showy array of rockets, his standing before them—in the short term, at least—was bound to rise, particularly in the eyes of other Arab countries, notably Iraq, which he regarded as an intense rival to lead the Arab world. Developing a rocket program was, in this respect, also about domestic and international politics—being seen to stand tall and being taken seriously by your various audiences. It was no coincidence that, according to an unpublished thesis on his speeches by a student at Beirut University, Nasser's favorite rhetorical words were "honor," "glory," "dignity," and "pride."[100]

In this respect, the rocket program served the same function as other policies and schemes of the Nasser era. The hugely ambitious scheme to build the Aswan High Dam, for example, which would have reclaimed a large area of the desert and increased Egypt's cultivable land by one-third, not just promised to enhance the dignity of the *fellahin* desert people but had also become an unmistakable emblem of the regime, an unmissable symbol of its sophistication, progress, and, despite its dependency on foreign funding, of Egypt's independence.

So it was very revealing that, in July 1956, the American decision to withdraw an offer to fund the Aswan Dam was followed just days later by Nasser's announcement to nationalize the Suez Canal Company, using the proceeds to fund the project: feeling rejected and humiliated by Western powers over one issue, he sought to compensate by getting his own back over another. His sense of injured pride was undoubtedly inflamed even more because of the way in which Washington had phrased its message: Nasser's appeal for financing the dam, announced the U.S. State Department, was not viable because of the "weakness of the Egyptian economy" and "the instability of the regime"—references that the infuriated president took as a grave insult against his country and his own rule.

For the Israelis, if Nasser enhanced Egyptian prestige then he would become more dangerous: "[T]he growth in Nasser's prestige is bound to make him want to destroy Israel, not by a direct attack but first by a 'peace offensive' and an attempt to reduce our territory, especially in the Negev, and when refused, he will attack us," wrote Ben-Gurion in the summer of 1956.[101]

But for Nasser, there was no better way of bolstering his reputation and defending his country against France and Britain as well as Israel than by instigating a new arms program.

CHAPTER SEVEN
Egypt Under Attack

F or Pres. Gamal Nasser and his staff, the evening of Wednesday, October 31, 1956 began more or less like any other. The president entertained important visitors most nights, and on that occasion the Indonesian ambassador had been invited to dine at Koubbeh Palace, the former residence of King Farouk. This was not where Nasser usually lived or where he liked to stay—he much preferred his modest house in the Manshia district of Alexandria—but Koubbeh was well suited to his steady stream of visitors from the world over.

Evening meals in the company of the Egyptian premier were a protracted affair, starting late and often continuing into the small hours. By the standards of international diplomacy, they were also modest, for long before his diabetes had been diagnosed, Nasser had always been a man of quite simple tastes, always opting wherever possible for traditional Egyptian dishes such as white cheese, fava beans, falafel, *tamiya*, and *mulukhiya*. As he was a devout Muslim, there was, of course, no alcohol. His only real indulgence was tobacco, and he got through several cigarette packs a day.

That evening, more so than most, the hosts and their guests certainly had much to talk about. For just two days before, on Monday evening, news had reached Cairo that Egyptian positions in the Sinai Desert had been bombed by Israeli jets and that, at the border village of Kafr Qasim,

Israeli border police had opened fire on a number of Palestinian civilians, killing forty-eight. Soon afterward, in the pitch dark, Israeli paratroops had seized a key strategic point in the Sinai Desert and were now threatening to advance.

But shortly after six o'clock, while the visitors and their hosts were talking over drinks and well before the start of their meal, a series of enormous roars and explosions suddenly shattered the genteel calm and tranquility. Such was the force of the explosions that the entire building shook and the ground trembled beneath them, as the terrified guests looked at each other in stunned silence. Nasser was not one to show any sign of panic—he had once continued delivering a speech, imploring his audience to stay calm, after a would-be assassin had fired eight shots at him—and he coolly left the dining room, running up the stairs and onto the roof to find out what was going on.[102]

In the dark he could make out British jets swooping over Cairo's airfields and airports before dropping high explosives, incendiary bombs, and napalm that blew up the Egyptian jets lined up on the tarmac. The roar of the jets as they attacked was loud enough but, together with the bombs they were dropping and the explosions they were causing, the noise was earsplitting and the scene terrifying. Just as the British premier Anthony Eden had been sitting down to dinner, entertaining King Faisal of Iraq, when on July 26 he heard the shattering news that Nasser had nationalized the Suez Canal Company, so, too, by a curious irony, was Nasser sitting down to dinner when Eden launched his military response three months later.

At first the Israeli attack, two days before, had seemed to Nasser and his generals like another hard-hitting raid, similar to those that had happened every so often in previous years. But now, as British planes swooped over Cairo's airfields, Egypt was plainly facing a coordinated attack that was more akin to invasion. The country was in grave danger. For this was the opening salvo of Operation Musketeer, the bid by the British, French, and Israeli governments to seize control of the Suez Canal.[103]

Almost as soon as the bombs fell on Cairo, Nasser personally took command of the battle, barely hesitating to order a series of retaliatory moves. Seizing the phone, he ordered his military chiefs to move what was left of his air force to the relative safety of the Sudan and Saudi Arabia, and to sink ships in the Suez Canal to stop any international traffic from moving along it. In the days that followed, as fears grew of an outright invasion of Egypt by the allied force, he also rallied his people with almost Churchillian rhetoric, vowing to fight for every corner of his country and promising to train guerrilla militia forces to stand up to the imperialist enemies. Some members of his entourage crumbled psychologically almost as soon as the attack began, notably his long-term ally and confidant, Gen. Abdul Hakim Amer, who appears to have suffered some sort of nervous breakdown and instantly advocated an immediate surrender. But Nasser himself, whatever private doubts he may have harbored, never wavered in front of others.[104]

Just a week later, the fighting was over. By November 7, Nasser's men had lost control of much of the Sinai Desert and the territory surrounding the Suez Canal, which had been seized by British and French soldiers who had made airborne and seaborne landings. But despite the rapid progress of their soldiers on the ground, the allied governments had faced ferocious political resistance from the outside world and, with the Americans effectively imposing economic sanctions on them, had been forced to respect a UN-sponsored resolution to halt the campaign. "It's rather like blowing up a balloon and then putting a pin in it," sighed a deeply disappointed British chief of staff. "I had learnt this lesson when I was dropped from the Marlborough XI on the morning of our match against Rugby [school] at [Lord's cricket ground]: there is always something else ahead."[105]

In the short term, Nasser had succeeded in surviving a determined and organized assault by three allied powers, and by doing so had seized an astounding political and diplomatic victory and won the adulation of the Egyptian masses as well as popular opinion across the entire Arab world. But it was not a success that could have brought him any real comfort. Far from it, the week-long Suez War gave him every reason to fear for his own security along with that of his regime, his country, and his fellow Arabs. More so than at any previous time since the Second World War, Egypt seemed deeply vulnerable.

This was partly because of the very mixed, and sometimes wholly unreliable, performance of the Egyptian military. True, there were a few times and places during the Suez War when and where Nasser's army stood their ground and fought well, but in general the three invaders had met very little resistance. At El-Gamil Airport outside Cairo, barely a shot was fired at British parachutists as they dropped, while their French counterparts were also untroubled by the defenders of Port Fouad, who were persuaded by two local European residents to put down their arms and surrender.[106]

It was, however, in Sinai that the Egyptian military had suffered real humiliations. Again, the record was mixed, for, confronted by a numerically strong, coordinated, and highly determined Israeli attack, a good number of Nasser's soldiers had shown a real determination to fight, notably in the central sectors, Umm Qataf and Umm Shihan, where the defenders gave the Israelis "a very tough time indeed."[107] And at Abu-Ageila, the Israeli Seventh Armored Brigade had "a very tough fight" against the Egyptians.[108] But the truth was that, despite numerous acts of real personal bravery, many officers had panicked and fled, sometimes forcing Nasser himself to give fighting units detailed orders for withdrawal. Within just days, virtually the whole Sinai Peninsula had fallen into Israeli hands. The president felt that he had been spared only because Washington had put huge pressure on the allied force to pull back, and that he had been defeated "by my own army," which should have performed far better.[109] As a leading Egyptian general later admitted in private: "Everyone knows [about] our battle experience and so-called victories in 1956. A load of bull. I was in Sinai, I saw what happened. It was a debacle. No coordination of any kind, conflicting orders or no orders at all—and then we just turned and ran, officers in the lead."[110]

Of course Egyptian propagandists did their best to paint a very different picture. One official cable even claimed, quite fictitiously, that "the job of annihilating enemy forces at Gamil airport has ended," while another stated that "the total number of aircraft shot down this morning up to the issuing of this communique is fifteen."[111] And naturally the president himself did everything he could to hide his country's vulnerability: "In the first twenty-four hours of the fight," he told a huge Cairo crowd on November 2, "[we] had inflicted disastrous losses on the Israelis, so that Israel could not, for two days, foolishly buzz around and boast, as she had done previously," while the subsequent military withdrawal had been "more successful than I ever imagined."[112]

To bolster Egyptian defenses, Nasser had a number of options. He could have simply cracked down on the fedayeen, stopping them from crossing the border and provoking such massive Israeli retaliation. But even if this had been wholly practical along such a large, porous border, Nasser felt sure that it would make no difference: other than Moshe Sharett, who was Israel's prime minister for nearly two years in the mid-1950s, there was no other leader in Tel Aviv whom Nasser trusted. He felt that none of them was interested in peace and all were merely looking for excuses to attack the Arab world and seize more territory. The only options would be to find new friends abroad, or to build arms at home.

The Egyptian leader could, of course, have built up closer alliances with other Arab countries, perhaps exploiting a common fear and loathing of Israel to unite them. But despite their extra demographic weight, this would have given little protection against the Jewish state, or Britain and France, because the other Arab states were equally lacking in up-to-date hardware. After all, even a concerted effort by Syria, Iraq, and Egypt against Israel in 1948, when the newly created state had been in its infancy and at its most vulnerable, had ended in bloody defeat instead of the outright victory the Arab powers had hoped for. The strong, bitter rivalries within the Arab world—notably between Egypt, Iraq, and Saudi Arabia—had in any case made all Nasser's talk about "pan-Arab unity" just a hollow boast. The Syrians, for example, rejected any proposal that failed to give them a leading position, mainly because they considered themselves more truly Arab than the rest. The Jordanians feared being relegated to the role and status of a large, second-rate tribe. The Saudis were also deeply conscious of their standing, and feared sharing their vast oil wealth, while there were vast, fundamental religious and ethnic tensions inside Iraq that could not have been accommodated within a larger state. "Arab unity" was, in fact, a myth.

After centuries of being subjected to foreign rule, most Egyptians were deeply wary of close alliances with other countries that might have unnecessarily compromised their freedom and independence. This was why, by 1957, Cairo was starting to become a center for national-liberation movements the world over, particularly from colonial territories in Africa. Almost every African nationalist movement—but notably those in Kenya, Uganda, Tanganyika, and South Africa—had an office in Cairo where numerous pamphlets were published and messages were broadcast that decried the injustices of their respective countries' colonial rulers. Groups such as the Afro-Asian People's Solidarity Organization also set up headquarters in the Egyptian capital and hosted well-attended conferences that issued strongly worded condemnations of Western imperialism.

If alliances with any states outside the Arab world were unacceptable to Cairo, then another option was to remain neutral and then try to win support and arms from one of the superpowers. If Egypt remained unaligned, Nasser reasoned, then neither Russia nor the U.S.A. would regard it as a threat. Instead it was possible that they might try and lure him into an alliance by offering to supply him arms or economic support first.

This helps explain why Nasser now strove to maintain a strict neutrality between East and West.

To some degree this is what he did, and with some success, after 1955, when he was greatly influenced by the Indian leader Nehru and, more profoundly, by Marshal Tito, the elderly Croat leader who first visited Cairo in February 1955. In the space of a series of meetings on the Nile, both Nehru and Tito are thought to have deeply inspired the Egyptian leader, fueling his deep mistrust of foreign alliances that could compromise his country's independence. Weeks later, Nasser attended a high-profile international summit at Bandung in Indonesia, where his foreign policy was dubbed and proclaimed not as neutralism but something less negative—positive neutralism. His country was unaligned, in other words, but still actually heading somewhere.

Nasser hoped to remain essentially neutral but persuade the Americans to send arms. On seizing power in 1952, he and his fellow officers had initially enjoyed considerable goodwill from Washington, where they were regarded as a potential ally against Soviet influence in the Middle East. Almost right away, Nasser had cracked down hard on the Egyptian Communist Party, imprisoning nearly all of its leaders. The U.S. administration had then shown its support and gratitude by sending him a "personal gift" of three million dollars, delivered in two suitcases that were personally couriered by a senior CIA agent, Miles Copeland, on behalf of President Eisenhower.

Nasser and Amer had at this time made a bid to buy arms from Washington but received a more complicated response than the one they hoped for. In return, the Americans had replied, the Egyptians had to sign up to a common defense agreement; otherwise, they reasoned, some of the best equipment could easily fall into the hands of an enemy. Yet this was exactly the type of restraint upon Egypt's national independence that Nasser wanted to avoid: he had built his career upon the rhetoric of Arab freedom and risked destroying his own credibility, as well as undermining his country's liberty, if he signed up to any such pact.

When the Israelis attacked Qibya on August 28, 1953, Nasser held back and instead appealed to the Americans to supply the arms he needed to defend his country. He immediately found supporters and sympathizers among some senior CIA officers, who argued strongly that such ties would help keep Nasser away from the Soviets: a detailed intelligence report on the man had described him as "vain, suspicious, confident, resilient, courageous, a risk-taker and obstinate"—exactly the sort of individual who might be susceptible to Russian approaches.[113] But the proposal met stiff opposition from the State Department, whose officers argued that the United States, along with Britain and France, had signed an international pact, the Tripartite Agreement, that prohibited the sale of arms to countries other than close allies.

After the Israeli raid on Gaza in 1955, Nasser tried his luck once again, summoning the U.S. ambassador, Henry A. Byroade, and presenting him with a list of all the occasions on which he had lobbied Washington for military support. "Up till now we have been asking for arms so that our army could be properly equipped. Now we are asking for them to save our lives. The situation has changed completely. Now I can't wait." His appeal seemed to be reaping rewards because some months later, in December, his finance minister, Dr. Abdul-Moneim Kayssouni, unexpectedly received a warm invitation to meet American leaders in Washington. Within weeks, on December 19, the U.S. administration offered Cairo a vast loan of $54 million—to be made quite unconditionally and without any strings attached at all—to enable the construction of a hugely ambitious hydroelectric program based on the Aswan Dam. And at the instigation of Washington, the Aswan Dam project would also get strong support from both London and the World Bank. Nasser was still wary because if the World Bank lent him money, then it would also have powers to supervise the Egyptian economy. But the deal fell apart in any case when it was effectively torpedoed by his many enemies, notably the Israelis and the French, who lobbied powerfully on Capitol Hill.

There was another reason any deal with the Americans would not have lasted long, had it been struck at all. The strong degree of mistrust between the two countries would have soon undermined it. When in 1954 the Egyptian authorities unearthed the Israeli spy ring that was carrying out Operation Susannah and hanged some of the perpetrators, the Americans responded by taking an overtly pro-Israeli line. Almost at once Washington canceled a new agreement on intelligence sharing and cooperation, and ended negotiations over the use of the waters from the River Jordan.[114] From this moment on, the Egyptian leader became supremely suspicious of any proposals put to him by the CIA team in Cairo.

Nasser's total refusal to enter into an alliance with the U.S.A., or any other Western power, may also explain why he alienated Washington in the summer of 1956 by granting diplomatic recognition to the communist regime in China. As he was well aware, there was scarcely any better way of infuriating the Americans. He also angered the Eisenhower administration by initiating talks with the Soviets, whom he regarded as possible suppliers of arms. For in July 1955, aware that Nasser was growing impatient with the Americans and was therefore susceptible to its advances, the KGB sent one of its best agents, Dmitri Shepilov, to Cairo.

Shepilov had the perfect cover to work for Soviet intelligence because he was the editor of the Soviet newspaper *Pravda* and was due to visit Cairo that summer to report on the annual ceremonies that commemorated the 1952 revolution. He patiently waited his chance, attending a series of meetings and interviews that were supposedly connected with his work, before he was at last granted a private audience with the president. This was his opportunity to put the Kremlin's proposals forward.

It was in the course of that meeting that he relayed a message from Moscow—the Soviet Union was willing to go ahead and send Nasser arms, using Czechoslovakia as a conduit. The timing of the move was superb because news had just leaked out that the French had sold six squadrons of their latest plane, the Mystère IV, to Israel, and because Nasser had just made his own unsuccessful bid to persuade Washington to increase its own arms supplies to Egypt. As a result, the tactic and the message worked brilliantly. Within days, Nasser went on radio to make a dramatic announcement that stunned his people: "The West refuses us the means to defend our existence," he announced, so "we have just signed an arms contract with Czechoslovakia!" It was this deal that had also caused so much alarm in Washington, prompting a serious rethink of policy that led to an offer of unconditional support for the Aswan Dam project.

A few months later, after Britain and the U.S.A. withdrew pledges to give their support, Nasser turned to Moscow for assistance in building the Aswan Dam. By the late 1950s the Russians were starting to find an even greater influence in Cairo than before. Large numbers of advisers and contractors began to arrive to work on both military and civilian projects, and increasing numbers of shops started to sell East European goods. High-level representatives from every corner of the communist world—including Fidel Castro and China's foreign minister, Zhou Enlai—were by this stage often visiting the Egyptian capital for talks. Ordinary Egyptians began to joke about the relationship. When, on a hot summer's day, a man was seen in Cairo with his umbrella up, a friend stopped and asked him why he was protecting himself against the rain. "Didn't you hear this morning's weather report?" came the reply. "It is raining in Moscow."[115]

Once again, however, there was a serious downside, partly because of the loss of national independence and partly because any deal with the Soviets could embolden the Egyptian Communist Party, which Nasser regarded as a serious threat. He had outlawed the Egyptian communist party soon after seizing power and had written a booklet, *Communism as It Really Is*, arguing that it was a dangerous, atheistic movement. Although he borrowed ideas from communism, notably his extensive program of nationalization within Egypt, his hostility toward it as a political force never wavered.

During a trip he made to Moscow, shortly after the political union between Syria and Egypt, a sharp diplomatic exchange took place between Nasser and the Russian leader, Nikita Khrushchev, that fulfilled the

Egyptian leader's worst fears about the threat to his national independence. The official Soviet translator told Nasser that Khrushchev wanted him to end his ban on the Syrian Communist Party, a request the Egyptian leader regarded as an outrageous intrusion of the sovereignty of the United Arab Republic. Nasser replied curtly and sharply, prompting a startled Khrushchev to blame the sudden confrontation on a translation error.

But although his personal prestige and Egypt's self-defense plainly mattered to him enormously, Nasser had allowed the CERVA project to dry up by the eve of the Suez attack in October 1956. Although he stayed in Egypt for a further two years, Rolf Engel resigned from the program in the course of 1955, while Voss left Egypt and returned home the following year. The program had been an expensive disappointment, one that had failed to produce a working battlefield rocket.[116] But at some point in the months that followed the allied attack on Suez, Nasser was ready to instigate a much more ambitious project to defend his homeland from foreign attack. Instead of developing an artillery rocket, he started to show interest in something that was vastly more expensive and technically far more demanding—the development of a ballistic missile.

There was one other project that seized his imagination. Egypt could also develop a jet fighter, he argued, that would not only help restore the balance of power in the Middle East, warding off Israeli attacks, but also hugely impress his Arab followers. It would be the first such jet plane to be developed in the Arab world, and would prove that the Arabs were just as capable of setting the pace as the superpowers. The Suez War, and the Qibya and Gaza raids, had proved beyond a doubt just how much Egypt needed this aerial support. In 1951, the British had placed an embargo on arms exports to the Middle East, and the Egyptians had tried their hardest to get around this by ordering some rather archaic aircraft from Syria. But Nasser and his military chiefs were well aware that these would have been worthless against the highly trained Israeli pilots, who were using the latest French jets, if they had confronted them. True, the Egyptians did have some Russian-supplied MiG jets, but these were not in full working order, mainly because Moscow had been refusing to send desperately needed spare parts.

To pursue such ambitious projects, he would have to start off by finding someone who could weigh the costs and assess their viability. To do this, he need to find an individual whose loyalty was absolute, who had good contacts in the military, and who knew something about the hardware that was required.

He found just such a man in Isam al-Din Mahmoud Khalil. Squadron leader Khalil, who was also the deputy chief of air force intelligence, was a stout middle-aged man, then in his early fifties, with wavy hair and a long, drooping mustache. His loyalty to Nasser and his regime had been proven beyond doubt during the Suez Crisis, when he was visiting Rome and was approached by a member of the exiled Egyptian royal family, Mehmed Hussein Khairi. The young prince had a simple but extraordinary suggestion: Would Khalil join a group of conspirators who were based in Cairo and poised to topple the Egyptian leader? Nasser, he continued, would be extremely vulnerable as soon as the Western powers struck back at him and now was Khalil's chance to end the existing political order in Egypt, ousting Nasser and replacing him with monarchical rule.

Khalil never had any intention of joining the conspiracy but did agree to meet again, this time in Beirut, where Khairi said he could introduce him to some other key players in the plan. The main contact here was a senior MI6 officer, using the name John Farmer, who promised Khalil high-grade intelligence information in return for his assistance in establishing the ring of conspirators in Cairo. Khalil responded by demanding substantial funding, without which, he argued, the whole operation would get nowhere, and insisting that he alone should be the main contact liaising between the British and the Egyptian ring.

This was the last that Khalil was to hear from his contacts until four months later, after the Suez Crisis, when the Restoration Plot was reactivated. Khalil claimed that he was then given a large sum of money—allegedly £166,500, all of which was supposedly donated by the Saudis—to arrange the assassination of Nasser and his senior officials. But, to the dismay of the conspirators, Khalil revealed the plot to the Cairo authorities as soon as he arrived, handing over every dollar of the money, which was used to help reconstruct the battered city of Port Said, the scene of much fighting during the brief Suez conflict. Hugely impressed, Nasser had subsequently rewarded and promoted his loyal follower, decorating him with the Order of Merit and awarding him a high level of responsibility to organize Nasser's rearmament program.

At some point during late 1958 or early 1959, Field Marshal Amer summoned Khalil to his office. Nasser had decided to set up a new military program, he explained, and Khalil would be perfect for the job. The organizing body would be called the Bureau of Special Military Programs, which would be responsible for the missile and aircraft factories that Nasser now hoped to build. Khalil would be given an unlimited budget to procure the hardware and to lure the foreign talent that was essential for the job. Khalil immediately accepted the offer, extremely eager and pleased to have this chance to help Nasser, his country, and his own career.

The Egyptian bid to develop long-range ballistic rockets had begun.

CHAPTER EIGHT
The Frustrated Scientists

One May morning in 1957, huge crowds of ordinary Russians gathered excitedly in and around Red Square in central Moscow to watch the annual parade by the Red Army and its air force. This year, however, a special treat was in store, one that could not fail to impress them as much as the foreign dignitaries and journalists who had been invited to watch the day's proceedings. For now was a good moment, estimated the party chiefs in the Kremlin, to unveil the Soviet Union's latest technological triumph, one that would bear unmistakable testimony to the supremacy of the communist system over its capitalist adversary.

Shortly after midday, the crowds fell silent in awe as a rumbling sound became louder until, as the ground shook beneath them, a wave of giant bombers thundered and roared overhead. The bombers were huge, measuring around 150 feet by 160 feet, and to the shaken foreign observers seemed at least as big as anything their Western adversaries could muster. And judging by the roar they made, their engines were perhaps vastly more powerful.

Over the next few days, as they pored over the photos of the flyby, Western defense experts quickly saw another aspect of the giant bombers, one that troubled them deeply. For the experts noticed that they had only four engines, all of which were turboprops, rather than jet engines. The use of turboprops was an impressive enough technical feat in its own right because they use far less fuel than their jet-driven counterparts, allowing a plane to fly much greater distances than it otherwise would. As a result, the Soviets now had a bomber that could strike anywhere in Western Europe without refueling. But what really bothered the NATO analysts was that if the Western air forces wanted to fly a plane of that size, then they would need at least eight such engines to power it. These engines would then be so heavy it would be virtually impossible to get the plane off the ground. In other words, the Soviets had surpassed their Western adversaries.

As they tried to solve the riddle of how the Kremlin had pulled off this remarkable technical feat, they may have guessed the answer. For the engine of the Tupolev Tu-95, or "Bear," was the offspring not of a native Russian but of a native Austrian who had been spirited away from his homeland at the end of the Second World War and forced to work for a regime that he'd despised ever since. In other words, "their Germans," as the comedian Bob Hope once quipped, "are better than *our* Germans!"[117]

His name was Ferdinand Brandner, and in 1945 he had been an important catch for the Red Army as it swept westward through the remnants of the Reich. By the end of the war, the forty-two-year-old scientist, a bespectacled, ruddy-faced giant, had acquired a huge amount of engineering experience that had been of immense use to the German war effort and promised to be of indispensable value to the Russians. For he had started his career designing train engines in the 1920s but become increasingly involved in the world of aircraft, joining Junkers in 1936 and subsequently working at its Dessau factory, where he had pioneered prototype engines, which by the time of the cease-fire were the most sophisticated jet engines in the world.

The Russians had been immensely eager to exploit his knowledge and experience, and that of his senior colleagues, and carefully drew up detailed plans to use it all. Anxious to avoid causing any alarm or panic among the scientists, they held a copious banquet for several hundred of the top names, complete with the best wines, vodka, caviar, and other luxuries that almost no one in Germany had enjoyed since before the outbreak of war. This, they reasoned, would put the scientists in a good mood before the news broke of what would happen next, for the next day, on October 22, 1946, the mass deportation of the prisoners began. In a brief and well organized movement, around five thousand key personnel and their families—a total of about fifteen thousand—were herded onto ninety-two trains, along with their furniture and other belongings, and taken off to Kuibyshev, on the Volga River, where they would be "voluntarily" starting work that had to be finished before they could return home.

This was just one part of the highly secretive Operation Osoaviakhim. For at the same time, the Russians had been busily dismantling entire factories and plants—the Bavarian Motor Works at Stassfurt as well as the Junkers plant at Dessau—and were starting to ship them, piece by piece, to Kuibyshev, where exact replicas were rebuilt. Given the delicacy and sophistication of much of the machinery, this was an immensely difficult operation, but the Russians had worked hard to familiarize themselves with it beforehand and had worked out exactly how to move it.

One of the scientists who was forcibly removed to the Soviet Union was Ferdinand Brandner, who was amazed to find that the factories had been rebuilt so precisely that even his desk, complete with his papers and instruments, had been put back in exactly the same way and at exactly the same spot within the replicated building. But that was where the familiarity came to an end. For the next few years, Brandner and his colleagues were housed in drab apartments that had been hurriedly built, in the space of just weeks, in a small village outside Kuibyshev, put under the constant watch of armed guards, and kept well away from the villagers and any other native Russians. It was here, in what became termed "the Junkers-BMW collective," that the scientists were expected to continue with their work and deliver impressive results for their hosts.

"Our first task," explained Brandner, "was to rebuild from memory and improve the jet engines on which we had been working in Germany. We were told we could return home as soon as we had finished."[118] Relying purely on their memory, and with no documents at their disposal to help them, the expatriates struggled to recall every technical detail of the highly advanced Junkers engine and racked their brains to remember the highly precise mathematical formulas that their work had depended upon (aeronautical engineering relies heavily upon a number of thermodynamic tables that reveal the characteristics of the heated gases that drive engine power, and at Kuibyshev the scientists worked tirelessly to reconstruct these tables).

A powerful, almost bullying, personality, Brandner often shouted at his subordinates to drive them harder, not least because he knew there was no chance of release and repatriation until they had finished the task at hand. He admitted that he was "a very unpleasant man for the Germans" but defended his actions and attitude: "What else could I do?" he asked. "There was much despair and I felt the only way to prevent despair was by working hard."[119] If the Germans could cope with Brandner's onslaught, then they still had to face the Russians, who devised an approach they called "the Defect System": if any piece of new machinery failed, went this rule, then the workers who designed and built it would have to fix it within a strict time frame or else face punishment.

Not surprisingly, the Germans worked furiously, all the more so because they were desperate to avoid the ultimate punishment—being imprisoned inside Russia even if their compatriots were released. But although, three years on, they had finished building a jet engine, there still seemed no end to their ordeal, for they were now ordered to start on their next, and supposedly final, project—the construction of a turboprop engine that could power a long-range bomber with 6,000 horsepower. "At the time, no such engine had been developed by any nation," wrote Brandner, but "with the energy born of hope we started work again." The engine was built within two years but still the Soviets wanted more, ordering their staff to double its power output, far surpassing what any other country had done.

Yet formidable though such a challenge was, Brandner and his fellow Germans succeeded in executing detailed design drawings for a new 12,000-horsepower engine within just three months and took merely another two years to put the design into production. Had any Western experts known of this extraordinary accomplishment, they would have been astonished. How had these Germans succeeded in outclassing the efforts of their Western rivals, they would have asked, when they lacked some of the vital components? "I don't think anyone in the Western world would believe so much could be accomplished in such a short time," as Brandner put it.

The answer lay partly in the brutality of the methods used by the Russians and partly in the supreme engineering skills of the Germans, and of Brandner in particular. Western engineers were later fascinated to learn of an ingenious method he developed of solving a problem that confronts every scientist working on a turboprop engine. This challenge is to keep to an absolute minimum the space between the turbine blades, which spin at a very high rate, and the engine that surrounds them. To avoid slowing the turbo down and reducing its efficiency, this gap should measure no more than a bare fraction—a few thousandths—of an inch. To get an exact fit, Brandner had to improvise. He did so by coating the engine lining with a ceramic mixture, leaving no gap at all, and then allowing the spinning turbines to mold a precise fit before the mixture dried. Brandner figured that this technique produced a much greater efficiency, around 94 percent, than any equivalent engine anywhere in the world.

Elsewhere in the Soviet Union, other German scientists were performing similarly miraculous feats for their "hosts." At the same time that Brandner and his associates had been busily working, several hundred Germans and their families had been forcibly moved to Gorodomlia Island, two hundred miles northwest of Moscow. It was here that they were forced to work on a new rocket that the Russians wanted to be far more impressive than the V-2, with perhaps as much as three times the range. To begin with, conditions on the island were extremely hard, and many of the expatriates were forced to put up without any running water and with only very basic sanitation. But this difficult start did not deter them from making rapid progress, and in 1949 they succeeded in developing the R10 rocket. The following year they pioneered the more sophisticated R14, which had a range ten times greater than the V-2 and a payload three times more deadly. Just as the Americans were making the most of the genius of Wernher von Braun and his colleagues to pioneer the first steps into outer space, so too were their Russian adversaries exploiting the expertise of their own German prisoners.

In the early 1950s, Moscow started to allow an increasing number of German scientists to return home. The Kremlin argued that many of their prisoners had by now served their purpose and it was becoming increasingly expensive to maintain them. Not all the expatriates were still alive, however. Out of the eight hundred fellow nationals who had started work with Brandner at Kuibyshev, five had committed suicide, two had gone insane, and fifteen had died of natural causes. By early 1955 all the surviving German scientists had left Russia and gone home.

After finishing his work for the Russians in July 1954, Brandner returned to Germany but immediately found, like so many of his contemporaries, that professional opportunities were extremely limited, particularly for someone with his high-ranking association with Hitler's SS. In particular, he was bitterly disappointed to have been turned down for a job with a German engineering company that had a number of contracts to supply NATO. True, he had found some work as a technical director of an Austrian company, Maschinenfabrik Andritz AG, which manufactured turbines for Austria's growing number of hydroelectric plants, but he had quickly found the experience unrewarding. Now, at the age of fifty-one, he knew that time was pressing on and he did not have infinite time to realize his lifelong ambitions.

In the postwar years, however, West Germany had nothing to offer. The Allied Military Control had prohibited German scientists from carrying out scientific research for military ends anywhere in the homeland. In other words, Brandner and his fellow compatriots would have to look for jobs elsewhere in the world.

Brandner's story was typical of thousands of other supremely talented, highly experienced scientific experts who had worked for the Nazi regime but discovered few options in the years that followed. Around a hundred of the top experts found work with the French government, which was anxious not to fall behind in the postwar race to develop the most impressive rockets. Because there was so much popular antipathy toward the Germans in the immediate postwar years, the French government came up with an ingenious idea to tempt the former Nazis to work on their behalf: the scientists would live on the German side of the Rhine River, renting homes that the French employers would pay for, and then be taken by bus every day to and from Saint-Louis, where the rocket installations were being set up. This arrangement, which was a central feature of their contracts of employment, worked well, and very few French citizens discovered anything of the Germans in their midst, or of their work on the secret project to build the Veronique missile.[120] For the next decade, two separate teams, one dedicated to researching missile guidance, the other to propulsion, worked in tandem to deliver results that would help push the French rocket program much further forward.

But by 1957, even this opportunity, limited at its height to only a few hundred scientists, was closing as the French government became disillusioned with the high cost and exasperating technical difficulties of developing rocket technology. The research programs, announced a government minister before the National Assembly in 1956, "have demonstrated the complex technical difficulties and the extremely high cost," and as result the government had concluded that "the medium- and long-range bomber will remain the most reliable retaliatory weapons for a long time to come."[121] The mass of redundant or underemployed former Nazi scientists, dubbed "the brain mercenaries" in some governmental circles, would have to look somewhere else to find opportunities.

There was a handful of other openings here and there. In Argentina, Pres. Juan Perón was eager to build up both the prestige and the military invincibility of his regime and started to make a proactive effort to recruit former Nazis with an expertise in engine and aircraft design. Aware that some of the scientists had dark pasts, he knew that an offer of political sanctuary would be a tempting one. In the late 1940s, a number of Argentinian agents, based at the embassy in Bonn, had started to actively headhunt suitably qualified experts, promising them lucrative opportunities if they relocated to Buenos Aires. Several hundred accepted the offer and were given fake passports before being smuggled into Denmark and then flown secretly to South America. Others were spirited out of West Germany along an underground route that ran through the Austrian mountains and northern Italy to the Mediterranean, where they could easily be shipped westward.

Yet once again, this professional opportunity turned out to be something of a disappointment. On arrival, the Germans found that the Argentinian infrastructure was extremely primitive compared with the highly organized and sophisticated standards they were used to, and operated on far too small a scale to absorb the sudden influx of immigrants. As a result, only a relatively small number, with specialized skills, were offered work, such as the gifted engineer Kurt Tank and Dr. Armin Dadieu, a former SS colonel and gauleiter who had been spirited out of Germany by the secret organization known as ODESSA that worked on behalf of wanted war criminals. The rest were forced to look elsewhere, and a few found openings in South Africa, Brazil, Australia, and New Zealand.

A handful of others did strike it lucky. Hermann Oberth, a native Romanian who had taken up German nationality as a young man, had worked as a technician at Peenemünde until 1943, when he was offered a chance to help build a solid-fuel rocket, joining a project that was being developed at Wittenberg on the River Elbe. Captured by the Allies in May 1945, the fifty-one-year-old had managed to cross the border into Switzerland, breaking a strict prohibition by doing so, and searched hard for work as an engineer. Penniless, and with barely more possessions than the clothes he wore and the suitcase he held, he was eventually able to find employment with the Italian navy, which needed his skills and experience at its experimental research establishment in the coastal city of La Spezia. It was here that he continued with his wartime work, developing a solid-fuel rocket before being recruited to work, alongside his former Peenemünde colleagues, on the American space program at Huntsville, Alabama.

But such stories of professional satisfaction and fulfillment were much more the exception than the rule. By 1958 there were still thousands of scientists whose experience, skills, and ambition were only matched by the level of professional frustration they felt. The majority were by this time approaching retirement age and wanted to make the most of the years that were left to them.

After the Second World War, an old saying, popular in the nineteenth century, had suddenly become fashionable again. A German engineer starting with just a piece of bread, went the adage, can make almost anything if given enough time. For the Israeli government, this would soon prompt an obvious, and alarming, question. For if Brandner and others had already performed miracles for the Russians and the French, what could he and his fellow German experts do if they went to work in the Middle East?

CHAPTER NINE
"Wanted: Specialist Engineers"

T hroughout the summer of 1958, a series of simple, single-line advertise-ments appeared in a number of German and Austrian newspapers. They were easy enough to overlook, and anyone who did notice them would not have been likely to give them more than a casual glance. "Aeronautical industry in North Africa requires specialists," ran most of the ads, which went on to specify an anonymous post office box number in Zurich to which any interested parties could send their replies.

Almost every day, a well-dressed businessman arrived at the central post office in Zurich, flashing his proof of identity to the staff and then checking for any replies. Like the ad he had placed in the press, he too was easily overlooked and unlikely to attract much attention. Of average height, quite thin, and black-haired, this youngish man—he was barely forty—looked like nothing out of the ordinary, although he was noticeably darker-skinned than most native Austrians.

His name was Hassan Sayed Kamil, and he was hard at work trying to recruit high-level staff to Nasser's emergent rocket and aircraft programs in as energetic, and as surreptitious, a manner as he could. He was well aware that he could easily have attracted unwanted interest from law-enforcement and intelligence agencies in Switzerland, Germany, and beyond. In his line of work, it was always best to keep a low profile, just in case of any trouble.

In a number of ways, Kamil was ideally suited to such a task. He was by training an engineer who knew a considerable amount about the caliber of people he was trying to recruit and what was required of them. Over the years he had moved into the world of professional arms dealing, cleverly using the depth of his technical expertise to make his way into this exclusive, if risky, world, brokering large deals for the Swiss arms giant Oerlikon before starting to work independently. He was also very well connected, a big plus in a business where you have to rub the right shoulders, because he had married into the German nobility when he was in his midthirties, and his wife, Helene, the Duchess of Mecklenburg, was a big help in getting the right European contacts. And, in a trade where loose talk could cost deals, he also had a reputation among his business associates of being a shadowy figure who said little about himself and who revealed little of his frequent and sometimes lengthy trips abroad, particularly to the Middle East.

He had another huge advantage when it came to the arms trade. The son of an Egyptian father and Swiss mother, he was a fluent speaker of both German and Arabic, the native languages of the country that manufactured arms and those that had an insatiable demand for them. With first-class contacts in Germany, Switzerland, and Egypt, Kamil had quickly come to the attention of President Nasser during one of his visits to the Middle East after the Suez Crisis in 1956.

Well paid by Cairo and, with Egyptian ancestry, highly motivated to help Nasser's cause, Kamil set to work in the spring of 1958. To begin with, he made good use of the Egyptian military attaché's office in Bern to establish a number of front companies, all registered with addresses in Zurich, that he could use to procure both the personnel and the hardware that Cairo so badly needed. Each of these front companies was focused on a different aspect of the arms program. So the Mechanical Corporation, better known as MECO, and the Machines, Turbine, and Pumps Company [MTP] were both geared toward securing supplies for Egypt's aviation programs, and Kamil used the cover they provided to make discreet approaches to a number of European firms that provided the spare parts for a new jet trainer.

Kamil's orders from Cairo were clear. Now that Moscow had vetoed Nasser's efforts to get ahold of Soviet rockets, Egypt would depend on foreign expertise not just to design the rockets themselves but also the physical infrastructure—such as test stands, laboratories, chemical mixers, and specialized machine tools—necessary to build even the most basic rockets. Getting ahold of the right people in the West would be challenging in the best circumstances, since such highly qualified experts would probably be tied down with existing professional and personal commitments and would not want to leave their jobs and homelands to start new lives in a wholly alien environment. And financing this whole operation—sending agents out to Western Europe and paying their expenses, as well as building the infrastructure and luring men of the right caliber to Egypt with considerable sums of money—would be hugely demanding for Egypt, even if Nasser was prepared to make sacrifices if need be.

Kamil's boss in Cairo was Isam al-Din Mahmoud Khalil, better known among his peers as General Khalil. In the summer of 1959, Khalil had flown out to Zurich to meet Kamil and to assist, and supervise, his recruitment efforts. He had dealt with European expatriates in Cairo before and, said one of his former associates, "knew how to argue with them."[122] The president himself was closely informed of all the main developments in the program and took a keen interest in what was happening on the ground.

Kamil and Khalil now worked out a detailed strategy for recruiting the engineering talent that Nasser so desperately needed. Numerous phone calls were made and they personally visited, or dispatched their agents to visit, leading universities, technical colleges, and research institutes across Europe in which some of the suitably qualified experts might already be working, or where the staff might at the very least give them some leads. Because the scientists sometimes developed new areas of expertise and moved in and out of the specialized areas that were relevant to the Egyptian programs, effective networking was essential if these headhunters were to have any real chance of quickly finding people with the necessary skills and experience.

The two men did not have to work so hard to devise a powerful sales strategy with which to tempt their targets once they had located them.

Nasser had granted the project a huge budget, which meant that they could afford to offer the top talent huge, tax-free salaries. What was more, they would be offered luxurious accommodations, including specially built apartments in a closely guarded living area that would be earmarked specifically for Western expatriates. The scientists would be absolutely safe, the Egyptian authorities promised them, and their identities, and their role in the missile program, would be kept a close secret. As an added bonus, they would be able to enjoy virtually constant sunshine and have easy access to the Mediterranean coast.

Kamil and his accomplices did not have to wait long to get the first reply to their post office box number, for within just days they had been sent an elegantly typed letter of inquiry from a name they knew well—Ferdinand Brandner. Kamil was quite familiar with the name and immediately called him at his home in the Austrian city of Graz to invite him to Zurich to discuss a way forward.

Always calm and impeccably mannered in social settings but, as he had proved at Kuibyshev after the war, capable of being a thunderous and bad-tempered bully in a work environment, the fifty-six-year-old Brandner met his contacts over coffee and told them of his recent plight.

Kamil was fully aware that, if he managed to recruit him, Brandner would be a very big catch. This was most obviously because of the technical contribution he would make, but Brandner could also offer the project a certain amount of prestige and superb contacts with other experts throughout Germany and his native Austria. He would know not only who had the relevant expertise but who might be tempted by Egyptian offers of a luxurious lifestyle and a high salary.

Brandner wasted little time in joining the project. He signed a five-year contract that gave him a a basic annual salary of ten thousand Swiss francs as well as an equity stake in Kamil's MTP company. Kamil triumphantly telegrammed the news back to Cairo. He had made it clear to Brandner what he wanted in return, and during their initial meeting he had emphasized how important it was that the Austrian use his networking skills to get the project going. Within just days his new recruit had started work, phoning or sometimes visiting colleagues, both past and present, from every stage of his professional career—including Dessau and Kuibyshev as well as Graz and a number of German technical colleges—who might be interested in this new professional opening.

While Brandner got in touch with his own contacts, Kamil and Khalil continued their recruitment campaign. One of the first ports of call was the German engineering giant Mercedes-Benz, home to many of the top engineers in Western Europe. Writing to various heads of departments, carefully wording their letters to avoid arousing any possible suspicion, they requested meetings to discuss "new career openings" in North Africa. Within a few days they had received a most encouraging reply, written by the manager of the Jet Engines Department, who offered to meet them at the central office in Stuttgart.

In the comfort of his office, Dr. Bruno Eckert explained courteously to his visitors that he had no wish to leave his job at Mercedes, which already gave him every professional satisfaction he could hope to have. But he could help them find the right people, he said, and point them in the right direction. In particular, they should be aware of an important and highly successful engineering program that was being conducted at a jet propulsion research institute in Stuttgart, where several leading authorities, all perfectly qualified with the skills that his visitors needed, were based.

The Jet Propulsion Study Institute in Stuttgart had been set up by the West German government in 1954 in order to resurrect a number of aviation research projects that had been shelved at the end of the war. The project quickly attracted a lot of business interest and, within a few months of being set up, was being backed by a good number of very generous, and high-profile, sponsors, including Daimler-Benz, several technical universities, and one regional authority within Germany, the state of Baden-Württemberg.

But besides the level of expertise and experience at the Jet Propulsion Study Institute, there was almost certainly another reason Eckert gave the two men this lead. For he was doubtlessly well aware that many of these scientists were deeply frustrated by the lack of government funding and, by extension, of government interest in their program. This was essentially because the West German government was still tied down by a number of postwar agreements that prohibited any research on its soil into rocketry, but in any case it also had more important priorities than designing and developing aviation engines, even if they were meant only to be used for peaceful purposes. As a result, many of these experts felt that their talents and professional careers were being completely put to waste.

In a series of meetings that began in November 1959 and continued over the next few months, General Khalil visited the institute and met a number of leading experts who showed considerable interest in the opportunities he outlined to them. Each of the three leading experts—Dr. Hans Kleinwachter, a guidance expert; Dr. Wolfgang Pilz, head of the propulsion department; and Dr. Paul Goercke, an electronics specialist—wanted to know more but also had reservations. What would happen, for example, if for any reason they were unhappy in these new roles and wanted to return? Or if Israel or any other country found out and created a fuss?

Khalil knew that if he could give them the assurance they needed, he would have a real chance of luring them to Egypt. For each of these three men had enormous talents and a wealth of collective experience to offer the rocket program but were now professionally and academically frustrated, having enjoyed huge opportunities and privileges during the war only to fall victim to a dearth of subsequent openings. Kleinwachter, for example, had a huge amount of experience in acoustics and radio communications but had felt professionally limited well before 1945. His real passion was in using acoustics to invent a guidance system for blind people, but he had been forced to spend the early part of the war in Dresden, researching ways of processing household refuse into pig food. After that he was drafted to the Eastern Front, where he worked on military communications.

Similar disappointments had befallen one of the leading lights of the Jet Propulsion Study Institute, Dr. Wolfgang Pilz. Described by contemporaries as "a propulsion expert who has deep blue eyes [and] the wavy silver hair of a matinee idol [resembling] a moody Werther of the Atomic Age," Pilz certainly looked the part of the German scientist he had played since beginning his career at Peenemünde in 1943.[123] Not much is known about his wartime career, but it is possible that he was involved in efforts to develop the highly sophisticated surface-to-air missiles that were code-named Wasserfall (Waterfall). After the war, he fell into British hands and was then ordered to participate in Operation Backfire, the top-secret launching of V-2 rockets from the town of Cuxhaven, on Germany's North Sea coast, in 1946.[124]

Pilz's postwar experience did not end there, for, together with over a hundred other fellow Germans, he was recruited by the French authorities to develop the embryonic Veronique rocket.[125] His area of specialization was missile guidance, a highly technical field that was then in its relative infancy, and he made a huge contribution to the French program, particularly in its initial stages, by devising ways of stabilizing the missile soon after takeoff, using cables and explosive bolts to do so.[126] But as the French government's interest in and funding for the rocket project began to diminish, Pilz had become disenchanted with his new employer and left in 1956. Although he later claimed that the local climate had made him "depressed," the real reason was more likely to have been a fall in pay and conditions, the result of a sudden collapse in government funding for the project.[127]

To begin with, he had held high hopes for his next employer, the Jet Propulsion Study Institute, which he joined within months of leaving France. But he was infuriated by the legal restrictions on research that were imposed by the West German government and by its total lack of interest in aerospace in general. There were several projects that fascinated him, notably the construction of a three-stage satellite launcher and a rocket similar to the British Blue Streak, but when he sent detailed proposals to the Bonn government for these projects, claiming that he could win huge foreign investment and earn large returns from exports, he didn't even receive a reply.[128]

His colleague at Stuttgart, Dr. Paul Goercke, had similar doubts about his own professional prospects. Middle-aged, with "benign features, close-cut grey hair and the square head of a physics professor," Goercke had also worked at Peenemünde during the war before moving on to the Veronique program. He had worked in Egypt some years before, contributing to Rolf Engel's rocket program, and was therefore less concerned than his colleagues by what might lie ahead, but he still wanted to ask his visitors a good many questions about what his prospective new role would involve.

Of course, Khalil and Kamil had both expected the scientists to have doubts and questions, and quickly assured them. Their contracts with the

Egyptian government, they countered, would initially just be part-time roles that would allow them to retain their existing jobs in Stuttgart, from which they could take extended periods of leave every couple of months or so. What was more, they would not have to declare the real purpose of their visits to anyone, since to all outward appearances they would just be giving lectures on space flight at the University of Cairo and undertaking "consultancy work" on rockets that were ostensibly only for meteorological purposes.[129]

These tactics worked, and soon Khalil had managed to persuade not just Kleinwachter, Goercke, and Pilz to join the program but also twenty of their technicians, notably Walter Schuran, Manfred Heide, and Peter Schulz, who had a great deal of specialized knowledge. Within the space of just months, Egypt's rocket program had taken big steps forward.

As each of them signed up, Khalil triumphantly informed Cairo of the enormous progress he was making. Yet even though each of these individual scientists was important enough in his own right, by far the biggest catch was yet to come.

Dr. Eugen Sänger, the fifty-four-year-old director of the Jet Propulsion Study Institute, had impeccable credentials to become a star contributor to Nasser's rocket program. As a young scientist he had quickly made his name in designing and modifying liquid engines, and using chemical powders to enhance the performance of rocket fuels. After he joined the German Society for Space Travel in the early 1930s, his talents were quickly recognized by the Nazi Party and he was soon offered a top-level research post in the German Air Ministry. By 1936 Sänger had started to make his name by pioneering designs for a high-speed projectile that would be capable of traveling vast distances beyond the hemisphere at supersonic speeds. In particular, he perfected a liquid-fueled rocket engine that was "regeneratively cooled" by its own fuel and moved at a speed that was, by contemporary standards, quite astonishing.[130]

The basic idea underpinning his design was that a rocket could reach the periphery of outer space and then remain there, without actually entering orbit, for considerable periods of time. Powered by specially designed diesel and liquid oxygen engines, and using new rocket technology, this suborbital projectile could be sustained in flight by "lift," the upward pressure from the density in the atmosphere that would push it higher in the same way as a stone that is thrown over water and bounces along its surface. This lifting effect would allow the projectile to travel in "hops," as it gained and then lost height before being pushed back upward again.

Not surprisingly, articles that Sänger wrote in the mid-1930s for the Austrian journal *Flug* (*Flying*) attracted immediate attention in the Luftwaffe, and in 1936 he was offered a chance to experiment with his designs at a top-secret site at Taeun, on Lüneburg Heath, in Lower Saxony. The development of a manned, winged plane that could reach outer space, his new sponsors emphasized, might be of real benefit to the Reich.

At the outbreak of war in 1939, this remained very much a drawing-board idea, one that had remained only at design stage, but whose conception had nonetheless attracted considerable interest in the German scientific world. But it was during the war that Sänger's revolutionary new design revealed its full potential. Pressed by the Luftwaffe high command to develop new war weapons, Sänger worked closely with his wife, Irene Bredt, who was a brilliant scientist in her own right, to find ways of converting his blueprint plan into an operational long-range bomber. This would have been a huge military asset, one the German air force painfully lacked. Above all, it would have been particularly indispensable in the event of any conflict with Russia.

By 1943 Sänger and his wife had developed their plans for a modified projectile, building a plane that they called Silbervogel, or Silver Bird. Propelled along a two-mile rail track by a rocket-powered sled, the plane would then be launched into the skies. Next, it would fire its own engine, which would take it to a ninety-mile altitude at a speed of around 13,700 miles per hour. After eight minutes its main engine would burn out and the plane would then descend back into the stratosphere where it would be "lifted" by the higher air density and bounce back to its earlier, higher altitude. The two scientists made careful calculations and figured that the plane would gradually gravitate back to earth, each "lift" being lower and shallower than the last, but that the Silver Bird would nonetheless still be capable of crossing the Atlantic with an 8,800-pound bomb and striking continental America before landing at a site somewhere in the Japanese-held

Pacific. By the end of the war, however, their plans for the Amerika Bomber had still not yet been formally commissioned by the Air Ministry in Berlin, or even progressed beyond fairly basic test stages.

Unlike Wernher von Braun and other high-profile former Nazi scientists, Sänger failed to find any postwar work that could compensate for the disappointment he must have felt, as a scientist, in watching Germany lose the war and his projects remain the stuff of dreams. Falling into Allied captivity after the war, he and his wife were recruited by the French Arsenal de l'Aéronautique in Paris to work as consultant engineers on a rocket research program. The work was well paid and the conditions were pleasant enough, but opportunities were very restricted. In the austere postwar years, the French government had no spare cash to work on the sort of hugely ambitious projects that the two Germans hoped and longed for. And, as Sänger later wrote, this was compounded by the political uncertainty that characterized France in the decade that followed the war: "[T]he frequent changes of government prior to the accession to power of General de Gaulle by no means encouraged continuity of current projects. For example, one evening we would convince Government representatives by a successful experiment of the suitability of a launching rocket with an alcohol-water mixture as fuel, only to be told next morning that a new government had again cancelled all liquid rocket engines."[131]

Sänger did turn down one prestigious postwar opportunity. This was presented to him by a former V-2 engineer, Walter Dornberger, who suggested working on a rocket-plane project for the Bell Aircraft Company. For reasons that remain unclear, Sänger chose not to get involved. He also had a narrow escape from a much higher-level, and more ambitious, project devised by Joseph Stalin, whose spies had heard about the Amerika Bomber. "Do you realize," Stalin had asked one of his leading scientists, "the tremendous strategic importance of machines of this sort? They could be an effective straitjacket for that noisy shopkeeper Harry Truman . . . the problem of the creation of transatlantic rockets is of extreme importance to us."[132] Stalin then dispatched a squad of secret police to kidnap the leading figures who were involved in it, but the scheme fell apart rather farcically when the head of the Soviet squad decided to defect to the West instead.

After working on schemes as grand as bombing New York with long-range supersonic jets, it was perhaps not surprising that by 1959 Eugen Sänger had become disenchanted with his work at Stuttgart, which he described to friends and colleagues as "modest" and "unsatisfying."[133] Over the previous three years he had found a certain amount of recognition for his work, having even been awarded a highly prestigious prize, the Hermann Oberth Medal, for his recent contribution to space research. But his name was wholly eclipsed by many others in his field, notably von Braun, who—he felt sure—had far less to offer than he did. He still wrote occasional articles for leading journals but that was not enough to escape the fact that his name was by this time sinking into oblivion. His sense of loss and disappointment was noticed by colleagues, one of whom observed that he regularly "fumbled around at the Institute with all kinds of things. But the hardware which everyone in this field is a fanatic for, he could not get in Germany."[134]

Now, fourteen years after the end of the war, Sänger may well have thought that his hour had come. Approached in Stuttgart by a suave and self-assured "Herr Doktor Mahmoud"—the name the Germans gave General Khalil—and offered a vast salary in return, Dr. Sänger jumped at his chance to build rockets for President Nasser. What was more, Khalil mentioned that Egypt now had plans to build a satellite and would much appreciate his input into that project as well.[135] Sänger could scarcely believe his luck; nor, for that matter, could those who had recruited him. It was usual in the engineering industry for the principal scientist to be offered a fee worth seven percent of the contract's total—and that would be enough to earn Sänger a lump sum of $2 million.

None of these scientists would have been specifically informed that they would be working on a military program producing rockets capable of striking Israel. They were told, and would have been able to convince themselves, that their project was only a civilian program to build a meteorological rocket. But, at the very least, they would have been aware that their work could have been put to dual use and could also contribute to the construction of a military rocket. Some of the scientists, like Sänger, probably looked away from this. Others, like Goercke and Kleinwachter, saw nothing wrong with such a military program and found counterarguments to justify their position.[136]

There was one other big name that the Egyptian recruitment team was hoping to draw. It was a name that everyone in Germany, and probably the world over, had by this time heard of and associated not so much with the Nazi regime but rather with the engineering genius that Hitler and his war machine had relied upon—Willy Messerschmitt. Through their contacts, Kamil and Khalil tracked the eminent German down and prepared to pitch a business offer to him that was too good to refuse.

Both men knew how important an acquisition the legendary German would be. Although reviled by his enemies either as an ardent Nazi or, at the very least, an amoral opportunist whose factories had employed slave labor in the most brutal conditions, Messerschmitt was nonetheless by any standards a brilliant engineer whose input into the German war effort had undoubtedly pushed the barriers of aviation knowledge a long way forward. From a remarkably early age, while still in his early twenties, he had been inspired by the sight of giant Zeppelin airships to design new gliders, and in 1921, at the age of just twenty-three, had built a new model that broke the world record by staying airborne for twenty-one minutes. Numerous other ingenious designs had followed, some of which were more successful than others. Then, in 1935, he got his first real breakthrough, winning an open competition to design a high-speed, single-seat fighter aircraft. The Bf 109, which later became so well known during the Battle of Britain, hugely impressed the Luftwaffe judges with its remarkable rate of climb and superb maneuverability. Some of his later wartime designs, such as the Me 262 twin jet-powered fighter with swept wings, which saw only fleeting action during the Second World War, were later considered by experts to have been years ahead of their time.

When in 1948 Messerschmitt was finally released from a three-year spell of detention and cleared by his British captors of any responsibility for Nazi crimes, he must have felt that, at the age of fifty, he still had considerable time to develop his constant flow of ideas and to pioneer more path-breaking inventions. Since aircraft production in their homeland was still banned, most German aircraft designers were looking overseas, mainly to South America or Asia, for new employment opportunities. Messerschmitt, however, was looking for something closer to home and in 1951 was offered a consultancy role in Spain, whose ruler, General Franco, was taking a close interest in the distinguished German's career. Messerschmitt's planes had played a crucial role in helping him to win the civil war in 1936 and now, more than a decade later, the Spanish ruler probably also had a strong personal sympathy for him.

Under the terms of a deal signed in 1951, Messerschmitt agreed to help build two types of jet-engined planes for the Spaniards. The HA-200 would be capable of reaching 800 miles per hour and carrying a cannon, and could be used either as a training aircraft or as a ground-attack aircraft. The other would be the HA-300, a jet fighter that the Spanish air force desperately needed. Messerschmitt had no qualms of conscience about getting involved in any of these projects: Spain was a neutral country and only needed the plans in the event of foreign attack or serious domestic unrest, or as a source of export revenue.

Yet promising though this project initially seemed, it was soon in trouble. In particular, the plans to develop the HA-300 supersonic fighter—the project that mattered more than any other to the Spaniards and to Messerschmitt himself—encountered all manner of unanticipated technical problems that Messerschmitt found no way to counter. He was unable to find a suitable engine for his design, without which the whole project foundered. The Spanish authorities were also alarmed by the escalating costs of wind-tunnel testing, which had to be done in Switzerland because Spain lacked any such infrastructure. Messerschmitt himself started to have doubts about the aerodynamics of his original design and was then dismayed to learn that his Spaniard bosses were revising their plans and now looking for a double-seater instead of the single-seater version he was working on. To add insult to injury, they were now more interested in a rival version put forward by his old acquaintance the world-renowned German aircraft designer and manufacturer Ernst Heinkel. He also started to quarrel with Spanish contractors, resenting their involvement in a project that he regarded, with some justification, as his own and missing other people's suggestions, even when they were constructive and conceivably improved on the ideas he had put forward.

In the summer of 1957, soon after a disastrous first test flight by a glider version of the fighter plane, the Madrid government finally brought the HA-300 program to a halt, prompting the German design staff to head back to their homeland in search of better opportunities. Yet there was some good news that did something to redeem the strong sense of failure Messerschmitt felt: a number of foreign countries, he was informed, were showing interest in his design, and the Egyptian government was particularly eager. In or around 1959, the Spanish government went on to sell the design of the HA-300 fighter to Cairo and by the end of November Messerschmitt himself had signed a contract that had been discreetly put before him by the two chief representatives of the Egyptian government. At a reported fee of one hundred thousand Egyptian pounds, the legendary German engineer, whose brilliant work had fueled the Nazi war effort for so long, was set to become one of Nasser's foreign experts.

In all, about two hundred German and Austrian scientists and engineers had signed up to Nasser's program by the summer of 1960. Most would be paid between three and four thousand Swiss francs every month, although the leading figures would be receiving double that, and half their salaries were to be paid in local currency in Egypt, while the rest would be converted into Swiss currency and forwarded to international bank accounts. There were also a good number of perks, including two months' paid leave every year, generous relocation costs from Germany to Egypt, and good schooling for their children, most of whom were signed up to start at a Protestant school for Western expatriates in central Cairo.

The Egyptian leader's plan to build long-range rockets was well under way.

CHAPTER TEN
The Mossad Reaction

As Egypt's recruitment drive of German experts continued in the course of 1959, Israeli spy chiefs were working hard to find ways of keeping pace with their enemy's plans and movements, knowing that a constant flow of first-class, up-to-date information was essential if they were to have any chance at all of foiling any threat that might emerge to the security of the Jewish state.

There was, however, one major obstacle that lay before them—the almost complete lack of information about what was happening inside Egypt. Their undercover sleeper network had been blown during Operation Susannah and would probably take years to replace: finding and training suitable agents was hard enough, but to place them covertly into a foreign country was a protracted, painstaking, and often highly exasperating affair.

The most promising and obvious starting point lay not in Egypt but in Germany, where Mossad had a well-established agent network, as it did in all European countries, and where it could monitor some of the activities of the expatriates with relative ease.

The man to whom the Mossad chiefs now turned was, at the age of just twenty-nine, something of a veteran of war, armed struggle, and espionage. After fleeing his native Poland with his parents, Peter Malkin had started a new life in Palestine and gone on to join the Jews' armed struggle to establish a homeland when he was just twelve years of age, in 1939. He learned quickly and impressed his elders in the Haganah, one of the underground movements that wanted to end the British mandate over Palestine so that a Jewish homeland could be established. After Israel won independence in May 1948, he served a stint in the army and was then recruited into Israeli intelligence as an undercover operative.

By the time he was approached by his handlers and briefed on the Egyptian rocket program, Malkin was supremely skilled at some of the arts his new mission would require. He had been closely trained, for example, in the difficult skill of reading the mind-set of various enemies. Sent to test the security arrangements of Israeli government residences and embassies in Eastern Europe, he "would spend long days wandering the streets or sitting in cafés and darkened movie houses, trying to get a fix on how people behaved locally, on how they thought and what they believed." He constantly prowled the vicinity of the possible targets, moving from one to another, "all the while probing, probing, trying to figure how I, as a terrorist, might contrive to breach local Israeli defences."[137] He found that such training was particularly instructive in helping him see how people of different cultures could sometimes behave: "I found it endlessly intriguing to note the ways in which entire cultures embrace specific attitudes and modes of behavior," he wrote later.

Surveillance was a particular specialty of the young Israeli spy. After several years in the field of active operations, Malkin knew, for example, that "not attracting attention to oneself is very much a matter of technique" and that "the casual eye takes more notice of someone moving than of someone who stays in place." He used this basic rule to keep close tabs on an insurgent who was based in a building in downtown Athens, devising a carefully timed routine with a Mossad colleague in which the front door never left their sight even though they could only be rarely seen as they walked around the surrounding area. A skilled and careful agent, he also believed, was just as expert in easing off a surveillance operation, knowing or sensing when his adversary might be getting suspicious, as in knowing what to do when the operation was in full swing.

Above all, he felt strongly that one of the keys to a successful spying operation was *over*preparation. Because he knew from experience the ways in which, in real life, there were "an astonishing number of things that can go wrong," he felt it was essential to work constantly, to the point of obsession, to rehearse every plan and prepare thoroughly for every eventuality he could think of. "I aimed to leave no detail unattended to, to have a solution at the ready to every conceivable problem, and an alternative solution, and an alternative to the alternative."[138]

Israel's spymasters assigned Malkin the task of monitoring Dr. Wolfgang Pilz and the team who worked with him. His orders were simple—to keep a close watch on each of them and find out as much as possible about what they were doing on behalf of Nasser, obtaining proof of their role that could be shown to Israeli chiefs. It was vital that no harm came to any of the German scientists under surveillance, since that would jeopardize what promised to be crucial sources of information.[139]

Malkin agreed to go ahead with the operation but did so only with reservations. He knew that the assignment might well be a long-term operation, perhaps lasting a year or so, during which time he would be away from his family and friends in Israel. And he was afraid that getting involved in such an important mission would drive him further away from the people who were—supposedly—closest to him, turning him even more inward rather than allowing him to open up to others. Years later he wrote how secret service work "took a devastating toll" on his personal life because "an agent spends his life keeping things to himself, covering up as a matter of course, not only with strangers but among friends, family, lovers, everyone who is not a part of his tiny circle of professional intimates. You lie so often that invariably you start to contradict yourself, forgetting the lies you've already told."[140]

But he also knew that he would react adversely to making any sort of visit to Germany. He had been there a few years before and thought he had noticed "an appalling level of indifference" that preyed on his mind and conscience. "There was definitely less shame or sorrow over what had happened than clear regret that the war had not been won, less concern with moral responsibility than annoyance that the matter was still being raised at all."[141] Always quick to look for aspects of a national character that explained the past and present, Malkin thought he found an explanation of German behavior: their attitudes toward "authority and personal responsibility," he felt, enabled them to exonerate themselves of any feelings of guilt.[142]

Right from the onset, the Israeli spy knew that he and his fellow agents would need "a degree of patience and perseverance, rare even by the usual standards of the business." A huge amount of painstaking surveillance work would be required in order to identify every member of the ring of German scientists and then to discover a great deal of information about their daily lives and routines. "Only then," Malkin wrote, "would we be in a position to know how best to get our hands on the research data, and, even more so, which of it was most likely to be of significance."[143] But though in these respects the mission promised to be a challenging one, the Israeli spies had some things in their favor, notably a well thought out and organized plan: extreme caution was of paramount concern and this meant that, to avoid any risk of being noticed, none of the agents would be spending more than a few hours shadowing one of their subjects. Instead, each would be given regular breaks from watching that particular target before starting another stint.

Above all, Malkin had at his disposal a team of highly trained and experienced agents.* Thirty-five-year-old "Meir" was, like Malkin himself, a veteran member of the armed struggle in Palestine and had immense experience in field operations, including missions to track down and summarily execute particularly notorious SS men. Though formidable in combat, he reputedly had a gentle nature and was said to have refused to participate in one of the most brutal types of training that agents had to endure—fifteen minutes of unarmed one-to-one combat against each other. Then there was "Jack," a specialist driver. He was expert at studying local traffic patterns in order to work out the best way to approach and then flee from target locations. "Jean-Claude" was an affable and unflappable, if rather forgetful, Frenchman whose language skills and nationality could be of great use in putting an enemy off the trail, while twenty-six-year-old "Hannah" was, as the only female member on the team, certain to prove an indispensable asset since she could play the part of a wife or girlfriend when the need arose.

However, Hannah's presence in the group naturally raised issues. One summer evening, Malkin and Hannah were on a surveillance mission,

---

* In his memoirs, Malkin only mentioned the first names of his team.

posing as a couple by walking together and holding hands. Then, wholly unexpectedly, Malkin suddenly found himself locked in a passionate embrace with her.

"Peter, why don't we share a room tonight?" she whispered in his ear.

"Don't call me Peter!" Malkin whispered back sharply, horrified that she had used his real name in the course of an operation.

Back at their base, Hannah told him that she wanted a relationship with him. She was lonely on active operations, she explained, and liked him very much. Malkin had deeply divided loyalties. On the one hand, he felt deeply drawn to her black hair and blue eyes, and to "the particular grace born of self-confidence" that he saw in her. But he knew that he could not let himself be drawn toward her: intimacy in the course of an operation was strictly against Mossad rules because it could create a conflict of interest. And he knew that he would be demoted or dismissed from the service, or from frontline action, when word got out, as he was sure it eventually would.[144]

After long months of patient and painstaking surveillance, Malkin and his team had acquired a detailed knowledge of Professor Pilz and his team. They had, he noted, "ascertained not only when they went to bed and got up but with whom, not merely how often they dined with which colleagues but what they liked to eat, not only how they traveled to work but, even more important, where they journeyed when they left town and for how long."[145]

Having established this wealth of background data, it was time to move a stage closer and find out more about what these scientists were actually working on. Malkin had by this time already broken into the apartments used by two of the scientists, including Pilz himself, but had found nothing that gave him any real clue. He discovered only a number of rather meaningless documents, which he photographed, alongside some phony passports and other fake IDs.

Getting hold of the information would mean breaking into one of the four research facilities—in Stuttgart, Cologne, Munich, and Zurich—that Malkin's team had located. Choosing a site involved careful assessment, weighing the risks of getting caught against the possible rewards such a raid could yield if successful. After some deliberation, the team decided to target Professor Pilz's laboratory in Cologne, situated on the second floor of a building in a quiet residential street. The group already had an excellent vantage point, since some months before they had rented a third-floor apartment that looked down at the laboratory from across a courtyard.

Soon Malkin was ready to move. He chose his moment carefully, knowing that Pilz was out of town, making one of his regular visits to Zurich, and that most of his colleagues had tickets to see Wagner's *Tannhäuser* at the local opera house that evening. Around midnight, when the windows of the laboratory and the surrounding apartments were shrouded by the dark and the sky was completely moonless, he stepped out of the courtyard window of the apartment. He made his way onto a narrow ledge and then inched his way toward his target destination, crouching below window height just in case someone happened to be looking out.

Highly experienced at this sort of work, Malkin now had no difficulty in prizing open a large French window, taking exactly five seconds with a large jimmy, before stepping into a pitch-black hallway. Moving down the stairs, taking care to keep close to the wall so the floorboards wouldn't creak, he went around a corner and was confronted by large double glass doors that led into the laboratory. Malkin felt euphoric, feeling sure that the doors were probably secured by little more than a basic lock that he was highly expert at breaking. But as he took a strip of celluloid from his pocket to carry out the task, he felt a huge force suddenly come crashing at the doors, sending a shock wave of terror through him. "I was overcome by dread," he later wrote; "I knew I was going to die."

Hearing loud barking, he realized that it was not an assailant confronting him but a large dog that was, fortunately, trapped behind the glass doors. Using his torch, he saw a huge black Doberman with immense fangs staring at him with its ebony eyes, snarling ferociously. Almost at once, Malkin was on his heels, praying that no one could hear its bark and that it would soon quiet down. Despite all their careful surveillance of Pilz's apartment, the Mossad team had somehow missed the presence of this daunting animal.

The giant Doberman posed a huge problem to Malkin and his team. How could they get past it and make their way into the laboratory? None of them had any idea how to proceed, and nor did their bosses in Tel Aviv, who were given constant updates on what was happening on the ground. After a great deal of deliberation, the spy chiefs in Israel could only suggest one thing—that the group get in touch with an elderly woman who lived in the Paris suburbs, and who trained dogs professionally. A survivor of the concentration camps, she was a good and trusted contact of the Israelis.

A few days later, Mme. Messmer was listening to the spy's story with a mixture of sympathy and amusement.

"You're sure it was a Doberman?"

"I'm not absolutely sure, [but] I think so. I can tell you that it was as big as a horse and it wanted to kill me."

"If you'd opened those doors, it would have."

But as Mme. Messmer considered her options, Malkin weighed in with an idea of his own. Messmer had a large collection of dogs, among which was a particularly fierce Rottweiler. Couldn't such a ferocious dog take on a Doberman, perhaps even just briefly? If so, would Messmer let Malkin take the dog with him to Cologne for a few days? Better still, would she make an impression of the Rottweiler's teeth that he could use when he got back home? Soon afterward, Malkin had arrived back at Cologne and was ready to put his ingenious plan into action.

If it was to work, precise timing would be everything. From their careful surveillance, the spies discovered that every day, between half past three and four in the afternoon, a secretary took the Doberman out in the streets for a walk. At three o'clock, their plan kicked off.

Closing his eyes and clenching his teeth, Meir thrust out his arm and bit his lip as Malkin took the impression of the Rottweiler's teeth, drew the fake jaws apart, and then clamped them down onto Meir's bare flesh, drawing blood. Meir winced, glad that the first and most painful part of the operation was over. He then picked up the Rottweiler's leash and headed to the street outside.

About half an hour later, exactly when they expected, Meir saw the secretary and the dog approaching. Then, as they rounded a corner and caught sight of each other, the two dogs suddenly jumped, straining at their owners' leashes with a ferocious, almost uncontrollable force, and instantly dragging the shocked secretary along with them. The dogs were now tearing into each other, gnashing their teeth, and barking furiously. Meir, shouting at them at the top of his voice, ended up on the ground as he fought desperately to prize them apart.

Shocked and startled by the commotion, passersby rushed to help, and when, after several minutes, they eventually pulled the dogs away from each other, Meir was screaming that he had been bitten by the Doberman. Pulling up his shirtsleeve, he displayed the teeth marks inflicted by Malkin some half an hour before, to "prove" it.

"That looks bad," one of the passersby said. "You'd better get to a doctor."

"What about the dog?"

"The dog should be put into quarantine," said another member of the public, whose voice was familiar. It was Jean-Claude, who had arrived exactly at this prearranged moment to make this specific suggestion. A policeman had by this time also appeared and readily, and thoughtlessly, agreed with the idea.

The plan worked brilliantly. The dog was taken to the police station and put into quarantine for the next forty-eight hours, enough time for Malkin to seize his chance and raid the laboratory before it returned. Breaking into the apartment later that day, Malkin was amazed by how much information was worth photographing. Besides a large number of letters and documents, he was also astonished to discover a blueprint for liquid-fuel rocket engines.

On that day, wrote Israel's great spy, there was, among the few who knew what had happened, "only jubilation, and raucous congratulations all around."[146]

Although things were proceeding well for the Israelis in Germany, infiltrating Nasser's infrastructure in Egypt promised to be a much more difficult nut to crack. Considerable patience, skill, and an element of luck would be required if Mossad was going to place a high-level mole within the Egypt rocket program.

But the spy chiefs in Tel Aviv now had a highly fortuitous stroke of luck. For at the same time Malkin was busily reconnoitering the scientists in their homeland, Israel's Military Intelligence service came across a remarkable Israeli citizen who seemed a perfect recruit for its special operations division, Unit 131.

Like Avri Seidenwerg before him, Wolfgang Lotz was highly susceptible to the advances of the Israeli secret service when its agents first made their approach. By 1958 the thirty-seven-year-old Lotz had a long military record behind him but had reached a stage when he knew that he would rise no higher than company commander, a rank he had attained during the Suez campaign in 1956, and that his duties were likely to become more and more routine and administrative as he became older. Twice married and twice divorced, he also found that life in general was becoming increasingly dull and that he was in urgent need of some new challenge.

The Aman chiefs knew that Lotz would be very interested in pursuing a new career. For Lotz was a highly valued rarity for the same reason as Seidenwerg—he had German ancestry and, what was more, a *highly visible* German ancestry. The son of a German father and Jewish mother, he was, in his own words, "blond, stocky and thoroughly Teutonic in gesture, manner and looks" as well as "a hard drinker and the very epitome of an ex-German officer."[147] True, he did not have much firsthand experience of the country, since he and his family had fled Germany in 1933, when he was just twelve. But he did have "an innate acting ability," which he perhaps had inherited from his actress mother, and this would allow him to play his chosen part with real conviction.

His military experience also meant that he was not likely to be easily unnerved and that he would know exactly how to play the part of a former soldier. For he had joined Haganah at the age of just sixteen before joining the British Army on the outbreak of the Second World War, forging his birth certificate in order to do so. But there was another reason his wartime service was now particularly valuable to Aman. For in 1942 he had been posted to serve in Egypt, where he could put his knowledge of the region, and of its languages, to good use in the war effort against Rommel's Afrika Korps. Speaking fluent German and passable Arabic, he spent a good deal of time interrogating captured German soldiers, extracting details from them about their units, senior officers, movements, and plans.

Lotz had other attributes that made him virtually unique. Although he had left Germany when still a child, he had always retained his German nationality, meaning that his passport and birth certificate were absolutely valid documents. Of course Aman could have forged these papers and invented some fictional identity, but what could not be faked was Lotz's other prize asset—the fact that he was not circumcised. So even in the highly unlikely scenario that someone did suspect this supremely

Aryan-looking man of being Jewish, he had an obvious counterargument. Finally, he was good at making friends—a huge asset in the world of espionage in which the ability to ingratiate oneself into selected circles is vital—since he had, in his own estimation, "a sort of bombastic charm" and was "an excellent raconteur and a good mimic."[148]

Despite such superb qualifications, the Aman recruiters may have initially wondered if Lotz had enough loyalty to the Jewish state to be fully trusted. After all, his father had been an Aryan German and his mother a nonreligious Jew who spoke no Hebrew and who had emigrated to Palestine, at great personal cost, only because she felt she had no other option at a time when the Nazi Party was coming to power in Germany. But a close look at his background would have been enough to dispel any lingering doubts. On arriving in Palestine, Lotz had changed his name to Ze'ev Gur-Aryeh and taken up a highly active role with the Haganah, during the British Mandate for Palestine. He had also spent three years smuggling arms, guarding Jewish settlements, and fighting Arab insurgents. His subsequent service in the Israeli Army had also been exemplary.

Astonished by the proposals put forward by Aman agents, Lotz hesitated, wanting to consult with a close friend, a high-ranking Aman officer, before making any firm commitment. His friend was unsure, pointing out only that new recruits either sank or swam in the difficult situations they inevitably found themselves in, but Lotz nonetheless decided to take the risk and join.

The training program he now began was both exhausting and intensive. He learned how to create and use dead-letter drops, where secret messages could be safely left and picked up; how to shake off hostile surveillance and to use codes to communicate with his handlers; and how to recruit potential spies and oversee their operations. The most basic rules in espionage—such as the compartmentalization of agents, who should know nothing about the wider network they belonged to in case they were captured—were drummed home. For weeks on end, he read a huge number of documents and books on Egypt that his trainers gave him, committing to memory numerous details that might, at some future point, come in handy. A great deal of time and effort was also spent on inventing a fictional, or semifictional, past, one that nonetheless drew upon the factual basis of his own life. Instead of his having left Germany in 1933—which he had actually done—the story would go that Lotz had continued to grow up in Berlin, leaving school at the age of eighteen before eventually joining Rommel's Afrika Korps. After that, the cover story continued, Lotz immigrated to Australia, where he lived for eleven years and pursued a new career, with considerable success, as a racehorse owner and breeder. Later, he had become homesick and decided to return to his homeland.

Like any other, this cover story had its strengths and weaknesses. On the one hand, he plainly had a much more detailed knowledge of Rommel's forces than virtually anyone, given his role in the British Army during the war. He also knew a lot about horses, because when he had arrived in Palestine as a child he had attended an agricultural school in Ben Shemen where he grew to love horses.

On the other hand, if someone had checked hard enough, he or she could have discovered that, even if his passport and papers were valid, he had not in fact had German citizenship between 1933 and 1958, when he reregistered, or that no one in Australia had ever even heard of him. But the Aman chiefs decided that it would suffice if he simply familiarized himself with Germany once again. He would have to spend at least twelve months there, they decided, in order to get highly familiar with every aspect of its culture and politics, its modern-day cities, and even such banal things as everyday expressions and household names. The country had been transformed so dramatically over the previous fifteen years or so that it was virtually unrecognizable from the one he remembered from his childhood. In the course of this twelve-month project, the Aman chiefs also wanted him to move around regularly from one address to another, partly because that would give him a broader knowledge of the country, but mainly because it would make his past much harder to check up on.

Lotz spent the second half of 1959 and the early months of 1960 building his cover story in Germany, at the same time that Malkin and his team were also active in the country. He started off first in Berlin, where he joined a riding club, and then moved to Munich, changing addresses frequently. Gradually, over time, he was able to train himself to think and react like a German nationalist who was out of place in, and highly critical of, the new Germany. Then, in late December 1960, he finally felt ready to move, and was given the green light by Tel Aviv to do so. He drove overland to Genoa and from there took a passenger ship that would take six days to reach Egypt.

Aman's daring plan to infiltrate the Egyptian infrastructure of Nasser's rocket program had begun.

CHAPTER ELEVEN
The Scientists Get to Work

In July 1960, completely unnoticed by anyone except a number of airport officials, a small private jet took off from Echterdingen Airport in Stuttgart to take its twenty-strong contingent of passengers to Egypt.

The passengers on board this particular jet, however, made this an unusually interesting flight. For among those being flown out that day was Dr. Paul Goercke, along with a number of other, more junior, technicians and specialists from the Jet Propulsion Study Institute. The other leading lights of the Egyptian missile program—Sänger, Kleinwachter, and Pilz—had already left, or were set to go, on different flights, partly to avoid arousing suspicion, partly because they had leave from the institute at different times of year. Now it was Goercke's turn. Like the others, he too would be delivering a series of lectures on space flight at the University of Cairo, but behind the scenes would also be working hard to push Nasser's space flight program forward.

Goercke stepped off the plane at Cairo International Airport and was driven by taxi through the streets of the capital. He immediately noticed that it was different from the place he remembered. He had spent a year in Egypt in 1954, when he had signed up to work as an electronics expert on Rolf Engel's rocket program, and had helped the Egyptians develop a national radar network.[149] But in the course of those few years Cairo had not only become more populous and teeming but also less cosmopolitan as its long-established European and Jewish populations, which had had a sizable and very visible presence until a few years before, had already started to retreat, looking elsewhere in the world for places of refuge where they could start a new life.

This exodus had begun in earnest after the events of January 1952, when "foreign" shops in the city, belonging to businessmen of mainly French, Italian, Greek, Armenian, and British origin, had been burned by angry crowds. But this was also when a new law had been introduced, although initially not strictly enforced, which compelled all businesses to have an Egyptian director or partner. The Egyptian authorities also found ways of actively encouraging non-Arabs to leave the country, although they never forced them to do so. Emigration rules were relaxed, allowing emigrants to take with them all their possessions and up to five thousand Egyptian pounds. There was then a further emigrant wave after the Suez War, when Westerners must have suddenly started to wonder what lay ahead and wanted to join the Egyptian Jews in leaving the country.[150]

This was not because the capital suffered as a result of the week-long allied campaign to seize the canal. True, there were some signs here and there that Egypt was at war: the policemen who guarded the city's banks, bridges, and other key installations were now always armed, wore steel helmets, and used hastily constructed sandbagged shelters. And every so often an Egyptian warplane flew high above the city streets. But while life otherwise just carried on more or less as usual for the people of Cairo, somehow the whole political scene seemed much less predictable than before. In particular, it appeared likely that the regime, or the Egyptian people, would be more hostile to any Western or Jewish influence, even though Cairo's "foreign" residents had been born and bred in Egypt and knew nothing of any other country, even those from which their ancestors had originated.

Within months of the Suez War, the European and Jewish populations had started to rapidly diminish and their influence to wane. Shops were staffed by native Egyptians, and restaurants served only traditional Egyptian food. The western suburbs where these populations had lived and worked for decades began to lose their very visible Western appearance as local Egyptians moved in instead, dressed in traditional garb such as the black *meliya*—long, shapeless gowns—that women wore. As a result, these streets had become not only more Islamized and Egyptianized but had deteriorated, reflecting the different standards of living of the various communities. Road and pavement surfaces became cracked, shops signs faded, buildings crumbled, and rubbish began to accumulate in the street.

There were a number of other, very visible, changes that Goercke could not have failed to notice as he made his way through the city's streets after a six-year absence. One of his abiding memories of the capital would have been the enormous number of beggars who infested the streets, all of whom were quick to spot and approach Western travelers. But soon after seizing power in 1952, the revolutionary government had moved to suppress them, using troops to round up huge numbers and ordering them to keep off the streets. This initially had only a very limited effect, since there always had been occasional and sporadic clampdowns, but by 1960 persistent efforts by the authorities meant that only the most determined beggars were left. The Cairo authorities had also cracked down equally hard on the hordes of prostitutes who proliferated in the streets and pestered passersby, particularly Westerners, as brazenly during the day as they did at night. This more stridently Islamist tone in the regime's rule showed itself in other ways too—for example, by the closure of several hundred sleazy nightclubs where some of the more revealing and erotic versions of belly dancing had long drawn numerous Western visitors.

Above all, Goercke would have observed the absence of the associates and friends he had made with his fellow Germans during his earlier stay. He had very pleasant memories of spending long evenings at the popular haunt of the German expatriates, the Löwenbräu brewery in the center of Cairo, where large quantities of traditional Bavarian lager were consumed on Friday and Saturday evenings. But by the late 1950s, some of the leading lights of this expatriate community had left the country. Dr. Wilhelm Voss, who had recruited Goercke into the Egyptian rocket program in 1953, had emigrated at the height of the Suez Crisis, and Rolf Engel had also returned to Western Europe, taking a job offer in Italy. Other central figures in the German expatriate community, such as General Fahrmbacher and Colonel

Beierlein, who had been a senior aide to General Rommel in North Africa, had also left by the end of 1959.

Yet neither Goercke nor the other star recruits to Nasser's programs would be alone. The new influx of German expatriates into the capital during 1960 promised to make the Löwenbräu busier than ever before, and most of the leading scientists were in any case accompanied by colleagues and associates from the Jet Propulsion Study Institute: Brandner traveled with a Germanic-looking engineer by the name of Naye and another scientist, Waldemar Schierhorn, who had lived in Egypt for some years and was very familiar with the country. Willy Messerschmitt was also accompanied by his own separate clique of engineers who had worked under him in Spain, while Sänger's team became known as Sänger Knaben (Sänger's Boys). This was a clever pun because the German phrase also means "choir boys," a fitting reference to the fresh, young faces of his assistants.[151]

Needless to say, not all of the German expatriates in Cairo had clean pasts. One of the doctors who was assigned to look after the scientists in their new surroundings was Dr. Hans Eisele, who was wanted in a number of countries for mass murder. During the war he had been a physician at several concentration camps, notably Dachau and Buchenwald, where he had conducted lethal scientific experiments on inmates, and had subsequently been condemned to death by two postwar tribunals. The sentences had eventually been quashed, and in 1952 Eisele had been released from Landsberg Prison, ready to start a new life, but had fled to Egypt in 1958 when new evidence came to light about his wartime activities. He was now starting a new and highly lucrative career as a doctor, establishing a large, affluent client base drawn from the rapidly growing community of Western expatriates. The experience of meeting Eisele, a "tall grey-haired man with a deeply lined face," was for some visitors extremely unsettling.[152]

When he was driven out of the capital after several days' rest, Goercke would have noticed other very striking changes. At Helwan, just outside Cairo, for example, he would have seen a giant steel mill standing on what, just a few years before, had been derelict land. By 1960 this had only just been built by its sponsors, the West German engineering firm Demag, which a few years before had won a highly prized contract to exploit huge quantities of iron ore that were buried under the deserts. The massive site attracted not just large numbers of scientific experts but also a huge influx of migrant workers who were housed in the sprawling blocks of apartments and houses that covered the surrounding area. This was the new face of Egypt—a rapidly industrializing country that had considerable natural resources and a plentiful labor force but that was nonetheless very dependent on foreign investment and skills.

Goercke's first destination was Site 36, an aircraft factory at Helwan, just outside Cairo, that had originally been built by the British. As he made his way through the security checkpoints, the German expert was taken inside to see the state of readiness of the apparatus. It was here that Messerschmitt would be working on the wings and the fuselage for his new supersonic jet plane, the HA-300, and developing his trainer aircraft, the HA-200. By this time the trainer had already been revealed to the Egyptian public, because a daring Spanish pilot named Dr. Estaban had flown fast and low over the Cairo crowds on Revolution Day in 1960. But this early version desperately needed some technical improvements and modifications—notably on its highly unstable landing gear—before it went into production.

There were two other main installations that Goercke and his colleagues would soon be taken to visit. One was an enormous, whitewashed factory, situated in the vast deserts surrounding the city of Heliopolis, which had now become known simply as Factory 333. In the days of British rule, the site had been designed and used as a hospital, making the most of the dry climate and sulfur springs to treat rheumatism, a common condition among expatriates. Then, in 1952, the four-square-mile area had been taken over by Rolf Engel's CERVA project and used as its headquarters. By the time the German scientists were taken on a tour in the summer of 1960, it was being used by a state-run engineering company to manufacture simple training planes for the air force but had never at any stage been used to produce rockets. Surrounded by machine-gun nests and encircled with barbed wire, this site, which the Egyptians called Thalathat (The Threes), was to be the very heart of the rocket program where most of the top people would be based.

The other was Site 135, at Helwan, twenty miles outside the capital. This was the home of huge hangars and wind tunnels that Ferdinand Brandner could use to test prototypes of his aircraft engines. Needless to say, this site, like the two others, was very closely guarded by heavily armed soldiers.

Goercke and his colleagues at Stuttgart had already extensively discussed his role in the weapons program long before they left their homeland. Goercke and Kleinwachter, it was agreed, were to contribute to the guidance mechanism of the rocket while Pilz would direct the engine-development department. Another colleague and veteran of Peenemünde, Walter Schuran, would contribute to the airframe design. All of the expatriates, moreover, were expected to spend a great deal of time training indigenous Egyptians in both the classroom and the factories where their work would be concentrated.

But though their roles had been discussed and detailed well in advance, nothing quite prepared any of the men for the reality of what their task would entail. Almost as soon as they arrived and were taken on an inspection of the proposed industrial and research sites, they were all struck by just how unsphisticated the Egyptian facilities were. All had expected to see workshops and laboratories equipped with high-precision tools, specialized machines, and toxic chemicals, but the main sites instead bore barely any resemblance to the relative sophistication they had seen and become used to in their homeland.

In the summer of 1960, each of these different sites was in a state that, by Western standards, was technically primitive. But Egypt lacked any industrial base of its own that was capable of manufacturing the high-precision components that were required to bring them even remotely up to scratch. So if the Egyptian rocket and aircraft programs were to have any chance of taking off, the German experts warned, then their patrons would have to make far greater efforts to acquire the relevant hardware, without which nothing much could be done. Supremely expert in their fields though they were, the Germans could only make the most of the materials that lay before them, and could not just conjure the materials they needed out of thin air. Yet a further difficulty for the Egyptians was that they had very few sources of overseas supply.

One such source was the Soviet Union, which had been Egypt's main source of arms over the preceding few years. On May Day in 1957, the Soviet military had paraded new missiles, the SS-1 Scud rockets, which had been quickly noticed by the outside world and may well have whetted Nasser's own appetite to acquire something as impressive. The Egyptian premier had then asked the Soviet leader, Nikita Khrushchev, if Moscow would sell any "intermediate-range rockets" but found his advances immediately rebuffed. Egyptian territory was so small, Khrushchev later claimed in an unconvincing response that didn't seem to address the issue, such weapons couldn't be used. Some months later he risked offending the Egyptian leader by claiming that the Cairo authorities couldn't be trusted with such weapons, which he said could cause "excitement" and lead to "undesirable actions."[153] The Soviets may not only have mistrusted Nasser, perhaps viewing him as an unreliable long-term partner in the Middle East, but also felt that supplying arms to him might have risked stirring up unnecessary tension with the United States.

Without Soviet support, General Khalil was forced to think up other ways of obtaining the hardware his project was dependent upon. Perhaps the most effective and simplest solution was to set up more front organizations in Western capitals that could provide the right cover for his procurement drive. And he had heard about just the right man to establish and run them—a former German army officer called Heinz Krug.

Able, driven, well connected in the engineering world, and highly motivated by the large sales commissions he was promised, Krug was well suited to his new job. He was also very familiar with the world the scientists lived in, having worked as a business manager and lawyer representing the Jet Propulsion Study Institute. By this time he had proven his skills as an advocate, as well as his interest in money, by representing Pilz, Sänger, Goercke, and other leading scientists before the Institute of Physicists in Bonn, which had challenged their right to work for Nasser. The experts were not breaching their professional obligations, argued Krug, because their activities were just "private secondary activity" and did not violate their contracts with their Stuttgart employers. For taking the case on and winning, Krug was awarded a huge sum of money—a twenty-percent share of a deal worth two million deutsche marks.

Hearing about the scientists' activities in the Middle East, Krug had professed to Kamil his own interest in Nasser's work and duly been signed up to run the European procurement operations. On July 14, 1960, he registered a new front organization that would be known as the INTRA Commercial Company, and named himself and a colleague, Dr. Elizabeth Habermeyer, as shareholders. Its official purpose was the "internal and external trade in goods of all kinds as well as the development of technical devices," which was a convenient euphemism for the acquisition of essential spare parts for Nasser's rocket and aviation programs.

By late fall, Kamil had succeeded in finding an office for the first of these new front organizations, as well as a director. Situated in Stuttgart, right next to the offices of Egypt's national airline, the INTRA office was run by Krug and Habermeyer, who were supported by an office staff of two. Krug worked furiously to get the company going and impress his Egyptian elders, prompting his office colleagues to refer to the company as his unofficial "bride," to whom his devotion seemed to be total.

An important part of his brief was to win the rights to foreign patents of rocket engines and guidance systems, bidding for them before other rival governments did so. But Krug also had some other responsibilities. He was, for example, tasked with exporting particular spare parts and obtaining licenses from the authorities in Bonn before flying them out of the country on the weekly United Arab Airlines flight to Cairo. There was nothing illegal about this, either under international or domestic law, but such operations were, of course, best hushed up in case the Israelis, or either of the superpowers, found out what was happening and tried to disrupt them. Using surreptitious means, Krug concentrated on acquiring the top items on the shopping list he had been given, such as special trays, measuring and testing equipment, machinery, and valves.

Another of Krug's tasks was to subcontract particularly specialized projects to privately run companies and laboratories throughout West Germany, finding and then employing individuals who were deemed to be particularly trustworthy. Within a few weeks of setting up INTRA, Krug had struck a deal with Hans Kleinwachter, and early in 1961 a

Swiss firm in Emmen began testing rockets in an aerodynamic tunnel for the benefit of the Egyptian government.[154]

At this stage, Messerschmitt's involvement in the aircraft program also became invaluable. He had by this time become a joint director of Kamil's company, MECO, and a branch of this company was set up inside the giant Messerschmitt factory at Augsburg. A number of key components for the HA-200 and HA-300, including the chassis and cabin, were designed and built there before being exported to Egypt, while a number of other leading German companies—including parts of the Siemens Corporation—also acted as leading suppliers to the Egyptian program.[155]

Beside coping with the stresses and difficulties of building up the Egyptian rocket program from scratch, the scientists had other issues to deal with. Many found the intense summer heat to be a serious distraction, while others succumbed to diseases that developed largely from poor hygiene. All knew that they could never afford to wholly drop their guard. All knew that the missile program could not fail to be of interest to Israel—even if it was only a civilian program they were working on—and that there was always a latent risk of assassination. On arrival, all of them were automatically issued pistols and special identification passes, and all were constantly accompanied by bodyguards.

There were, however, some mitigating factors. An entire floor of the luxurious Shepheard Hotel in Cairo was put at Messerschmitt's disposal, while all of the top scientists had the luxury of having air-conditioned villas in Cairo's wealthy suburb of Maadi or in Heliopolis, and privileged access to the exclusive country clubs in and around Cairo.[156] Brandner chose to live on the exclusive Zamalek Island, where he was given an entire floor, which comprised three separate apartments, of a luxurious building.[157] Pilz and Kleinwachter often rode horses in the desert around the Pyramids, went fishing together in the Red Sea, and regularly swam off the idyllic beaches of Alexandria, a favorite venue for tourists who were drawn to its palm-lined beaches and brilliantly lit cafés and shops. All of the scientists enjoyed Western foods and drinks that were specially shipped in to cater for them: in February 1962, Brandner, for example, made the most of such luxuries to host an impressive Rhenish Carnival at the Nile Hilton in central Cairo, complete with voluminous quantities of specially imported German beer.

By 1960, Western visitors who were familiar with the old colonial days were lamenting that in Cairo and elsewhere "the glitter of the old days had gone" but noting that the country as a whole still had a great deal to boast. The bazaars, mosques, and gardens, wrote Britain's diplomatic representative at the time, were still "places of enchantment," and the Germans also had access to the old colonial clubs—once the exclusive preserve of Westerners but now full of upscale Egyptian nationals—where tennis courts, swimming pools, and golf courses still retained their colonial aura.[158]

It was here that they rubbed shoulders with Egyptian military officers, foreign diplomats, Egyptian and foreign journalists, academics, and professional men, and their families, joining many of them in long games of bridge, or watching an annual tennis tournament in which the Italian star "Nicky" Pietrangeli often took part, easily defeating a succession of opponents.

A Western journalist who was given exclusive access to the scientists around this time compared their "opulent" lifestyle to those of "aristocrats," writing:

> [T]he German scientists, engineers and technicians who work for Nasser today live in an atmosphere . . . of luxury. . . . After hours they lead a carefree, fun-loving life . . . at carnival time they nostalgically caroused at a "River Carnival" party in the Nile Hilton Hotel. The blond giants loafing in the sun or diving off the high board at the Heliopolis Sporting Club look like incongruous leftovers from *Afrika Corp* days. With their air-conditioned penthouses, their sports cars and their special imports of sausages and other delicacies from Hamburg, they are the inheritors of the opulence of King Farouk's days . . . the three rocket men are coddled specialists who know they will always be in demand, like the German princes who once filled the vacancies on European thrones.[159]

Central Cairo, c.1953. Parts of the capital had changed little for centuries.

A typical demonstration in the streets of central Cairo, c.1953. It was Nasser's supreme affinity with the Arab masses that deeply alarmed planners in Tel Aviv as well as in Western capitals.

Cairo c.1955. The young Egyptian leader, Gamal Abdel Nasser, waves to adoring
Egyptian crowds.

Isser Harel, the legendary head of Israel's foreign intelligence service from 1951 until his resignation in 1963. Operation Damocles was devised and executed at his instigation.

Revolution Day, July 1963: Cairo crowds surround one of the regime's long-range missiles.

On Revolution Day, Egyptian soldiers parade in front of regime missiles c.1965.

On trial for his life before a Cairo court, the captured Israeli spy Wolfgang Lotz talks to Egyptian officials.

After his capture, Israeli spy Wolfgang Lotz demonstrates how he hid his radio transmitter in a set of bathroom scales.

But if the German scientists had now embarked on their project in earnest, making the most of their generous salaries and pleasant working conditions, so too was the Israeli secret service starting to enjoy successes of its own. For at the same time that Goercke and his colleagues had begun their work on the Egyptian military programs, Mossad had succeeded in inserting another agent, by the name of Shaaltiel Ben-Yair, into their midst.

Ben-Yair's story came to light when, around 1959, he suddenly phoned an old acquaintance, Amos Keinan, from the Jewish underground in Palestine. The men had lost touch nearly a decade before, but Keinan immediately recognized the French-speaking voice at the other end of the line and the code name—Charlie—that Ben-Yair had been assigned all those years before. Astonished, Keinan arranged to meet him on a tourist boat on the River Seine and catch up with his news.

By meeting Keinan and telling his former comrade of his story, Ben-Yair was committing a huge, and quite uncharacteristic, breach of security. But he deeply trusted Keinan and was willing to take the risk. His story was certainly remarkable. After Israel's independence in 1948—the last time the two men had seen each other—he had been unemployed and drifted but in 1955 had followed other members of the underground into the ranks of Mossad. As a youth he had spent a good deal of time in France, learning the language fluently by the time he returned to the Middle East in 1942. It was this familiarity with France that had made him useful to Mossad when its operations chiefs began to look for new ways of infiltrating Egypt.

In the course of 1959, Ben-Yair had assumed the identity of a "Francois Renancoeur," a Belgian citizen and international authority on cattle, and put his Jewish past behind him: "[E]ven if you shout to me in the middle of the night in Hebrew I would not wake up," he told Keinan. Having established this identity, he had received an invitation to visit Cairo to advise the government on how to look after its livestock. But the loneliness of his work there drove him to break the rules and make contact with old friends. "Once a month I come to Paris for one evening, going to Brussels the next day and from there to Cairo. I have no one to talk to," he explained.[160] How much he disclosed to Keinan about his true role in Egypt remains unclear, but by 1960 he appears to have become one of Israel's most daring operatives in

Egypt, single-handedly mapping Egyptian airfields and feeding information to Tel Aviv about military installations.

The German scientists had attractive salaries and working conditions, but with agents like Ben-Yair close by, they could hardly afford to drop their guard.

CHAPTER TWELVE
Mossad Watches the Egyptians

While the German scientists were busy at work, and enjoying a certain amount of luxury in their spare time, Wolfgang Lotz was embarking on his bold mission to infiltrate Nasser's rocket and aircraft programs. He had arrived in Cairo at the end of 1960, feeling thoroughly miserable and lonely in his new surroundings; but, like any other professional spy, he was determined to press ahead with his mission.

Lotz himself may have been astonished by the remarkable ease with which he now accomplished his most vital goal, upon which the whole success of his enterprise turned—his ability to build up relationships with the select few who had firsthand knowledge of, or even direct involvement in, the military programs. Since he was posing as a horse breeder, his obvious starting point was the capital's main riding club, preferably one that was used by senior figures in the government, the military, and, if at all possible, by the German expatriate scientists themselves.

Wasting almost no time, he was personally driven by his hotel manager, just two days after arriving in Cairo, to the capital's leading riding club, one that was owned and run by Egyptian cavalry officers. On arrival, Lotz casually strolled around, watching the horses and their riders, and waiting for the right moment to strike up a conversation.

It was at this point that the Israeli agent started to make his first contacts within the closed world of the Egyptian military. As he watched the horses, he was approached by one of the riders, who was puzzled, and probably very pleased, by the unexpected presence of a Westerner. Lotz ran through his well-prepared cover story, explaining that he was a German horse breeder with a particular love of Arabian thoroughbreds and adding that he couldn't resist the temptation of visiting the club.

The rider was a dark-skinned, clean-shaven Egyptian man in his forties by the name of Youssef Ali Ghorab, who was general of police in Cairo, and the honorary president of the club. Ghorab showed Lotz around the grounds, introducing him to a number of Egyptian officers, and as they discussed their common interest, finding so much to talk about, the two men quickly established a good rapport.

Within a matter of days, they had started to ride together and to share drinks and meals. Lotz was soon a regular visitor to the general's house and became very good friends with his family, often bringing with him expensive gifts that he thought strongly appealed to the Egyptians' more acquisitive instincts: "[T]he Egyptians were like greedy, avaricious children," he wrote, although he was also aware that "if I failed to keep them sweet they could easily cut up rough."[161]

The Israeli spy was now well positioned to make the most of Ghorab's contacts and knowledge but would have to do so in as subtle and clever a way as he could. "An introduction here, a telephone call there, licenses, permits, recommendations—they all served the real purpose of my stay in Egypt very well indeed."[162]

Six months later, in the summer of 1961, Lotz returned to Europe, flying back to Paris—a favorite rendezvous for the Israeli secret services—where he secretly met up with his boss in military intelligence's Unit 131. Carefully folded and hidden away in an inside pocket was a detailed report about his journey, the people he had met, his general impressions of Egypt as a country and, of course, some information he had obtained about the rocket and aircraft programs.

Lotz made contact with his handlers in the highly cautious way that he had been taught, going to a public pay phone in the street to call a memorized number. "After I'd given the code word, I was told to meet a friend at three o'clock in a certain café," he recalled. "In fact, three o'clock at café X meant two o'clock at café Y."

The intelligence chief was very pleased with Lotz's progress and in return handed over a large sum of money. The spy chief had something else to offer Lotz, something that was now set to become indispensable in his mission—a tiny radio transmitter that he could hide in the heel of a riding boot, where a cache had been cleverly hollowed out. To use the transmitter he would need to refer to a special code book, the key to which was to be found on the pages of a manual about horse breeding that he would be taking with him. He had some other invaluable necessities with him as well, including a packet of high explosives that he smuggled past customs in the hollowed-out bottom of a case of French cheese. Lotz was now ready to continue with his mission in earnest, and his immediate objective was simply to obtain as much detailed information about the German scientists and their work as he could.

Besides the transmitter and the explosives, Lotz would have one other huge asset when he returned to Egypt a few weeks later—a wife at his side In early June he had boarded the Orient Express and happened to move into a compartment that was occupied by a "tall, extremely pretty blue-eyed blonde with the kind of curvaceous figure I always had a weakness for."[163] The long eleven-hour train journey brought the two together and just two weeks after meeting her, at the end of which "we were madly in love," he proposed marriage. He had already been through two marriages and two divorces but had not lost his appetite for more, having felt intensely lonely in his first few months in Egypt and not wanting to return alone. In any case, he knew that in Cairo a married couple would arouse far less suspicion than a forty-year-old bachelor, who might have been suspected of having a secret family life and commitments elsewhere. It was usually much easier for a couple to ingratiate themselves into other people's social circles than a single person.

But Lotz was taking a huge risk by failing to tell his bosses about the relationship, the marriage, and his wife's presence in Egypt. Invaluable though he was as an agent, he simply could not afford to get on the wrong side of his employers by keeping the matter silent, starting a new life in Egypt with his wife, Waltraud, at his side, before revealing the truth to his bosses. He also broke another of the most basic rules in the intelligence world, or at least in the world of Israeli intelligence—that of telling his wife about his true business in Egypt. During his training, he had been repeatedly warned about the huge risks of sharing such information and had been given examples of agents who had paid the ultimate price when their real identities were exposed by those who were closest to them. Often, the spy trainers had emphasized, such betrayals had not been made deliberately but were simply the result of careless words or remarks that were ventured quite innocently, often in unlikely venues such as dinner parties. Lotz's move was all the more risky because his wife was German and had no reason to feel any loyalty to the Jewish state, something that would have infuriated Lotz's handlers had they known of his indiscretion. Yet Lotz claimed that he was so desperate to return to Egypt with his wife at his side that he was willing to break such vital rules.

After taking their honeymoon in Vienna and Venice, Wolfgang and Waltraud prepared to return to Egypt, three months after he had left. This time he was well prepared, and eight out of his seventeen suitcases and crates contained gifts for his Egyptian friends, including Western luxuries such as electric mixers, Swiss watches, tape recorders, and electric razors, which were extremely hard to find, and consequently extremely expensive, in the Arab world. He was also well funded and could now afford to rent an attractive apartment on the island of Zamalek, where he was looked after by a number of Sudanese *boab*, or gatekeepers, who guarded him and his wife, performed a number of household tasks, and "reported to the [Egyptian] secret police on everything that went on in the house," wrote Lotz, "how the tenants lived, how they spent their money, what they spoke about among themselves, who came to visit them, what mail they received, and so on."[164]

While Lotz was working hard to infiltrate the Egyptian rocket and aircraft programs, the German scientists were pressing ahead with their plans. By early 1961, there were as many as a thousand employees working at Factory 333 alone, including over a hundred foreign scientists, engineers, and technicians, who were by now starting to turn their blueprint plans into crude prototypes that could be tested.

The scientists and their bosses had also encountered a number of unexpected delays and obstacles that were seriously hampering their plans. The most urgent problem that had confronted them in the summer of 1960 was the lack of vital spare parts, but over the next few months an increasing number of the parts started to arrive, courtesy of the various front companies that had been set up in Germany and Switzerland. Willy Messerschmitt was also able to use his extensive network of contacts to get hold of several ejectable seats—essential for Brandner's supersonic-aircraft program—and some French-built engine components. Top engineers from Mercedes-Benz, such as Dr. Eugene Neher, and from the technical universities at Aachen, Munich, Berlin, Vienna, and Graz had also signed up to join the Egyptian programs.

Yet by the end of 1960, progress on both the missile and the aviation programs was still very slow, far more so than either the scientists themselves or their Egyptian sponsors had hoped or planned for. The HA-300 jet plane, for example, had originally been designed to use an engine, the British-built Orpheus, which the German experts were quickly dissatisfied with. It was just not powerful enough, argued Brandner, and, to add insult to injury, the British company that manufactured it was also demanding a "crazy price" to supply a new one.[165] But to replace the Orpheus would mean designing a completely new engine, and this was, of course, a supremely challenging task given Egypt's total dearth of high-quality precision engineering.

Brandner, by his own admission, was "an idealist and a fanatic of technique" and, true to form, devoted himself wholeheartedly to his new scheme, alongside a young fellow German, Karl Bauer, a former national paragliding champion who had worked for Telefunken, the German communications company, before arriving in Egypt.[166] As models, they used the engine of a French Mirage, supplied to them by Messerschmitt, as well as a British Orpheus, and by early 1961 they had made good progress on building the supersonic new engine, now tentatively called the Brandner E-300, that he had specially designed for the HA-300.

But Brandner desperately needed to test his new engine in flight, since the various experiments he had performed on it gave no real indication of how it would work in practice. The trouble was that the jet fighter was by now only at its prototype stage and was nowhere near ready to take flight. And the Egyptians sorely lacked any jet aircraft that could be easily fitted with the new design, which was specifically geared to the HA-300.

The breakthrough that Brandner so badly needed for his aviation program came from another German engineer, Kurt Tank, who had been recruited into the program in the summer of 1960 by his longtime acquaintance Willy Messerschmitt. Tank was a sixty-two-year-old veteran soldier of the First World War and a highly successful aircraft designer before and during the Second, but after 1945 he too had struggled with professional disappointment and failure. Having tried and failed to interest several governments with his aircraft designs, he was eventually hired by the Argentinians to work at a research institute in Córdoba, using a pseudonym to protect his true identity. But after the fall of Pres. Juan Perón in 1955, Tank was forced to leave the country and look elsewhere for work, returning to his homeland along with a handful of other German expatriate engineers. Quickly approached and commissioned by the Indian government, however, he moved to Bangalore, where he helped to build the first Indian jet fighter, the HF-24. By a stroke of amazing good luck, he had decided to power this plane with the British Orpheus.

Brandner knew quite a lot about Tank's work in both Argentina and India, and on learning of his recruitment into the Egyptian program had a clever idea. If Tank could arrange delivery of an Indian HF-24, then Brandner would simply be able to replace its Orpheus engine with his own E-300 model, and could then have the flight test that was so crucial. This flight test would allow the HA-300 Egyptian jet program to make some very real progress.

Yet there were numerous other obstacles that would have to be overcome, notably the almost complete lack of engineering skills among local Egyptians, without which the relatively small number of Western experts lacked the support they needed. "Egyptian engineers are being trained and schooled by the Europeans," wrote one Western journalist who reported on the story, "both in the classroom and in on-the-job training procedures."[167]

Meanwhile, the engineers who were working on the missile program were confronted by a huge obstacle of their own—the complete lack of a reliable guidance system. It was all very well being able to launch a rocket into the atmosphere, but unless it landed where it was supposed to—which was right on the top of an enemy position, striking it with pinpoint accuracy—then it was a virtually useless piece of equipment. Both Goercke and Pilz had a lot of experience in designing guidance systems, since they had both worked on the French Veronique program after the war. But the system used in the Veronique project—known as the wire-guidance device because the rocket was fitted with wire cables that stabilized its flight—was not much help for a more powerful and sophisticated military rocket of the sort that the Egyptians were now building.[168] At best, it offered just a temporary reprieve.

Aware of this major deficiency in the program, Pilz decided to utilize the same guidance system that the Nazi scientists had used for the V-2 rocket. This system was extremely accurate but exceedingly difficult to build, dependent as it was on a complex mechanism of pendulums, gyroscopes, and control systems. Yet even utilizing the technology pioneered twenty years before promised to be immensely challenging because none of the German expatriate staff in the rocket program had had any direct experience in the specialized field of V-2 guidance, having only a very basic knowledge of how it worked.

Meanwhile, Nasser was kept constantly informed of the scientists' progress, or lack of it, and was anxiously waiting for real progress to be made, particularly since the funding of such a hugely expensive project was not unlimited. He desperately needed to bolster his prestige before the Arab masses at a time when it was at a new low. For it was at this time that Syrian officials had announced that, just three years after joining, they wanted to leave the United Arab Republic and secede from joint rule with Egypt. Nasser had prided himself on being a "leader of the Arabs," but now his rhetoric seemed more hollow than ever.

Nasser was prepared to be patient over the military programs, but a sudden development now took him, and the rest of the Arab world, wholly by surprise. For early in the morning of July 6, 1961, the Israeli government announced that it had successfully launched a "multi-stage, unguided rocket," which it called the Shavit 2, seventy-five miles into outer space. This was not a military rocket, emphasized the government announcement, but was only designed for meteorological research, such as "ionospheric weather testing." Outside the inner circles of the Israeli government, no one had previously known that Israel had any capabilities in rocketry, and the announcement was a huge surprise to the outside world and, for the neighbors, enemies, and rivals of the Jewish state, a very unwelcome one.

Exactly why Israel launched this rocket, and why they did so at this particular moment, remains unclear. Some Israeli commentators felt sure that its purpose was political, since it could have potentially given Premier David Ben-Gurion, who personally attended the launch, a short-term electoral lift in the parliamentary elections that were due on August 15.

But Ben-Gurion also reputedly told his cabinet colleagues that the launch had taken "the wind out of the sails of President Nasser."[169] This may have been the reason the rocket was named version 2 when in fact there never had been a first version: domestic audiences would have known this but a foreign power, like Egypt, would have been given the impression that Israel's own program was more advanced than it really was. This suggests that Tel Aviv's real interest may have been to undermine Nasser: Israeli intelligence may have figured that the Egyptian leader intended to stage a special military display on July 23, to mark the ninth anniversary of the 1952 revolution, and wanted to spoil his propaganda coup. The Israelis had no reason to suppose that this would include any missile launches but probably thought that it would involve some of the Soviet planes and tanks that Nasser had taken delivery of.

Just a few weeks beforehand, Nasser appears to have heard unconfirmed reports about Israel's preparations for the launch, and he then made a desperate last-minute move to beat them to it, hoping to launch his own rockets just before Israel did the same. In June 1961 his agents approached NASA and one of the leading American companies that dealt with rocketry, the Zimney Corporation, and urgently requested delivery of a number of rockets that would be all ready, in technical terms, to be launched into outer space. Washington, however, instantly vetoed the Egyptian request.[170]

Nasser was forced to swallow his pride, for Israel had beaten him in the race to be the first Middle Eastern power to own and launch rockets into outer space. The Egyptian premier knew that his prestige would diminish in the eyes of the Arab masses if he was seen to have failed to keep pace.

It was therefore a matter of his own political career, as well as the security of his country and of the independent Arab states that looked to him as a savior and a protector, to forge ahead with his own missile program.

Under pressure from his president, General Khalil now summoned Eugen Sänger to his office and showed him photographs of the Israel rocket. Anxiously, he asked Sänger about its design and whether it could be used for military purposes. Sänger calmly reassured him, replying that he was sure it could only be used for meteorological purposes, but Khalil was still not convinced. The missile program would have to make more rapid progress, he replied, if Egypt was to avoid falling behind in the race into space.[171]

CHAPTER THIRTEEN
The Egyptians Press Ahead

B y launching the Shavit 2, Israeli chiefs were hoping to do more than just steal the limelight from the Egyptian premier. For by the summer of 1961, the Mossad chief Isser Harel judged that he had enough information on the Egyptian rocket and aircraft programs—supplied courtesy of agents such as Malkin and Lotz—to approach the West German government and voice his concerns.

Harel's first move was to personally approach his old acquaintance from the world of intelligence, his West German counterpart, Reinhard Gehlen. The Mossad chief flew directly to Bonn and within just hours of arrival had arranged to meet Gehlen at his office. Using some of his information about German expatriate activity in Egypt that his spies had provided, he accused Gehlen of deliberately ignoring the issue. Surely Gehlen must know about what his fellow Germans were doing in Egypt, he argued strongly, and surely he could do something to stop them from continuing? Gehlen retorted that Germany was using the scientists to gather intelligence on Egypt, but Harel did not believe him. "I want them stopped and stopped now," he demanded. "I am not interested in long-term efforts. For us there is only the short term. The long term can mean after their rockets have fallen on our heads. In the long term we are dead men." He finished the meeting by warning Gehlen that the Israeli secret service was ready to take the matter into its own hands unless the West Germans took some definitive action of their own.[172]

There was one reason Gehlen was being very ambivalent, and perhaps not entirely truthful, about the matter. For at this time West Germany was in the awkward position of not wanting to alienate either the Israelis or the Egyptians, knowing that one wrong move could serve Soviet purposes at a time when Cold War relations between East and West were very tense. In particular, the construction of the Berlin Wall, which started in August 1961, had created a real crisis between the two German states.

On the one hand, Gehlen had become increasingly concerned about the growing communist infiltration of the Middle East at a time when President Nasser had openly shown signs of leaning away from Washington in favor of Moscow. As a result, he had started to regard Israel, always quick to emphasize its credentials as a Western-leaning democracy, as an important regional ally for West Germany and other NATO allies, one that it could not afford to alienate. This gave Harel a huge negotiating advantage, which he doubtlessly knew he could exploit to the full: unless the German government made more effort to help Israel, he may have hinted, then Israel could not do its utmost to help the West.

On the other hand, if the West German authorities clamped down too heavily on the scientists, then they risked pushing the Egyptians further toward the Soviets. This was partly because Cairo might react spitefully, strongly resenting foreign—particularly Western—interference in its own affairs. But it was also because Nasser, who was so unpredictable, might fear that he would never be able to develop his own rockets and therefore be more susceptible to suggestions of a Soviet alliance. West Germany may also have felt that the presence of the German scientists on Egyptian soil could have strengthened the bond between the two countries.

Over the next few weeks, the Israelis stepped up their efforts to lobby the Bonn government, and in doing so they were joined by a number of French officials, who were equally concerned that the Egyptian leader would present a much more dangerous threat to their grip on North Africa if he succeeded in developing a missile capability: the insurgents in their French colonies, they argued, would step up their activities, viewing the missiles as a shield that could protect them from retaliation. In October 1961 the

West German foreign ministry relented and agreed, in principle, to take some action against the scientists, although they left open the question of what steps they were going to take and how they were going to persuade the scientists to renounce their overseas careers.

The Bonn government started with the biggest name among Nasser's recruits, Eugen Sänger. One October day a team of government officials visited the former Nazi scientist at his office in Stuttgart and asked him to provide a detailed account of his work in Egypt. Sänger replied that he had merely used forty-eight days' paid leave from his regular job, out of an annual total of seventy-two, in order to give lectures to Egyptian scientists and students. He added that he had already notified the Bonn government of his activities in Egypt and there was nothing illegal, or immoral, about what he was doing. But this was not enough to satisfy the Bonn government, which now judged that Israel's case was the more pressing. In early November the federal minister of transport wrote to Sänger and demanded his resignation from the Jet Propulsion Study Institute. The reason, argued the minister, was that his work for Nasser "exceeded the extent of the subsidiary work his contract [with the institute] permitted him to undertake" and that he was being "politically unwise" by working for the Egyptians.[173]

It is possible that the Bonn authorities also tempted Sänger by offering him lucrative contracts within Germany if he pulled out of Nasser's project. Whatever was being said behind the scenes, the government's tactics worked, for just days later Sänger canceled his Egyptian contract. He allegedly sold his equity stake in the missile-acquisition business, which had been earning him a large sum of money, and resigned from his work in Stuttgart. He instead took up a consultancy role for Junkers and became director of a new department of space research that was being opened at West Berlin Technical University, posts that the government may have been instrumental in helping him secure. True, his salary was now a relatively meager two hundred thousand marks, less than a third of what he expected to make from the Egyptians, but at least he had some peace of mind.

Now that he was no longer working for Egypt, Sänger gave a series of press interviews about the work he had undertaken there. He defended his actions resolutely, emphasizing that he had always been working "on nothing else but peaceful rockets" that were "more a matter of prestige for Nasser." Any military program, he continued, would demand a great deal more research and development, which Egypt was not committed to. He also claimed that the Egyptian program was in any case not a sophisticated one: "[A]lthough in principle the rocket could be launched into an inclined flight, there is no way of knowing with accuracy where it will impact . . . so I can't imagine how it would be used for military purposes."[174] He added that it was the Bonn government that should ultimately take the blame for what was going on. As a British newspaper reported: "German scientists [Sänger] said, would never have gone to Egypt if the Federal Government had been able to offer them the chance of real research at home. 'For my collaborators, there were no practical opportunities for rocket research,' he said. 'In Egypt, one was helped greatly.'"[175]

Various other pieces of information emerged during his interview, such as his revelation that the Egyptians had promised its recruits the vast sum of two million marks if they succeeded in producing a rocket, one quarter of which would have gone to Sänger himself.

But while Sänger bowed out of the Egyptian enterprise, his other colleagues involved themselves even more. Pilz and Goercke resigned their jobs in Stuttgart and moved instead to Cairo, while Krug and Kleinwachter stayed behind in West Germany to continue with their work for the INTRA procurement company and at the various research laboratories in Germany and Austria. Pilz now took over Sänger's position as the chief program manager, while another expatriate scientist, Walter Schuran, stepped into Pilz's position as head of the propulsion-systems department. All of these experts may well have calculated that they had more to gain financially by doing so: by the end of 1961 INTRA had become a highly profitable business, so much so that Pilz and Goercke had both been eager to become equity partners in the enterprise.[176]

But although the Egyptian rocket program had lost its star name, it was nonetheless making quite rapid progress by the end of 1961. Pressed on by Nasser, more factories and infrastructure were being built, including the large Kader Factory in Heliopolis, where guidance systems were probably designed and built, and another unidentified facility, where liquid fuel and explosives were produced.[177] A Swiss company was also conducting wind-tunnel tests on the prototypes, while U.S. intelligence services conjectured that an Egyptian front company was working hard to acquire Western-built range instrumentation equipment.[178]

By this time, the project's engineers were no longer merely designing blueprint plans; they had started to build and then test basic prototypes. A number of rocket tests were now carried out, with varying degrees of success. One such test, held in May that year, was watched by the president himself, while in July a high-altitude research projectile exploded after lifting a mile into the atmosphere.[179] Engine and flight tests were regularly conducted at a test site near Wadi El Natrun, one of which, according to Lotz's very mischievous report, nearly killed Field Marshal Amer, the head of Egypt's armed forces: "[T]he rocket turned around in mid-air and nearly landed on the head of Marshal Amer," he reported, with tongue firmly in cheek, "who was seen running for his life."[180]

The Israelis were not alone in noticing that the Egyptians were now making progress in their rocket and aircraft programs. The CIA had an office in Alexandria whose staff had for some years been tasked with tracking the movements of Egypt's Whiskey-class submarines and surface ships at the nearby naval base of Ras el-Tin. But at the end of 1961 the staff were also instructed to look out for any signs of rocket launches—such as vapor trails in the sky or any anecdotal reports they came across—and feed the information back to the CIA headquarters at Langley, Virginia.[181]

The Egyptian test launches were also picked up by the international media, whose interest in the program had been aroused by the controversy over Eugen Sänger. In November 1961, the Cairo correspondent of a leading British newspaper reported that a number of "successful" rocket experiments had been conducted over the preceding few months, and three months later claimed that a rocket flight test had been witnessed by "thousands" in Cairo. The journalist added that officials at Cairo International Airport had clearly not been informed about these tests since they had closed the airport for two hours while they investigated the incident.[182]

As the Egyptians conducted more test launches in the course of 1962 and more information came to light about their activities, foreign governments were in a position to make some tentative assessment of what the scientists had achieved. Such developments were of course of particular interest in Washington, where the military capabilities of every state in the Middle East were always carefully monitored, and where the Defense Intelligence Agency (DIA) now began to make a preliminary assessment of Egyptian progress. The DIA experts had information not only from their own sources in Egypt but also from the West Germans who, as NATO allies, were more than happy to pass on whatever facts they had about the activities of their expatriate citizens.

The DIA felt sure that the Egyptians were working not on any peaceful program to send satellites into outer space and gather information on the weather, as Sänger had claimed, but on a surface-to-surface missile that was intended to counter Israel's own capabilities. They also felt sure—and were quite right in thinking—that the Egyptian designs borrowed heavily from the French Veronique program, which so many of the German staff in Cairo had once worked on, although the Egyptian versions were much more powerful and had longer ranges.

In particular, the American analysts knew that the Egyptians had developed two distinct types of missile. They estimated that the smaller of the two—which Cairo called al Zafar—was about seventeen feet long and two feet across, and was a "single stage, liquid fuelled, unguided rocket, developed from the design of a French sounding rocket." In their view, it probably had a "maximum" range of two hundred miles, although they emphasized that if it was carrying a warhead, then the effective range would be so much less, perhaps as little as just thirty miles, that it would be virtually useless as a weapon.

The American analysts also thought that the other prototype missile—called al Kahir—was essentially a much larger version of its sister rocket, measuring closer to twenty-five feet in length and three feet across, and with a slightly longer range of about 250 miles. This larger missile, they continued, was "generally similar" to an "improved" German V-2 rocket, although it also shared some of the technical hallmarks of the Veronique design.

But at this stage the DIA was completely unaware of the biggest single technical flaw in the German designs—the complete lack of a guidance mechanism without which the missiles, no matter what their range, could not be accurately directed at their target destinations. They did not know just how limited the Egyptian missiles were in this respect and how desperately, and vainly, the German experts were at this point striving to find a convincing solution to this vast technical challenge.

Although he was doubtlessly well aware of such severe technical limitations, Nasser was nonetheless desperately eager to launch one of the rockets in full view of the general public in time for the annual July 23 commemoration. Of course that year, 1962, was a particularly special occasion since it was exactly a decade since the historic coup that had toppled King Farouk, and Nasser wanted the event to be particularly momentous.

Soon the scientists gave him the news he wanted to hear. The rockets would be ready to fly on July 23 after all. At some point, however, he seems to have lost his nerve. Knowing that something might go spectacularly wrong, he decided to test fire the rockets not on July 23, in front of huge crowds, but a couple of days in advance. That way, instead of risking a live performance that could end in disaster, he would be able to hush the whole thing up.

This was a wise move, for by the late summer of 1962 the Egyptian leader had every reason to feel concerned about the lack of technical progress of both the rocket and the aircraft programs. The plans for the HA-200 and HA-300 were not moving as fast as the Egyptians had hoped, not least because by this time Willy Messerschmitt was making only irregular visits to Cairo, spending most of his time at his corporate headquarters in Augsburg. This was not enough to iron out some of the technical faults that he and his team had detected in the design of the fuselages of both the HA-200 and 300. Messerschmitt's first move had been to recommend that a number of leading scientists at the Site 36 aircraft factory should be sacked, including Dr. Fritz Hentzen, the head of the development department. General Khalil agreed, aware that Messerschmitt would have the contacts and influence to fill the posts that would be vacated.

Exactly what lay behind these dismissals is hard to tell, but allegations of incompetence seem unconvincing: Hentzen, for example, was undoubtedly a very skilled and experienced engineer, whose numerous wartime accomplishments had included the development of the Me 323, the giant transport plane. Whatever the reason, heavily armed Egyptian guards made a show of force, parading in front of the two aircraft factories while the terminated engineers were escorted off the premises. During the summer, an Austrian scientist by the name of Dr. Schoenbaumfeld took over the directorship of the aircraft factory from Hentzen, while a German engineer, Dr. Stang, was recruited from the German company Siebelwerke to replace another fired employee. Altogether, fifteen Germans were let go, even though their contracts had not yet expired, and most of these individuals went on to file lawsuits against MECO in Swiss courts, claiming that their four-year contracts had been unjustly broken.

But though Nasser was concerned by the flaws and failings in the rocket program, he was nonetheless eagerly anticipating the tremendous impact on domestic and international opinion the launches would inevitably have. For he felt sure that the rocket and aircraft programs had been kept largely secret from the outside world, even if the U.S. and Israel doubtlessly knew that he had commissioned some kind of scientific research program and had a strong interest in rocket and missile technology.

For all the efforts of Wolfgang Lotz and the furor surrounding Sänger, the Egyptian president was exactly right. By the middle of July 1962, no one in Israel was taking the Egyptian rocket program very seriously—Mossad had devoted only very meager resources to following and assessing it—for the simple reason that no one thought it had advanced very far. The Israelis did not know that the Egyptians had started building rockets the previous year and by the summer of 1962 had produced about thirty of them. Nor did they have any idea that the Egyptians were already testing engines for liquid-fuel rockets. In Israel, a handful of newspaper commentators had also periodically picked up the story but given it little attention. Uri Dan in *Maariv* predicted that Israel's own satellite launch in 1961 would have military repercussions, but expected a large influx of Soviet guided missiles into Egypt. And the *Haaretz* journalist Ze'ev Schiff wrote simply that German experts were working on rockets for the Egyptians but elaborated no further.

Above all, Israeli analysts had not guessed that the Egyptians even possessed their own factory where they were designing and manufacturing these rockets. With hindsight, this should have been obvious, because there was no reason to suppose that the only country that could have supplied

Egypt, the Soviet Union, had done so. As one historian of Israel's intelligence service has written, "[I]t is almost impossible to understand why no one in Tel Aviv was able to piece together all the information they possessed and come up with the assumption, based on pure logic, that there had to be a factory somewhere in Egypt designing and manufacturing rockets." Not only did Israel not know about the factories, but it had no idea what type of rockets were being produced there, how advanced the program was, when the first tests had been conducted, and with that results.

But the simple fact was that the Israeli intelligence services completely failed to see what would happen next.

CHAPTER FOURTEEN
Celebrations in Cairo

In the early afternoon of Saturday, July 21, 1962, most ordinary Egyptians were eagerly awaiting what the state-run media had promised would be a very special announcement. For the past few hours, Cairo radio had been playing an unremitting blast of militaristic music, a virtually unheard-of gesture, and everyone expected some quite dramatic news to break at any minute.

It was just after one o'clock that the music suddenly stopped and the audience's patience was finally rewarded. A spokesman for the Middle East News Agency announced that a number of long-range rockets had been successfully test fired at a remote desert site, accurately hitting targets that lay more than 350 miles away. As a result, he continued, the country had now formally entered "the missile age" and stood at the forefront of international efforts to develop missile technology.

Always quick to exploit a propaganda opportunity, the government had been preparing for this carefully chosen moment long in advance. Almost at once, a closely choreographed sequence of events got under way, one that included, in the bigger cities such as Cairo and Alexandria, mass youth rallies, gymnastic displays, water shows, boat races, and fireworks. A specially chartered plane even flew low over the capital, dropping biscuits and candies, while a new mosque was dedicated to Saladin, the scourge of the Christian crusaders, whose example latter-day Egyptians could now perhaps hope to emulate. Even a new postage stamp was commissioned, portraying an Egyptian missile soaring into outer space, while across the country large numbers of people danced to a hymn that had been specially composed to commemorate the great occasion.

The announcement was no empty boast, for the firings had taken place in full view of the world's press. A number of Cairo-based journalists had been invited to watch a "spectacle" in the desert, although they were given no clues to what lay in store, and early that morning a fifty-strong contingent, mainly from Eastern Europe, had left the capital by bus. They were taken on a three-hour journey into Egypt's Libyan Desert, joining a procession that was led by a number of chauffeur-driven limousines, escorting the president himself and his senior generals. When they reached their destination, a strip of desert lying sixty miles north of the capital, the journalists were escorted to an observation stand while the leadership moved into a dugout. They were told to expect a dramatic event and braced themselves, hoping that the proceedings would be finished well before temperatures soared to their unbearable midsummer highs.

Shortly before ten o'clock, on that Saturday morning, the ground had shaken amidst a deafening roar as a rocket rose into the air and then disappeared into the blue summer sky, surrounded by a huge cloud of thick smoke. As one of the journalists wrote, the missiles pierced "a long, white cloud bank and later, in plain view, slowly arched to the north—toward the Mediterranean."[183] Thirty minutes later, another missile, quite identical, was launched, followed in turn by another interval and then another launching. In all, four such missiles were test fired over a two-hour period, giving the journalists, as well as their Egyptian hosts, an impressive, unforgettable, and somewhat terrifying reminder of the realities of modern-day warfare.[184]

The next day, the state-run Egyptian press was hyped up, as one Western observer in Cairo put it, into "a state of frenzy." One newspaper, *Al Gomhuriya*, spoke triumphantly of how the tests represented the country's future "glory," while others heralded the huge amount of prestige that the missiles would bestow. After earlier military failures, "we have recovered faith in ourselves," ran one article in *Al Akhbar*.

Such reports merely added to the spirit of festivity that was to reign in Cairo for another two days. For the dramatic events of that summer day were in fact just the start of a much wider celebration, one that encompassed the anniversary—in particular, the tenth anniversary—of the birth of a new political order. Ever since they had so dramatically toppled the king, Farouk, during the Free Officers' Revolution in July 1952, the leaders of the new regime had sought to commemorate their people's "liberation" with a series of lavish processions by Egypt's land forces and flybys by its air force. But that year's events were to take place over a three-day national holiday, and were set to be even more impressive than those of previous years.

There had occasionally been similar scenes of real jubilation before in Egypt. Just four years previously, in February 1958, there had been wild public celebrations of folk song, dance, and music to celebrate a new political unity between Egypt and Syria. Under the terms of the deal, the two independent states would merge as one distinctive entity to form the United Arab Republic. This pathbreaking new venture, Nasser and the media had proclaimed proudly, heralded the dawn of a new era for the Arab people. But the "unity" of the two countries had never been more than superficial, and a number of experts had thought, right from the onset, that even this superficial veneer of unity would soon vanish. They were proven right, for the "union" formally disintegrated in September 1961, when Syria declared its independence. Nasser would have to do something else, something spectacular, if the Egyptian masses were going to maintain their high regard for their leader.

A few Egyptians may have privately harbored similar doubts about the latest announcement when, on Sunday, July 22, more than three hundred thousand people flooded into the capital's Republic Square to listen to their president speak about the events of the previous day as well as about the more general progress their country had made over the past decade.

This was the moment that the crowd, the people of Egypt, and those of the much wider Arab world had waited so long for. For in places as far afield as Beirut, Damascus, and Tunis, busy cafés and restaurants usually came to a standstill to hear the Egyptian premier. But now, in the summer of 1962, when Nasser was still basking in the glow of pan-Arab fascination, he was at the height of his popularity. His picture seemed to appear

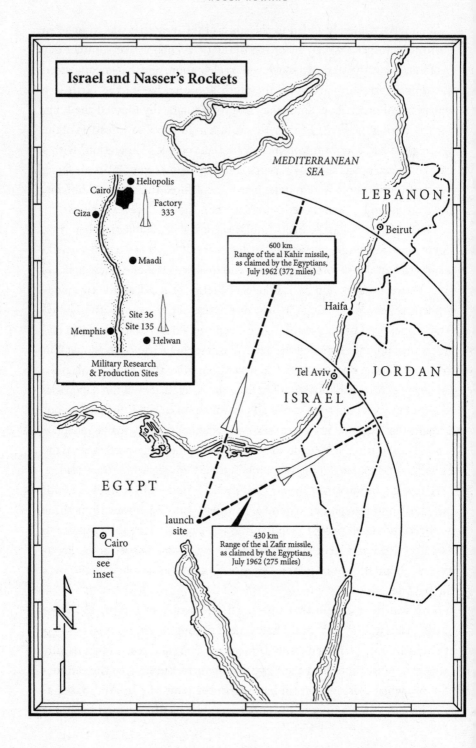

Israel and Nasser's Rockets

MEDITERRANEAN
SEA

LEBANON

Beirut

600 km
Range of the al Kahir missile,
as claimed by the Egyptians,
July 1962 (372 miles)

Haifa

Tel Aviv

JORDAN

ISRAEL

EGYPT

launch
site

430 km
Range of the al Zafir missile,
as claimed by the Egyptians,
July 1962 (275 miles)

Cairo

see
inset

N

Cairo
Heliopolis
Factory
333
Giza
Maadi
Site 36
Site 135
Memphis
Helwan

Military Research
& Production Sites

almost everywhere, the dark-haired man in his mid-to-late thirties with a broad, appealing smile, hawk nose, jutting chin, and dusky eyes that somehow had a greenish light like those of a gazelle, according to some contemporaries, or like those of a tiger, according to others. In Iraq the secret police had grown weary of trying to stop his followers from pinning up his portrait. In Syria rival political leaders tried hard to emulate him and prove that they had his approval. Demonstrations had broken out in Saudi Arabia among civilians who chanted his name and proclaimed a pro-Nasser agenda. Typical of this adulation was the scene in Riyadh four years before, for example, when witnesses watched in awe and astonishment as "tens of thousands rushed forward cheering wildly, breaking the police barrier, desperate to touch the God-like figure."[185]

It was not just his admirers and followers who were now waiting with bated breath, but his rivals and enemies elsewhere in the world. For Nasser was a man who, over the preceding few years, had aroused more fear, trepidation, and loathing among his Western enemies than almost any other figure since the end of the Second World War. At the rostrum in the Palais Bourbon and from the dispatch box in the House of Commons, Nasser had been castigated as "the new Hitler," "the insolent plunderer," "the barking dictator" who would "disgorge" whatever he swallowed. One of his enemies in the Middle East, President Camille Chamoun of Lebanon, even spoke regularly and powerfully of Nasser's "threat to Christianity."

A decade after he had seized power in the bloodless military coup orchestrated with a number of fellow officers, the forty-four-year-old Egyptian president had acquired a mesmeric speaking style, one that was widely admired and emulated across the Middle East, and which exerted enormous sway over his listeners. Part of this was perhaps due to his enormously powerful personal presence—he was a large man, at six feet tall and over two hundred pounds—which those who watched and heard him may have sensed. "When he rose before the microphone, he reminded one of a statue from the Cairo museum, in heavy, high-relief granite," as one Cairo-based French journalist later wrote. "The influence he exerted over men like Hussein or Arafat, whom he dominated with his sheer bulk, was in part due to that stature, on which he knew how to play with magnanimity."[186] By 1960, contemporaries were wondering if his speaking skills were just starting to wane—six years in power had been enough to take the best of him—but his grip and aura were still nonetheless enormous.[187]

He had, above all, also acquired a close affinity with the Egyptian masses, and with his fellow Arabs throughout the wider region. Part of this was due to the various heroic parts he had personally taken over the preceding years, in actions that he had subsequently trumpeted loudly and exploited to the full. He boasted about how he had orchestrated the coup on that fateful night ten years before when, during the night of July 22, he had personally led several infantry battalions to seize a number of key installations in Cairo, notably army headquarters, the airport at Almaza, the main radio station, and the central telephone exchange. Tanks had then surrounded Ras el-Tin Palace in Alexandria and a proclamation read out over the radio stating that the country was being "put in the hands of men in whose ability, integrity, and patriotism you can have complete confidence."

Everything had then happened with dramatic speed. The young thirty-two-year-old king quickly abdicated, agreeing to "submit to the will of the people" and surrender to the Revolutionary Command Council, before cramming as much as he could into his personal yacht and sailing for exile in Italy. Egypt was now set to become a republic, ending a monarchical tradition that extended back to the times of the pharaohs.[188] Of course, Nasser and his propagandists kept quiet the less romanticized version of events, overlooking how he had been stopped by the police on his way to supervise the coup because the taillights of his car were faulty, and how later on he had almost been arrested by his own men.

Nasser had many other strings to his bow of which he, and his followers, felt immensely proud. In 1948 he had fought bravely against the newly born Israeli army, saving his entire battalion from being overrun after leading a heavy Egyptian counterattack during which he was shot in the stomach and bled heavily. But his legendary status was due also to the perception that he had bravely asserted Egypt's sovereign rights during the Suez Crisis six years before, first by nationalizing the Western-owned Suez Canal Company and then by resisting the subsequent British- and French-led efforts to seize the canal from his grasp.

The Egyptian president, a highly experienced and accomplished speaker, had a penchant for long speeches and a distinctive style of delivery. In his slightly curious, almost metallic-sounding voice, which was deeply resonant in public as well as charming in private, he started off at his characteristically slow initial pace, speaking in a plain, clear style, using a moderate version of Arabic that avoided any dialect and which every member of his audience would therefore understand. There was a long preamble as he got himself going, trying to gauge the audience's mood before establishing a communion with the crowd's collective heart and mind along with doing what he did so supremely well—making each person in the audience feel as though he were talking to him or her directly, in the same personal manner as a close friend.

Initially, much of his speech was full of the usual alliterative references to the *wihdat al saf*—"unity of ranks" among the Arabs—to the "flag of freedom," and to "the Arabs from the Atlantic to the Gulf," references that proliferated within every one of his major addresses. He had a habit of emphasizing such terms to a degree that seemed, to the Western ear, quite exaggerated but which reflected a cultural habit of the Arabs, who equate repetition with sincerity. Nasser was apt at judging his audience's reaction to the particular phrases he used, discovering which ones meant most to them and which he should concentrate on in order to make the greatest impact.

Eventually the Egyptian leader came to the core of his speech. Since the overthrow of Farouk and his regime, he continued, the country had taken great strides forward. Above all, he argued, "we are no longer defenseless" in the way they had been six years before when, during the Suez campaign against British, French, and Israeli forces, "we had no weapons." When "in 1955 we made arms deals with Czechoslovakia and the U.S.S.R.," he continued, "that was one stage of our preparedness." But now, he thundered, "we have new weapons. You will see them in a military parade tomorrow." With typical flamboyance, he also referred to a hidden arsenal, telling his followers that "you will not see all of my new weapons. Some will remain secret."

The following day, Revolution Day, much of the city came to an almost total standstill, as if in eager anticipation. This was ordinarily a bustling, glowing, vibrant, and extremely noisy city of around four million—no one knew the exact number—but now, on this all-important national holiday, large areas were eerily quiet, even deserted. Office blocks were empty, shops were shuttered, and the street vendors had vanished. The roads were normally thronged by the dense traffic of taxis, streetcars, and buses as well as the cars, largely antiquated and worn-out, that sometimes wove their way through a mass of camels, donkey carts, pedestrians, and water buffaloes. But these roads, too, were largely abandoned.

The procession began midmorning, before the intense summer heat became too intense, and for two hours a vast collection of military equipment was driven through the streets of the capital. In the true style of Moscow's May Day parades, President Nasser stood on a reviewing stand and watched a steady procession of Russian-made tanks and artillery pieces rumble past, while well-drilled soldiers in full ceremonial uniform marched before him and a succession of supersonic jets roared overhead. This year was more impressive than its predecessors, however, since the planes overhead were the latest Russian fighters and bombers, newly delivered courtesy of Moscow.

It was a familiar routine, one that the crowd watched and loved every year. And a day that, in their eyes, bore special testament not just to the foreign oppression and exploitation that had been cast aside a decade before but also to the astonishing successes to which their charismatic and extraordinary leader had subsequently led them. Here was a man, they felt, who six years before had defied Great Britain, France, and Israel over the future of the Suez Canal, successfully fending off their mighty military attack and keeping Egyptian honor intact. Here was their chance to see and hear their great leader, who seemed to have elevated their country to dramatic new heights, as well as to take a look at the new weapons he had promised to show them.

Then, shortly after midday, the crowd's patience was rewarded, and they were not disappointed. Loud applause suddenly broke out when a number of small, stout jet aircraft roared over the masses. On the loudspeaker someone announced that these planes, a version of the HA-200, were the first-ever jet fighters that were entirely Egyptian built, an engineering feat that was an unmistakable sign of the country's independence. Two years before, just one solitary such plane had flown overhead, but now they were twelve strong. The previous day Nasser had emphasized during his speech that he would soon be opening a factory for the production of "Egypt's own jet planes," and the flyby gave extra weight to his words. Then came a procession of twenty flatbed trucks that were driven slowly through the central streets. Each was guarded by soldiers who stood rigorously to attention, and each was carrying one of two types of missile, one noticeably smaller than the other.

The crowd could not fail to miss the huge Egyptian flags that each and every one of these missiles had been draped in. They would not, however, have been able to see the names that the Cairo authorities had bestowed upon them and which had been inscribed into their metallic coats. The smaller of the two was called al Zafar, which was, as the DIA had estimated, about seventeen feet long and two feet in diameter, while the larger missile, longer and thinner in shape, had been labeled al Kahir, "The Conqueror." Their names were announced by loudspeaker as they were led through the streets, immediately becoming buzzwords for the Cairo crowds, who instantly latched on to them.

Nasser and his military chiefs knew that this would be a perfect moment to boast about the future achievements of his newly armed Egypt. At a press conference held on Saturday at the desert town of Wadi al-Natrum, near the test-firing site, he had announced that he would soon be mass-producing the missiles, each of which, he proudly asserted in truly nationalistic spirit, had been, and would continue to be, manufactured in Egypt. But when a journalist asked the president the purpose of the missiles, Nasser preferred to take a less direct approach, responding by posing his own question. "What," he asked, "is the purpose of a rocket?" Sidestepping the issue, he argued that what mattered much more than their purpose was "the range they reach." When a Middle Eastern reporter pressed him about the range, the president gave a revealing answer. The missiles had a 250-mile range, he claimed, and could therefore strike anywhere "just south of Beirut." In other words, the Jewish state and every inch of its territory—the distance between Port Said and southern Israel being only about 150 miles—would be within their ambit.

On the day of the parade, two days after the press conference, he made even clearer references to his enemy. Standing alongside his defense minister, Field Marshal Abdul Hakim Amer, Nasser announced boldly that the rockets, as well as all the other armaments exhibited at the Revolution Day parade, were being amassed for a war against Israel. "I want the world to know," he announced, "that we will not allow Palestine to remain in the hands of Israel. As the world has seen, we are getting ready." And after taking the salute from Egypt's armed forces, alongside his president, Field Marshal Amer was even more direct: "The enemy facing the Arab world is Israel, an overtly aggressive imperialist base, threatening peace." What was more, he added, "our enemy," the Jewish state, "spares no effort to obtain modern armaments to guarantee its military supremacy." But now, he continued, "the United Arab Republic air force has full command of the skies in our area. Its armed forces are the strongest in Africa and the Middle East."

An editorial in one local newspaper claimed that "the staff of the Israel embassy in Paris mourns and the Jews of New York are frightened," and the news of the development of long-range rockets that could potentially target Israeli cities was also picked up by much of the world's media, with the missile launches reported by papers such as the *New York Times* and the London *Times*.[189] But one German newspaper took a slightly different angle and made a startling revelation. According to the Munich-based publication, Nasser's new missiles had originally been purchased from the United States but then substantially modified and developed but not by native Egyptians—no one pretended that Egypt had any real native expertise—or in the country of the missiles' origin. Instead, this had been undertaken by a number of German experts who had been recruited from their homeland through "Swiss firms" and were now based on Egyptian soil.[190]

Just seventeen years after the end of the war, this had an obvious significance. In particular, why were German experts, rather than those of any other nationality, involved in the Egyptian project? Was it because they had unique experience in this line of work, experience that they were now looking to make good use of? In any case, were not some, or perhaps many, or even all, of those involved likely to have had some involvement with the Nazi regime, including its highly successful efforts to develop the long-range Vergeltungswaffe (V-1 and V-2) rockets?

CHAPTER FIFTEEN
"Little Isser" Raises the Alarm

Although the association of the Third Reich with Nasser's rockets was, of course, always bound to have a huge symbolic importance in Israel, it inevitably had a particular resonance in the summer of 1962. For less than two months before, the trial of one of the most notorious Nazis, the SS officer Adolf Eichmann, had been brought to a close, culminating in his execution in the Israeli city of Ramlah on the night of May 31. The year-long trial of Eichmann, one of the key perpetrators of the Holocaust, in which around six million European Jews had perished, had resurrected deeply disturbing memories for a nation whose entire national myth was concentrated upon the tragic story of persecution. Hundreds of prosecution witnesses, many of whom were concentration-camp survivors, and thousands of documents detailing Nazi plans to eradicate worldwide Jewry were brought to the forefront of public attention not just in Israel but throughout the world. And among the Israeli general public specifically, such memories, both relatively recent as well as extremely traumatic, could only heighten an underlying fear of persecution in general as well as concerns about an older generation of German citizens in particular.

This meant that, in the summer of 1962, even the mere suggestion of ex-Nazi scientists helping Nasser, a sworn enemy of the Jewish state, to build long-range rockets, which could conceivably be armed not just with conventional explosives but perhaps with gas, germs, and, maybe one day, even nuclear warheads, would have filled many ordinary Israelis with horror. One individual who read the reports in a Munich newspaper with an overwhelming sense of alarm was a middle-aged Israeli man, based in Tel Aviv, by the name of Isser Harel. At his simple wooden desk, surrounded by huge piles of papers and encircled by the cigarette smoke of his secretary, Dvora, who sat at his side, he began to look through the reports of Nasser's missile tests and the subsequent display of the missiles at the Revolution Day parade.

It was Harel's business to know about these matters, and to respond in an appropriate way to any such threat he deemed them to pose. For the past decade he had been head of Israel's foreign security service, Mossad—"The Organization"—and it was his professional responsibility, as well as a matter of personal conscience, to detect and eliminate any possible or actual threat to the security of the Jewish state.

To most outsiders, fifty-year-old "Little Isser" did not perhaps look the hugely important and impressive part he played, being of diminutive stature, at barely five feet tall, and having enormously large ears that seemed to stand out, even from a distance. He had a reputation for wearing worn-out, even quite shabby clothes, mainly because, in the words of one of his leading spies, he was "thrifty beyond reason, ascetic in his personal tastes," and had a "legendary" disinterest in traditional comforts. His office was equally unimpressive, being so "sparsely furnished, altogether lacking in distinction, [that] the room might have housed the most aggressively unimaginative middle-management functionary."[191] With a dread of spending taxpayers' money, this was the same man who made his agents stay in cheap, downscale hotels and who once refused a luxurious suite at Israel's Paris embassy, asking instead for a single bed in a small back room. Every bill his agents submitted and wanted to claim on expenses was inspected rigorously. Typically brusque and humorless, and with an irritating habit of constantly biting his nails, he was not everyone's personal cup of tea.

But those who knew him, and who scratched beneath the unimposing exterior, saw his true mettle. When his piercing blue eyes were fixed in a stare, his interlocutors saw and sensed the sheer force of his determination and the intense, suppressed energy of a man who did nothing halfheartedly and for whom "there could be no compromise with what he considered evil."[192] It was quite in character that Harel had walked away from a kibbutz in 1943, thirteen years after first starting out, because of a tiny perceived slight that others would perhaps have thought nothing of.[193] And this was the same man who expected all others to have a private life as utterly unblemished as his own, and posted security officers in every Israeli embassy to keep a watchful eye on wandering diplomats who might be open to bribery.[194]

He was also undoubtedly gifted with great charisma—"as commanding a figure as any I have encountered," as one of his chief spies later wrote—as well as a wealth of experience in intelligence matters. He had, after all, started his involvement in this shadowy business in his late teens, soon after arriving in British-controlled Palestine from Russia, where he had been born, as Isser Halperin, in 1912.[195] Joining Haganah, the Jewish paramilitary underground movement, almost on arrival in 1930, he had helped to run the Shai, its intelligence service, and quickly impressed his elders. Soon after the end of the Second World War, as the British began to beat a retreat, he was given responsibility for one of its internal departments and kept close tabs on various Jewish "dissident" groups, such as Irgun, the Stern Gang, and the Communist Party, building up a secret registry of their members, methods, and goals.

Of course, after such a life story, Harel not only had huge amounts of experience in his field but also a strong sense of just how much antipathy confronted Israel in the Middle East and therefore how fragile its position actually was. From his late teens, along with all the other Jewish settlers in Palestine, he had been confronted with the hostility of the indigenous Palestinian population and been involved in numerous skirmishes and full-scale battles with Arab militias. As soon as the British had pulled out of Palestine and an independent Jewish state had been declared, in May 1948, he and his fellow Israeli citizens had been forced to take up arms against the Arab armies that had worked together to crush the new state that had emerged so suddenly in the Middle East. At times these Arab armies came within a whisker of winning some decisive victories against the Jewish army. Through Israeli eyes, it also seemed that their homeland had subsequently been under near constant attack by insurgents, known as fedayeen, and was now threatened by an Egyptian dictator who was not only very unpredictable but, since receiving a massive supply of arms from the Soviet Union in 1955, was already becoming dangerously powerful.

But by the time Nasser was test-firing his missiles in the Egyptian desert, that day in July 1962, Harel must have felt that he was the right man to deal with any emerging threat. By this time, after all, he did have a lot of impressive credits to his name. He had, for example, masterminded an exceedingly successful operation to bring thousands of Moroccan Jews to Israel, personally traveled to the southern Sudan to assist pro-Israeli rebels, and also helped King Haile Selassie of Ethiopia, a long-term ally of the Jewish state, to crush an attempted coup against his rule. He had also succeeded brilliantly in winning new friends in very high places: when in 1954 he first met the U.S. secretary of state, John Foster Dulles, Harel was able to gain his sympathy and convince him that Israel was America's true friend in the Middle East. It was as a result of this meeting that, eight years later, Mossad had a good many of the latest spying gadgets—such as up-to-date listening and tracking devices, and remote-operated cameras—in its possession.

But his greatest coup was undoubtedly the operation to find, seize, and abduct Eichmann from Argentina and spirit him back to Israel for trial. "We *will* bring Adolf Eichmann to Jerusalem," he told his team members, hammering his fist down with full force on a table to give his words unmistakable emphasis, as they assembled in his office for one last briefing on April 27, 1960. It was under his guidance that Mossad located the elusive German in Buenos Aires and then brilliantly executed a daring plan to seize him.

In the course of this mission, Harel had shown some of his greatest attributes as a leader. For he had personally taken part in it, accompanying his fellow agents to the Argentinian capital, setting up an operational headquarters at a series of cafeterias—which he walked to and from—and personally ensuring everything went according to plan, for he did not want to miss out on the intense excitement of such a special undertaking. The mission gave him extensive hands-on experience in difficult operations, much more than most of his counterparts in other foreign intelligence services could probably have boasted. Given the risks of capture and subsequent interrogation, this was a huge personal risk for the head of any foreign intelligence service to take. His strong desire to be involved in every aspect of the organization showed itself in all sorts of ways—inside the office, he even answered phones and took messages for colleagues—but it was most striking because of his wish to personally travel alongside some of his operatives and escort them on operations.

Harel's reputation long predated the Eichmann operation. In 1952, David Ben-Gurion, the prime minister and Harel's close supporter and confidant, thought so highly of him that he urged him to retain control over Israel's domestic intelligence service, Shin Bet, as well as Mossad, until a new head was appointed the following year. Harel agreed, and in these roles he earned the unique honor of having overall responsibility for two quite different, and even antagonistic, organizations. By doing so, the unusual title and rare distinction of HaMemuneh (the Responsible One) was bestowed upon him, a title that he adopted in public when he once gave testimony at a trial and the judge asked him how he would describe himself. Among many circles, the name subsequently stuck.[196]

He also commanded considerable loyalty from most of his agents, perhaps partly because he was flexible and forgiving when the circumstances arose. "Isser was a very stern taskmaster, prepared to forgive mistakes, even rather serious ones," wrote Yitzhak Shamir of Mossad's Paris bureau, "but never lies, disobedience, a defaulting of any sort (whether money or even marriage was concerned), talkativeness, inaccurate reporting or any manipulation of fact."[197] And when Harel himself scrupulously followed the standards he set others, then he won considerable respect for doing so.

Yet Harel also had his critics who were not shy about alleging that he had made more than his fair share of mistakes. Some onlookers questioned, for example, his involvement in the somewhat peculiar case of Joselle Schumacher. Joselle was a young Jewish boy who was being raised in Israel not by his parents, Russian émigrés who had started a new life in Israel in the 1950s, but instead by his grandparents, who gave him a highly orthodox Haredi upbringing. But when his parents decided to return to Russia, wanting to take all their children with them, the Haredi community took Joselle and hid him from them.

Mossad had become involved in this case just months before the Nasser missile crisis had erupted. As the Schumacher episode became a huge issue in Israel, one that exposed deep religious divisions inside the country between traditionalist and more liberal Judaism, Little Isser stepped in and offered to help his great ally and supporter, David Ben-Gurion, who was under huge political pressure from liberal political parties to find the child and return him to his parents. By the end of July, around forty Mossad agents were deployed on a case that many within, and outside, the organization felt had nothing at all to do with its real purpose—collecting foreign intelligence on existing and potential threats to Israel, making an assessment, and then acting on it.[198]

Even Harel's fellow agents, though usually loyal, were willing to admit that, said one, "the man was so in love with the idea of clandestine activity that often, to my mind, he seemed to go out of his way to complicate matters that were essentially simple."[199] His Eichmann kidnap strategy, for example, was a "curious and highly complex plan . . . in which he would spend most of his waking hours wandering the cafés of the Argentine capital in a pre-determined pattern."[200] His very enthusiasm and intensity had a positive side but "could also make working for him a royal pain."[201] And, like most successful careerists, he was egotistical to a degree that could cloud his judgment and hinder his working relations with colleagues, particularly in rival departments. And there were occasions when particular projects, notably the Schumacher case, appear to have gripped him with a degree of obsession, a dangerous weakness that also threatened to warp his vision.[202]

That morning in July 1962, as he read the reports in the international press about German connections with Nasser's rocket program, Isser Harel would have been wondering about the various types of danger that their development presented to Israel. He would doubtlessly have imagined weapons of mass destruction raining down on his homeland, or a radical regime seizing power in Egypt that would have been even more audacious and less rational than its current leader. Or he may have wondered if such a missile could fall into the hands of a radical insurgent group, which could disappear after firing it, perhaps at the very center of Tel Aviv or another big

Israeli city, and which would not therefore fear the retaliation that would inevitably follow. Or he might have considered the possibility of a foreign enemy making a preemptive strike against Israel's own military sites. Perhaps, too, the high command in Cairo might calculate that Egypt, being so much bigger than Israel, could survive an armed confrontation much better than its neighbor.

And he would, of course, have wondered how best to deal with this new threat to the security of his homeland. Would it be necessary for Israel to launch its own preemptive strike in the same way it had done eight years before, when it attacked Egypt before it received and made use of a massive supply of new, Czech-supplied arms?[203] Would diplomatic pressure be enough, particularly if the United States weighed in on Israel's behalf? Or was there some other alternative, one that mixed threats and intimidation to back up a political solution?

Like his many enemies and some of his allies and friends, both within Israel and outside, perhaps he was wondering if any new strategy he devised and executed would follow the path laid down by his many successes, or if, on the other hand, his personal failings would show themselves and lead him to make some serious errors of judgment.

What Harel undoubtedly felt, as he weighed his options, was a sense of disappointment at the international reaction to the missile tests. Most American newspapers reported the development without any comment or opinion, and even then devoted only limited amounts of space, usually just single columns, to the stories. Other newspapers downplayed the story by quoting the doubts expressed by Dr. Sänger, who did not think that Nasser's rockets really had a range even remotely as impressive as the Egyptian leader claimed.[204] A CIA assessment, published on July 22, described the launches merely as "by and large a propaganda stunt of the kind in which Nasi [sic] excels," adding that "the launchings actually have little significance in terms of any real scientific or military capability."[205] And in a briefing to McGeorge Bundy, President Kennedy's special assistant for national security affairs, the State Department argued that the "latest development" did not "significantly" alter the regional balance of power, although it did concede that the launches were "a psychological coup for Nasser vis-à-vis his Arab rivals as well as Israel."[206]

On the surface, Israel's initial reaction was similarly muted. The *Jerusalem Post* commented that Cairo's new warplanes, bought from the Russians, presented a "far greater threat to Israel than any ballistic rocket in an experimental stage," while the cabinet ventured no official comment. Other Israeli commentators conceded that Nasser had achieved a propaganda success, although they played down the military effectiveness of the "experimental" rockets.

But underneath the superficial veneer of calm that they too tried to portray, Israel's leaders were now locked in heated discussions. There were some high-ranking military men and politicians who argued that there was no need for unnecessary alarm and there was a real danger of overreacting. Maj. Gen. Meir Amit, the director of Military Intelligence—a rival of Harel's who was the head of an organization that was also a rival of Mossad's—downplayed the development, arguing strongly that Nasser's missiles as yet posed no real threat to the Jewish state, especially since, he pointed out, the Egyptian program had encountered serious technical obstacles that its scientists were "nowhere near solving."[207] His moderate tone was echoed by Deputy Defense Minister Shimon Peres, who wanted to take a low-key approach to deal with the development: Israel was already locked in discussions with the Bonn government, he emphasized, and could not afford to alienate the West Germans by getting angry with them over the activities of a handful of their nationals who were working as expatriate scientific staff in Egypt.

Others, however, were far less complacent and regarded the Egyptian rockets as a serious potential danger. And almost everyone agreed that Mossad should at the very least have predicted the event, no matter how much importance it merited. Almost as soon as the news broke, Israel's various security chiefs were busily engaged in a bout of angry fingerpointing at those they deemed responsible for failing to foresee what Nasser had done, while loudly denying any responsibility themselves. Some accused the intelligence services not of failing to gather information about Egyptian activities but of being too casual about Nasser's missile program, perhaps because they felt that the second-rate, "no-name" German scientists he had recruited were not of sufficient caliber to produce significant results, or at least produce any quite so quickly. Surely Mossad had completely underplayed the sophistication of the Egyptian project, which was all the more unforgivable when Israel completely lacked any ballistics program of its own? "What are we spending our intelligence budget on," asked Amit caustically, "if we get our information from a public speech of President Nasser? All we need for that is a portable radio."[208]

In other words, despite all his earlier successes, Harel's reputation and his career were suddenly on the line. So, too, was the reputation of the organization he had created and nurtured. He and his boss, David Ben-Gurion, had already suffered enough criticism in the course of the year when the Israeli press mocked the failure to find Joselle Schumacher, and to take yet more, so soon after, would have been too much. But why, his critics were now asking, had he devoted as many as forty agents to finding Joselle Schumacher—whose fate hardly mattered at all to Israel's national security—while overlooking much more important issues? The new head of Israeli Military Intelligence argued that "these other operations took up so much effort that I had to tell my superiors." He added that he hadn't been "prepared to continue . . . when there was such a very severe shortage of information because of the diversion of our resources."[209] Not only that, continued Meir Amit, but Harel was unapproachable: "[H]e was really the man who knew everything," Amit told a sympathetic colleague, "but he couldn't bear any criticism."[210]

Knowing that his many rivals and enemies within Israel were snapping at his heels, and desperate to save both himself and Mossad, Harel had decided to respond within days of the news breaking. He was sure that only an active, aggressive, and hard-hitting approach would succeed in neutralizing—before it was too late—what he regarded as a rapidly emerging threat to the security of the Jewish state and in restoring some lost honor to Israel's famed foreign intelligence service. His every instinct—and he was ultimately a man who trusted his instincts and whose work was guided by them, rather than on any technology and hard analysis—told him that the developments in Egypt presented a grave threat to the country he loved.

In his view, Israel had to hit back with force. Operation Damocles had to proceed.

CHAPTER SIXTEEN
Operation Damocles

Days after the Egyptian missile parade, Hassan Kamil, the Swiss-Egyptian director and joint owner of two front organizations that procured vital hardware for Nasser's rocket and aircraft programs, hired a private jet to take him from his holiday home on the island of Sylt, in Schleswig-Holstein, to Düsseldorf. At the very last minute, however, he changed his plans, deciding to spend another day on the island to meet a particularly pressing deadline. But his thirty-seven-year-old wife, Helene, the Duchess of Mecklenburg, took the flight and headed for home.

His last-minute change of plans turned out to be a fateful decision, for barely an hour after takeoff, as it passed over Westphalia, the plane plummeted to earth and exploded on impact, killing his wife and the pilot instantly. Investigators subsequently failed to find any explanation for the crash, and in the end attributed it to mechanical failure.

Although the fate of the plane still remains an unsolved mystery, it is certain that Isser Harel had moved extremely fast to deal with the Egyptian military programs, which he regarded as a dire threat to his country's security. Within just days of Nasser's missile tests, he had set up a special team devoted to monitoring and countering the threat and had started to work more closely with Unit 131 in Military Intelligence, under whose command Wolfgang Lotz, one of Israel's very few active agents in Egypt, fell. Harel was convinced that, once again, German citizens were plotting to wipe out the Jews, and he was determined, above all, to use whatever means were necessary to stop the German scientists from helping the Egyptian leader build weapons that could potentially pose a serious danger to the Jewish state.

But officially, at least, he would have to win the backing of the prime minister, David Ben-Gurion, if he was to unleash any campaign of intimidation or even assassination against those involved. Although the chiefs of Israel's intelligence services, like those of any country, had some discretion to act without the approval of their political masters, Harel could not, of course, arbitrarily conduct a campaign that, if discovered, would plainly have profound repercussion for Israel's relations with at least two other states.

The key meeting between the two men took place on August 16, three weeks after the missile tests. The spy chief pressed for immediate and hard-hitting action against both the scientists and the West German government. Ben-Gurion should not hesitate, Harel argued strongly, to raise the matter with the West German chancellor, Konrad Adenauer, and urge him to clamp down on the activities of the expatriates.

Harel initially promised Ben-Gurion that he would have all the relevant facts about the rocket program on his desk within three months of the rocket launches but he managed to beat his own deadline by more than eight weeks. He may have failed to pick up on the existence of Egypt's own rocket-production site, but his spies had now taken just three days to locate Factory 333.[211] On that hot summer day in August, he met the prime minister and presented him with two documents, at least one of which had been obtained by Wolfgang Lotz, who would have handed it over to his spy handlers in Paris some weeks before.

One of these documents contained microfilm of the Egyptian guidance systems, crucial material that gave the Israelis clear proof just how much trouble the scientists were having over the issue. But the other was far more important and controversial.[212] This was a letter penned on March 24 by Wolfgang Pilz to Kamil Azzaz, the director of Factory 333, in which he asked his employers to allocate a large sum of additional expenditure for the purchase of spare parts and equipment for five hundred "Type-2" and four hundred "Type-5" rockets.[213] In the eyes of the Mossad director, this was clear and unarguable evidence of the size and scale of the emergent Egyptian threat: it was plainly not just about Nasser's personal prestige but instead had an obvious military purpose.

Harel was not used to having his advice and recommendations rejected by Ben-Gurion, but the prime minister remained unconvinced and was still swayed by the much more moderate tone of the Mossad chief's great rival, Maj. Gen. Meir Amit. Not only was the Egyptians' program plagued by technical obstacles, Amit continued to emphasize, but they lacked a warhead with which to arm the rockets. And even if they could design and build such a weapon, he went on, they would face overwhelming pressure from both the Russians and the Americans not to proceed with their plans, let alone use the weapons on the battlefield. In other words, Amit reiterated, Nasser's program was only a potential danger, and in no way an immediate threat. It was worth keeping a close eye on but no more.

The Israeli prime minister also much preferred the far more temperate manner of his deputy defense minister, Shimon Peres. Unlike others in the cabinet, notably Foreign Minister Golda Meir, who made Israel's relations with the United States a top priority, Peres wanted Israel to develop closer relations with France and Germany on the grounds that these two countries might be prepared to support Israel's emergent nuclear program. He was very alarmed by Egyptian ambitions: "[T]he rockets the Egyptians have launched constitute a serious threat to Israel," he argued, adding that "the advent of these modern weapons has radically changed the nature of the danger that lies in wait for us and the measures we have to take to protect ourselves from it." But in his eyes the use of force was at this stage unnecessary and heavy-handed.[214]

Above all, Peres and Ben-Gurion did not want to do anything that might endanger their new relations with West Germany. In Israel there was a long-standing parliamentary law forbidding diplomatic relations between the Jewish state and West Germany, whose name, in the eyes of this generation, was synonymous with collective responsibility for wartime atrocities. In practice, this prohibition had not always been respected. For example, in late 1955 a number of Israeli arms-purchasing missions in Paris had bought spare parts directly from their German manufacturers instead of going through French resellers. But such moves were always bound to provoke a parliamentary furor about the creation of a "Fourth Reich," and any new effort to build a rapport with Bonn was now certain to arouse a political uproar in the Israeli capital at a time when Ben-Gurion was working hard to hold a coalition together.

Twelve years after the Second World War, both leaders had very different ideas. They were fascinated by the possibility of building close relations with West Germany, which seemed to offer an enormous commercial opportunity for Israeli businesses as well as a potentially very important political and strategic ally for Tel Aviv. Ben-Gurion knew, for example, that Israel could not depend just on the French for military supplies. That would have left it at the mercy of a new government, hostile to Israel, that might conceivably take power in Paris. Like any other country, Israel had to diversify its sources of supply, and West Germany, which supplied the French armed forces with a lot of spare parts, was an obvious choice.

Peres had gotten matters under way in October 1957. First he persuaded the French defense minister, Jacques Chaban-Delmas, to probe his counterparts in Bonn and find out how receptive they would be to any overtures that Israel might make. Chaban-Delmas had approached his opposite number, Franz Josef Strauss, and received a broadly positive response. The German minister agreed to meet an Israeli delegation, although he knew how tricky this would be since such contacts were forbidden not under German law but by the decree of the Israeli Parliament.

The team of Israeli representatives that flew out of Tel Aviv's international airport a few weeks later, in the middle of December, did so under a veil of complete secrecy, flying first to Paris and then driving through thick snow to Strauss's private home in the Bavarian town of Roth. A long day of intense discussion then proceeded between the German minister and the team of Israeli representatives, headed by Peres, who was flanked by Asher Ben-Natan, a director of an Israeli armaments department, and Gen. Chaim Laskov, the chief of staff. Peres argued powerfully that West Germany had a "moral" obligation to help the Jewish state, as well as a strategic one.

Peres's path-breaking diplomacy reaped some material rewards, for in late June 1959 a German magazine, *Der Spiegel*, reported that the West

German army had signed a deal to buy a large quantity of Israeli rifles, which had proved their worth during the war with Egypt over Suez three years before. The magazine's journalists did not know, however, that, in return, the West Germans had agreed to clandestinely ship to Israel a large amount of surplus and obsolescent arms. Bonn wanted to establish new export markets and saw such deliveries as the first step in doing so, calculating that sending relatively antiquated armaments would not make any difference to the balance of power in the Middle East. It wanted, however, to keep the deal as secret as possible from both the Arabs and its NATO allies, and the deliveries were sent indirectly, via third countries, and under false bills of lading. Soon Israeli soldiers were being covertly trained in the use of these new weapons at training camps in Bendsburg and Munsterlager.

In the summer of 1962, after the Egyptians had test-fired their rockets in full view of the outside world, Peres did not have to push his prime minister hard to persuade him to use heavy diplomacy to lean on the West Germans, and with Ben-Gurion's approval, the defense minister now contacted his West German counterpart. On August 17, Peres sent a cable to the Israeli Trade Mission in Bonn asking its officials to personally relay a message to Strauss that fully explained Israel's concerns.

The Israeli minister deliberately took a quiet, low-key approach, subtly questioning Bonn's self-proclaimed ignorance of the scientists' activities and gently reminding Strauss that their work for Nasser was seriously endangering the good relations between the two countries. He stated simply that the Egyptian rockets were causing a great deal of uneasiness and anxiety within Israel and that there was no doubt that German citizens had been involved in their development and production. He asked Strauss to say whether he believed German citizens had the right to manufacture weapons of war that could be used in a region as volatile and tense as the Middle East, and asked him if he was embarrassed by the fact that Germany was effectively assisting the Egyptians to destroy Israel. At a time when the Eichmann trial had brought so much horror about the Holocaust to light, he felt confident that his message would be a powerful one.

Strauss's reply was full of good intentions and general assurance but short on specific details. Of course Bonn wanted to curb the scientists' activities, he assured Peres, but it had no legal powers to do so when every West German was entitled to a basic freedom of movement. In any case, there was no need to feel undue concern: none of the German experts were leaders in their field, and Wolfgang Pilz, the leading name in the Egyptian program now that Sänger had moved on, was "absolutely below the current standard of his field."[215] His rather dismissive comments about the quality of the scientists seemed to reflect a greater attitude prevalent among both the leadership in Bonn and the wider scientific community. The renowned German physicist Carl Friedrich von Weizsäcker, for example, told a journalist that the expatriates were working "for three reasons. First, because most of them were Nazis; second, because they'll do anything for money; and third, because none of them is in the top rank of his particular specialization, and so can't pick and choose."[216]

After Peres informed him of Strauss's lackluster response, Ben-Gurion was swayed by Harel's hawkish tone. He was also pressed to take hard-hitting action by the foreign minister, Golda Meir. At the same time she had met a leading German official, Prof. Franz Bohm, who had recently visited Israel and pressed home the same point about the scientists' essential freedom of movement. Exasperated, Meir strongly backed the Mossad chief's proposals. Harel should be allowed to pursue his "own methods," she argued, and there should be "all-out war against the scientists, as if they were fully fledged Nazis."[217] The head of military intelligence, Meir Amit, still felt sure that the threat was being exaggerated but reportedly did not object to the proposal that Harel now put forward—a campaign of intimidation and assassination.[218] Ben-Gurion now concurred and Harel had won the day. Operation Damocles could officially proceed.

Meanwhile, over in Cairo, Wolfgang Lotz had been busily stepping up his efforts to infiltrate the Egyptian rocket program. Word had quickly reached him, through the regular messages that he picked up on his secret radio transmitter, of Nasser's successful rocket launches and he knew that the Egyptian program had now been pushed right up the list of Tel Aviv's priorities.

Although by the late summer of 1961 Lotz had already been highly successful in establishing his cover story, he found some unexpected support from an unlikely quarter. For it was at this time that he was introduced to a former high-ranking Nazi by the name of Dr. Johann von Leers, who was living openly in the Egyptian capital. Von Leers had been, and remained, a rabid anti-Semite and was still wanted by the West German government, having been a close former associate of Hitler's propaganda minister, Joseph Goebbels. Although he had nothing to do with Nasser's military programs, Lotz was eager to meet him, for von Leers was very closely networked with many of the German expatriates who were involved in the rocket and aircraft programs.

Soon after being introduced to von Leers at his pleasant, and heavily guarded, two-story villa in Cairo, Lotz realized that he was enjoying a remarkable stroke of good fortune.

"I have an excellent memory for faces. I happen to remember yours very well," smiled the former propaganda chief. "We met only once, at some conference at Wannsee . . . I remember you distinctly, looking very smart in the black uniform of an Obersturmbannführer.[219] Don't deny it, my dear boy. I am happy you are one of us and I will keep your secret."

Lotz was astonished but also rather amused that von Leers was convinced that he was not a veteran of Rommel's army, as he claimed, but in fact had a much darker secret—that he was a formerly high-ranking officer in Hitler's SS and was desperate to conceal his true identity because he had war crimes to hide. Provided he denied this claim instead of admitting it—which would not have been quite consistent with a dark secret to hide—then word would gradually go around the German community that he was "one of them" and could be trusted.

By the summer of 1962, Lotz had already become highly adept at prizing information out of all manner of unsuspecting friends and acquaintances. He was good at inviting Egyptian officers to his home and making the most of their secret fondness for alcohol. "The drink makes them careless," as he told his new wife, a total novice to the arts of espionage.[220] Above all, he pretended that he could not speak a word of Arabic, even though he had acquired a reasonable knowledge of the language during his wartime days in North Africa. As a result, his Egyptian guests would often talk away in his presence, wholly unaware that he was able to follow much of their conversations. And when he was in the company of individual officers, he found that some of them would open up to him with surprising ease.

This was partly because, as a friend of General Ghorab's, he was above suspicion, partly because, as a supposed veteran of Rommel's army, he was considered to be an expert on military matters, and partly because many of the Egyptians were particularly keen to impress a Westerner.

On occasion he was able to get first-class information about the rocket program directly from the horse's mouth, ingratiating himself into the conversations of his "fellow" Germans. At one dinner party he made his way to a particularly noisy and cheerful group of revelers who were gathered around a piano, which was covered in bottles of spirits and lager beer. One of those present was the scientist Alois Brunner, whose bloated face, noted Lotz, was by now redder than ever. He was locked in discussion with a fellow scientist.

"And I'm telling you the last test was a success," he shouted. "There's nothing wrong with the blades, nothing whatsoever. If it wasn't for the way you geniuses make a mess of anything you touch, we would have it up in the [air] and in serial production in six [months'] time. Because of your lot it's still in the experimental stage."

Lotz knew immediately that this exchange could prove to be very revealing.

"It's easy for you to talk, Brunner," retorted his interlocutor, another engineer by the name of Schonmann, "and still easier to put the blame on others. You know just as well as I do where the fault lies. It's local labor, local so-called engineers, the delay in shipment of parts and a million other things. On top of all that you have the authorities tying us up in red tape. It takes weeks or months just to. . . ."

"Don't give me that!" Brunner shot back. "In my planet everybody is strictly on the ball!"

At this point, as voices were raised slightly, the Israeli spy interjected and broke the tension by introducing his wife into the room. But even such a relatively brief snapshot of their conversation was enough to reveal some of the problems and issues that were plaguing the Egyptian military programs by the late summer of 1961.[221]

Within a short space of time, Lotz had also worked out a particularly clever way of observing the movements of the Egyptian army. He was soon a regular visitor to a racecourse where, on each visit, he would mount a fifteen-foot-high observation tower that had been built in the very center of the track so that trainers and owners could watch their horses. Like every other visitor, he always took a powerful pair of binoculars with him to get a better view. His real interest, however, lay not in his horse but in the huge Egyptian military base that lay right next to the track. "Turning a little to the right I was able to spot almost anything that went on inside the armoured base," he wrote. "If tanks or armoured vehicles were moving out, I could clearly see the direction they were taking, and later I would follow in my car to check out their exact destination . . . at a glance I was able to determine the nature of a convoy, to assess whether I was watching an operational move, a unit going on manoeuvres or into training, armoured vehicles being taken to the repair shop or whatever."[222] In particular, Lotz knew that in the event that Egypt was ever preparing for war, this base would be alive with constant activity for days before the outbreak.

Now well funded by his spy chiefs, Lotz could also afford to rent a good-size farm, complete with paddocks, stables, and even a racing track. Although it was only a short distance from the capital, just ten miles, there was another reason it was so useful for his spying mission. One day, he wrote, "we were riding stirrup to stirrup at a slow walk [when] suddenly there was a great roar, not unlike the sound of a jet fighter taking off, and my stallion shied slightly."[223] The roar had come from the nearby missile range where the scientists were carrying out advanced tests on their rocket prototypes. Lotz made the most of this superb location. During the summer of 1962 he began to notice that the rockets were being fired more often than ever, and he always carefully noted the exact times of the various launchings as well as the frequency.

By this point he had also started to use a new transmitter, larger and more powerful than the earlier model he had hidden inside his riding boot. The new version was concealed in a specially made bathroom scale and was far more reliable and effective than the one it replaced. Early every morning, at a prearranged time, Lotz would pull out the transmitter in the bathroom—the only place where he had some privacy from his servants, whom he could not trust—and send and receive short messages to and from his bosses in Tel Aviv.

Yet there was one major problem lying at the very heart of the reports that Lotz was beaming back to Israel. For although he was a brilliant host, hugely successful and adept at winning friends in the circles that mattered, he appears to have confused the drunken boasts of his friends and acquaintances, made during long evenings at his home or at various bars, with hard, reliable facts. When he triumphantly transmitted the "intelligence" back to Tel Aviv, he either believed these boasts, or else just wanted to please his bosses, particularly when he needed to justify the enormous bills he constantly presented them with to cover his expenses. Whatever lay behind it, his misleading reports exaggerated the sophistication of the rocket program and explain why Harel was so concerned about the "threat" to Israel he thought it presented, and why he was therefore so determined to press ahead with Damocles.[224]

Meanwhile, Isser Harel was not wasting any time. Within hours he was on a flight to Paris to make contact with the handpicked agents who would be carrying out his plan, and to personally brief them on the importance of the mission and how to go about it. He wanted to use the Paris-based agents for the operation because they were so experienced, while he would personally supervise and manage events from a roving headquarters that would make its way across western Europe as the campaign against the German scientists evolved.[225]

The head of Mossad's Paris office was Yitzhak Shamir, who used the cover name Samuel Singer. Shamir was a highly experienced intelligence operative who had joined the spy service after fighting the British army, prior to Israel's independence in 1948, as a member of the notoriously violent and ruthless Stern Gang. Like his boss, Agent Shamir had his strong points: after years of armed struggle against both the British and the Arabs, he had developed a deep asceticism that allowed him to live uncomplainingly in difficult, sometimes rough conditions, and he was formidably driven and dedicated to his job. "Shamir was an introvert, thorough and hard-working, you could always rely on him," as one of his Mossad colleagues later recalled, while cautioning that "he did not come forward with brilliant ideas."[226]

Chief among his team were a German-born Jew by the name of Joe Ra'anan—also known as Joe Reisman—who had joined Mossad five years before after serving in air force intelligence, and Herzl Amikram, another veteran of the Stern Gang. Taking every precaution to avoid arousing suspicion, Harel met his star agents in a series of cafés in the city center. "Eat the cake because otherwise we'll look suspicious," the Mossad chief reputedly told them.[227]

On the morning of September 11, 1962, at around ten thirty, a dark-skinned man calling himself Saleh, reckoned by one eyewitness to be of Middle Eastern origin, walked into the office of the procurement company INTRA in Schillerstrasse in Munich. The director, forty-nine-year-old Dr. Heinz Krug, had returned there a few days before after making a short business trip to Egypt, where he had met with his colleagues and bosses in the military programs that he was working on behalf of. Krug now met his visitor and talked with him in his office for half an hour or so before they were seen by a flight attendant, who worked in the Egyptian airlines office next door, leaving the building together.

At first this seemed like any of the other business meetings that Krug regularly had with his clients, who were nearly all suppliers of the special-ized engineering goods that were vital to the rocket and aircraft programs. But the following day Krug's wife phoned the police to say that he had gone missing; after an intensive three-day manhunt, officers eventually discovered his Mercedes, locked, mud-splattered, and drained of gasoline, in the Munich suburb of Solln. At about the same time, an anonymous caller phoned the police and reported Krug's death, giving no details about what had happened, before hanging up.

Krug's body was never found and, as far as the German police were concerned, he had simply vanished without a trace. For weeks, rumors per-sisted that he had been kidnapped by an Israeli team or by an international gang that had auctioned him to Israel for a very large sum of money. But no clue to his fate was ever found. Mossad's complicity in Krug's disap-pearance, no less than in the unsuccessful attack on Kamil, has never been conclusively proven, but almost certainly this was just the beginning of Operation Damocles.

In the meantime, Harel had recalled the brief but very effective cam-paign waged in 1956 by the head of Military Intelligence, General Yeho-shafat Harkabi, who had sent letter bombs to two of the Egyptian officers he deemed to have been responsible for organizing fedayeen insurgents and sending them into Israel.[228] Harel wanted to try something similar, and, on his orders, Lotz appears to have handed over a small but lethal packet of high explosives to a contact he met in a Cairo restaurant.

On November 27, some weeks after Krug's disappearance, Wolfgang Pilz's twenty-year-old secretary, Hannelore Wende, was sorting mail at Factory 333 in Heliopolis when she came across a large, bulky airmail envelope that was addressed to her boss. Sent from Germany, and using as a return address the offices of a well-known barrister in Hamburg, it seemed nothing out of the ordinary. In any case, all the scientists had friends and family back in Germany who would mail them all manner of things. But when Wende opened the parcel, a huge blast tore through the office as an incendiary device exploded in her face, blinding her permanently in one eye and damaging her hearing. Pilz himself was badly shaken, though completely unharmed.

The following day, before the Egyptian authorities had time to take adequate countermeasures, another large package marked "specialized literature" was sent to Brig. Gen. Kamil Azzaz, the director of Factory 333. Again, it did not get near its intended recipient, but the explosive device inside tore through the building, killing five Egyptians and injuring six others. The Egyptian authorities quickly investigated the package but found that the return address—supposedly that of a Stuttgart book publisher—was entirely fictitious.[229]

Mossad doubtlessly knew that the chances of eliminating any of the intended recipients were very remote, since nearly all incoming mail to their business addresses would have been opened by more junior staff members. And having lost their initial tactical advantage of surprise, they had also forfeited their best chances of killing any of the scientists—inside Egypt, at least. For the Egyptian authorities now allocated more security personnel to guard the expatriates and their families, and started X-raying all incoming packages. On November 29, two more parcels arrived from Stuttgart, but both were intercepted by the Egyptians and found to be packed with explosives.

But killing top officials and scientists was not at this stage Harel's main aim. Much more important, in his eyes, was to frighten the German expatriates and dissuade them from continuing with their work, and in this regard Mossad's tactics were doubtlessly vastly more effective. After the plane crash over Westphalia, word had already gone around that Kamil had been deliberately targeted by the Israelis. Now, within the space of just two days, the lucrative, exotic, and trouble-free existence of the German scientists must no longer have seemed quite so appealing.

Security was stepped up, and the scientists, who had always carried their own revolvers, were given regular target practice under the supervision of Egyptian soldiers. Whenever they stepped outside the closely guarded compounds in which they worked, they now did so under the watchful eye of specially trained bodyguards who were commanded by Oberfeldwebel Walentein, formerly a leading member of Hitler's Waffen-SS. Some of the scientists, including Pilz, moved home every few months and none of them appeared in public. If journalists wanted to interview any of the scientists, they had to submit written questions instead of putting them forward in person, and when Pilz and Goercke appeared on Egyptian television, they were shown with their backs turned "for security reasons." Specially trained members of the Egyptian security services worked full-time at Cairo's central post office, personally supervising the inspection of every parcel that was sent to the factories, taking extra care with those sent from Europe.

At the same time, Harel started another letter campaign, somewhat less violent but perhaps just as effective, against the scientists. Around fifty letters were now written to some of the leading names in the research programs, warning them of dire consequences, for Israel as well as themselves, if they continued. Personally posted in Cairo by Lotz, who acted as a courier, the letters bore Egyptian postmarks that Harel hoped would make the recipients think and feel they were being constantly watched.

A typical letter ran like this:

> Dear Doctor
>   The work you are doing on behalf of the Egyptian govern-
> ment may have a significance in this part of the world which you
> may not even suspect . . . there can be little doubt that once the

weapons systems you are helping to build have been perfected, they will be used in order to wipe Israel from the map. The government of Israel does not believe that it will ever successfully be able to appeal to Egyptian self-interest. It is dealing with a leader and with a government hell-bent on war—irrationally holding to the belief that it will emerge unscathed from the resultant conflagration. . . . I believe, however, that I may be able to appeal to your own sense of self-interest in the hope that I can persuade you to resign your work here and return to Europe. [Otherwise] individual Israelis worried for the security of their country must seek out and, if necessary, destroy individuals of other nationalities whose work could reduce the dream of 2,000 years to ashes.

I beg of you as a fellow scientist to heed what I say most seriously.

This letter, my dear colleague, must, I regret, go unsigned.[230]

But some of the other letters were more direct, and one of the scientists, by the name of Heinrich Braun, received this message:

We are writing to tell you that your name now appears on our blacklist of German scientists employed by Egypt. We would like to think that you care for the safety of your wife, Elizabeth, and your two children[,] Niels and Trudi. It would be in your interest to cease working for the Egyptian military.[231]

The letter was signed "The Gideonites," a reference to the Old Testament hero who resisted the invasion of Israel by nomadic tribes spearheaded by the Midianites.

At the same time, the Israeli authorities started to move on another front as a result of Nasser's successful missile launches. They now decided to greatly accelerate their own rocket program and to try to catch up, and overtake, the Egyptians at their own game. One of those responsible for this decision was a military chief, Ezer Weizman, who pointed out, "we started working on the [MD-620 Jericho ballistic missile] in 1962 . . . we started when [Abdel] Nasser fired his [Zafar]. . . . in July 1962." Weizman added that after the launch "we convened a meeting at 12 midnight. I was Air Force Commander, Shim [Peres] was Deputy Minister, and everyone got into a panic. . . . [T]his helped develop the [Jericho] missile."[232] In early September 1962, after weeks of negotiations at the Ministry of Defense, Shimon Peres asked the French company Avions Marcel Dassault to carry out a feasibility study that would assess the viability of a surface-to-surface ballistic missile for Israel. The French hesitated but agreed to continue deliberating upon the matter, and in the meantime the Israelis pressed ahead with their covert nuclear program, to the consternation of the Americans.[233]

What is certain is that the relationship between Egypt and Israel was rapidly becoming one of sharply escalating tit-for-tat reprisals. Israel had probably launched its Shavit rocket because it knew that Nasser would eventually be firing his own missiles. But this then prompted the Egyptian leader to drive harder to acquire the rockets that Israel feared. Nasser and his generals also knew something about Israel's nuclear program and wanted to accelerate their own missile program to counter it, just as Israel had accelerated its ballistics projects after the test firing in July 1962.[234]

But Mossad was not interested in who was to blame. Isser Harel only wanted to stop the program, and those who were driving it, dead in their tracks.

CHAPTER SEVENTEEN
Damocles Continues

One day in late October 1962, a large, thickset, dark-haired Austrian man, in his early forties, turned up unexpectedly at Israel's embassy in the Austrian capital, Vienna. He had made no prior appointment to meet any of the staff but nonetheless insisted on talking to a high-level diplomat who dealt with political matters. Intrigued, a desk officer agreed to talk with him in private, although he had no idea what to expect.

"My name is Otto Joklik," the visitor announced, "and I can give you information on the work I have been doing for the Egyptian military projects."

Astonished by what he had heard, the startled diplomat called a colleague to join him and sat back to listen to what the mysterious visitor had to say.

Joklik's story was certainly remarkable. He had been born and raised in Salzburg, he told the Israeli official, and during the war had served in the German army before retraining as a professional scientist. In the course of his work in Austria he had gradually acquired considerable expertise in the medical uses of gamma rays and cobalt-60. His skills and knowledge must have come to the attention of Egyptian scientists, he continued, because the previous year he had been unexpectedly approached by a Colonel el-Din, who was working for General Khalil's network in Western Europe. He was asked to work on behalf of President Nasser's regime, which wanted him to try to obtain cobalt-60 from West German, Canadian, and Indian sources on its behalf.

Joklik said he had then traveled to Egypt to take part in the project, which he initially had known nothing about. But, he continued, he had quickly become aghast by what he found. Wolfgang Pilz, for example, had asked him to obtain radioactive sources for a secret weapons program, while Egypt's malevolence toward the Jewish state had become obvious to see. He was, he exclaimed, "horrified at being part of a plot to exterminate Israel" and as a result had decided to flee the country, leaving there just days before arriving at the Israeli embassy.

The Israeli officials were astonished at the quality of the information Joklik was able and willing to offer them, but first wanted to be absolutely sure that he was a genuine source of information instead of an Egyptian ruse, assigned to put them off the scent. Within hours Mossad had decided to take him to Israel, where he could be closely questioned by a specialist team who would know for sure just how authentic he was.

Once in Tel Aviv, Joklik stuck to his story and elaborated on it further, his revelations confirming all of Mossad's worst fears. The Egyptians, he continued, were not only building surface-to-surface rockets but also constructing lethal warheads that the rockets could deliver. There were, he claimed, two distinct programs to develop these warheads. One project, code-named Ibis, was a bid to fill the warheads with radioactive waste "composed of cobalt-60 isotopes and strontium-90." This was, he reiterated, a scientific effort that he had personally been involved in. The other, known as Cleopatra, was a program to develop a simple atomic bomb, using highly enriched uranium obtained from Dutch or West German centrifuges.

"When these rockets land on Israeli soil," the Austrian continued, "they will spread deadly rays that will infect the whole region for months, if not years."[235] The Egyptians, he added, were allocating considerable resources to the project and had already succeeded in buying a large amount of cobalt from West European sources. It had then been smuggled abroad by the Egyptian Airline Company, which had forwarded it to a Cairo doctor, who claimed, quite plausibly, to need it for her work. But had the German authorities looked into the matter more carefully, asserted Joklik, they would have discovered that the doctor was in fact the sister of General Khalil, the director of the Egyptian armaments program.

Not everything Joklik said was of particular interest to the Mossad chiefs, or even struck them as especially reliable. He claimed, for example, that he had once overheard General Khalil discussing a plan to bribe British pilots to defect to Egypt, taking their planes and nuclear cargoes with them. The Israeli spies were unconvinced by this but nonetheless felt sure that the man was essentially trustworthy and that the bulk of his information was accurate: he had, they judged, been directly involved in the Egypt program, and had helped Nasser to develop the lethal warheads he described.

At the same time, events elsewhere in the Middle East seemed to be confirming everything Joklik was warning the Israelis of. The setting was Yemen, where the Egyptians had become involved in a vicious dispute between various tribes and the ruling regime. For, in the course of 1962, word had been going around that Egyptian planes had used poison gas to bomb a number of villages, and if such reports were true, then the conclusion seemed to be obvious. Not only were the Egyptians barbaric and ruthless enough to deploy such lethal tactics, but they had also used scientific expertise—and probably the expertise of the German scientists—to make and manufacture the materials of bacteriological and chemical warfare.

Mossad had a few other indications of what the Egyptians might be planning, all of which were consistent with Joklik's story. They were particularly alarmed by reports about a German chemist, by the name of Matthilde Rosenfelder, who had arrived in Cairo on a mysterious business trip, and they also knew about the presence in Egypt of a former concentration camp doctor, Dr. Hans Eisele, who might have had enough expertise, and interest, in bacteriology to help the Egyptians. They were also aware of, although much less alarmed by, the apparent communication between the Nasser regime and a leading German atomic scientist, Professor Wilhelm Groth, who, during the Second World War, had studied ways of manufacturing uranium at relatively low cost. In particular, the spy chiefs in Tel Aviv wondered why a man who had refused to cooperate with the

Americans after the war had nonetheless sent a representative to Cairo in 1960. It was plausible although unlikely, they doubtlessly thought, that he was interested in selling a centrifuge, used to enrich uranium to a high enough standard to build an atomic warhead.

There was another, simpler reason Joklik's revelations seemed utterly convincing to the Mossad chief, Isser Harel. To him it seemed very doubtful that the Egyptians would go to so much trouble and expense to build a long-range missile that would then be fitted merely with conventional explosives. If that was all they wanted to do, it would have made much more sense just to use a Soviet-supplied bomber to drop the bombs, since a warplane was far cheaper and quicker to acquire—and, above all, much more accurate—than a missile. So it followed that Nasser must have had something else in mind, such as using the missiles with WMD warheads, as Joklik had claimed all along.

Above all, the Egyptians had previously approached a number of countries to win their support for building an atomic reactor. Although such a civilian reactor would have been designed to provide its people with a source of energy, Israel feared that it could conceivably be used to manufacture a warhead. It was thought that the Egyptian vice president, Abdel Latif Boghdadi, had raised the subject of atomic energy with his German counterparts when he visited Bonn in 1961 but found that Professor Ludwig Erhard, the minister of Economic Affairs, had immediately blocked it.[236]

None of these arguments was entirely convincing. There was no reason warplanes could not drop nuclear as well as conventional bombs, and both the Soviets and Americans had their own planes designed to drop nuclear payloads. This suggested that Nasser might have wanted the missiles more for personal prestige than because of any battlefield consideration. And although Egypt had shown some interest in atomic energy, that was perfectly understandable: its population and industry were growing rapidly and it had no indigenous sources of energy to keep them supplied. Provided the proper safeguards were followed—and the West Germans undoubtedly would have followed them—there was no reason the construction of an atomic reactor would have allowed the Egyptians to build an atomic warhead.

It was quite possible that Egypt had acquired British stocks of mustard gas that had been stored in the desert during the Second World War and then left behind either in 1945 or in 1954. By the early 1960s Cairo could also conceivably have acquired the capability to produce more.[237] But, again, the Egyptians did not need rockets to deliver such a lethal agent. Planes or simple artillery would have been just as effective. Using a rocket to deliver such a payload is technically far trickier, and would have meant developing specialized reentry vehicles, a release mechanism, and cluster munitions, and there is no evidence that the Egyptians tried to do any of these things, even if they had wanted or needed to do so.[238] Most experts also agree that, at some point in the decade that followed the 1956 war, Egypt probably considered developing nuclear and radiological weapons but made no real effort to pursue such a hugely ambitious program. "The Egyptian inability to acquire a rudimentary nuclear capability in the face of active Israeli nuclear pursuits," as one defense analyst has written, "remains a puzzle for proliferation analysts."[239] Experts point out that there is no reason to suppose the Egyptians showed any serious interest even in a civilian nuclear energy project, let alone a weapons program.

But for Isser Harel and the Mossad directors, two things followed from these alarming revelations. On the one hand, they were determined to keep their new information as quiet as possible in case it caused a mass public panic that led to political hysteria and poor decisions. Harel also stuck rigidly, even obsessively, to one of the most basic rules of intelligence work—the rule of compartmentalization. This was one reason—though considerations of professional rivalry and jealousy doubtlessly also crept in—he and his fellow Mossad chiefs wanted to keep Israel's various other spying agencies, notably Meir Amit's Aman organization, wholly in the dark about the existence of their new intelligence source.

The other conclusion drawn by Harel and his team was that it was more important than ever to step up the campaign against the scientists. Operation Damocles was now a top priority. Harel looked at his list of targets and selected his next victim—Dr. Hans Kleinwachter, who was due to return to Germany from Egypt for a few weeks. Yitzhak Shamir's assassination squad was instructed to execute Kleinwachter as soon as detailed surveillance of his movements in his home town of Loerrach had been carried out.[240]

Harel did have methods to deploy besides brute force. In particular, he estimated that some of the German expatriates in Egypt would be more inclined to take heed not of explicit threats by the Jewish state but of the gentle advice of their fellow nationals, especially former Nazis. All that was required was to find just such an individual who might play the part.

Though this seemed a very tall order, the Mossad chief thought of someone who just might, perhaps, be coaxed into taking his side. Otto Skorzeny was not only a former Nazi commando with a formidable reputation but was also personally acquainted with senior members of the Egyptian regime, on whose behalf he had worked some years before. Harel therefore drew up an audacious plan to win him over. Despite severe misgivings on the part of some of his Mossad colleagues, who objected strongly to collaborating with a former Nazi, Harel dispatched a team of agents to Madrid to meet Skorzeny. Posing as a group of NATO representatives, and brandishing forged papers and passes, the Israeli agents tried their utmost to persuade him that it was in the interests of Western security for the German scientists to leave Egypt as soon as possible. Their effort failed, however, because Skorzeny did not want to get involved in any aspect of the scientists' work. Mossad would have to find other ways of ending the Germans' involvement in Egypt after all.

Back in Jerusalem, the mysterious Austrian defector, Otto Joklik, was starting to raise eyebrows. Despite Harel's best efforts to keep Joklik's existence and revelations a secret—although it was unclear quite why "Little Isser" wanted to do so—word of this new source of information had eventually reached the Ministry of Defense. Given the vast importance of Joklik's claims, Shimon Peres immediately demanded that he should be brought before a ministry interrogation team, one that was quite separate and independent from the board of Mossad officers who had originally confronted him. Harel refused; but when Peres went directly to Ben-Gurion and threatened to resign, the Mossad chief was forced to relent.

Peres instructed Benjamin Blumberg, one of his most trusted—and mysterious—officials, to conduct the debrief. Blumberg was the head of the highly secretive Science Liaison Bureau, widely known in government circles by its Hebrew acronym, Lakam. This was a very specialized department within the Defense Ministry, which was entrusted with gathering and assessing scientific and technical intelligence material, particularly on nuclear issues, which were its specialty. Its experts undoubtedly had a far greater knowledge of the matters Joklik claimed to be expert in than the Mossad interrogators whom he had originally met. But when Blumberg's team interviewed Joklik, they did not have to wait long to reach their conclusion. Within a very short space of time, they felt sure that his claims, and his supposed qualifications, were fraudulent and fictitious.

But by this stage, Isser Harel's trust in Otto Joklik had grown considerably, and Peres and his team were unable to stop Harel from now actively deploying the scientist on Mossad operations. In one sense, such a decision was understandable. Harel knew that, as a native Austrian, Joklik would arouse far less suspicion than his own agents, and he would be an indispensable asset in Mossad's operations. True, Joklik was not a trained spy, but then he would not be working alone. A Mossad team would always be backing him up, and he would be operating closely alongside a professional agent, a thirty-three-year-old operative by the name of Joseph Ben-Gal. Yet on the other hand, Joklik was not a Jew and there was no reason to suppose he would have any loyalty to Israel. And if Peres and Blumberg were so sure his claims were false, how could he be trusted ever again? Harel was nonetheless undeterred and remained determined to use Joklik on the next round of Operation Damocles—the attempt to dissuade Dr. Paul Goercke from continuing with his work.

Harel was well aware that Goercke's contribution was vital if the Egyptians were going to overcome the major technical flaw in their plans—the total lack of a reliable guidance system. Harel's plan was not to directly target Goercke, who lived and worked in Egypt, where he was now very closely guarded. Instead, his idea was to put pressure on his twenty-five-year-old daughter, Heidi, who lived in Freiburg, on the Swiss-German border. If his daughter implored Goercke to stop his work and return home, then Harel felt sure he would do so.

In early 1963, Mossad undertook close surveillance of Heidi Goercke's movements and worked out a plan that was put into action in the middle of February. One evening, as she left her office, where she worked as an attorney, and began to walk home, Joklik suddenly emerged from a doorway and started to walk alongside her.

Needless to say, she was extremely unnerved at being approached so abruptly and unexpectedly by a man who had appeared, quite literally, out of the dark. She tried not to let her panic show as he started talking, telling her in a quiet, soft-spoken voice that he knew all about her father's work in Egypt and adding that Israel was quite determined to stop him from continuing with it. All he had to do, Joklik went on, was to renounce his work and he would be safe. "If he does not come back he will be killed," warned Joklik darkly, claiming that he "wanted to give him a chance."

Joklik then quickly pulled away, leaving the terrified young lawyer to carry on with her journey home alone. But she had not heard the last from the mysterious Austrian scientist. A few days later, the phone rang at her home and she heard the same voice uttering a simple message: "If you love your father," said Joklik, "come on Saturday [March 2] to the Three Kings Hotel in Basel at 4:00 P.M., and I will introduce you to my friends." Joklik was trying to persuade her to cross the border into Switzerland because he did not want to risk being arrested in Germany, where the authorities would, he thought, be less sympathetic to the Israeli threats against their own citizens.

By now seriously alarmed, Heidi Goercke got in touch with an enigmatic figure known only as Sameh, who appears to have been an Egyptian agent, based in Basel, acting as an intermediary between the Cairo regime and the German scientists. Ostensibly based in Cairo as a physician, and naturally keeping his links with the Cairo regime quiet, Sameh was not afraid to inform the police of what was happening.[241]

A joint police operation was now launched between the Swiss and German forces, who spent the next two weeks preparing a trap for the Israeli agents. Their first step was to trace Joklik, whom they found living in a flat in Zurich, and also to detect his accomplice, Joseph Ben-Gal, as he crossed the border from Italy. Brandishing an Israeli passport that identified him as an official of the Ministry of Education in Tel Aviv, and saying very little about the purposes of his journey, the fair-haired, mustachioed young Israeli man seemed casual and relaxed on arrival. But Swiss police were suspicious enough to follow him. When he made his way to the Three Kings Hotel, they knew they had their man.

Now the police were ready to close in. Instead of advising Heidi Goercke not to go, they planned to lie in wait and secretly watch the proceedings before moving in to arrest the agents. So in the early afternoon of that March day, several police cars waited behind the Basel hotel, waiting for the two spies to arrive. Passersby were warned to move on to prevent being caught in any crossfire. Inside, a number of detectives waited in the lobby, hiding themselves behind newspapers and trying their best to look inconspicuous. A number of microphones and tape recorders had also been hidden near the table, at the side of the hotel lounge, where Heidi Goercke had been asked to sit. At a carefully chosen location a few hundred yards away, Mossad's operations chief, Joe Ra'anan, was aghast, watching the police prepare for the arrival of the two Israeli agents but by this very late stage quite unable to warn them of the trap they were about to fall into.[242]

Heidi Goercke turned up at the appointed hour, accompanied by her twenty-one-year-old brother and another man, whom she introduced to the two waiting men simply as a friend. Then Joklik and Ben-Gal began to talk, apparently oblivious of the fact that their every word was being bugged, and for the next hour told her what they wanted her to do. Israel had nothing against her father, they emphasized, because he was not and never had been an active Nazi, unlike Wolfgang Pilz, whom they regarded as a one-time political sympathizer of Hitler's. They only objected to Dr. Goercke's work on behalf of the Nasser regime. And if she was willing to travel to Cairo to persuade him to stop his work, they continued, they would pay for her expenses to do so. Heidi Goercke hesitated, refusing to give any firm commitment. Then, nearly four hours after they had arrived, the two men got up and left.

The Swiss police now followed the two Israeli spies as they left the hotel. They both headed for the railway station and caught the six o'clock train to Zurich, where they stopped off for a drink at the Kongress Haus hotel before parting. It was at this point that the police stepped in to arrest them. Plainclothed officers stopped Joklik on the railway platform and asked him to accompany them to the police station, while Ben-Gal was arrested near the Israeli consulate. The German authorities were kept closely informed of what was happening, and immediately submitted an extradition request on the grounds that the threats had been made in Germany and that the two men were suspected of the attempted murder of Dr. Kleinwachter just two weeks before. The Swiss and German authorities kept the arrests quiet for another two weeks until, on March 19, it was officially announced in Basel that two Israeli agents had been arrested and charged with "attempted coercion."

Operation Damocles was about to be exposed to the outside world.

CHAPTER EIGHTEEN
Hysteria in Israel

As soon as word reached Tel Aviv that Joklik and Ben-Gal had been arrested, Little Isser moved fast to limit the damage. Two secret service agents were facing criminal charges in one European country and were also wanted by another for attempted murder. This was a political, diplomatic crisis of huge dimensions for Israel, one that could quite easily shake the Ben-Gurion government and gravely dishonor the reputation of the country. For the spy chief, this could very easily be the end of his professional career.

Because the story of Mossad's undercover work in Europe was about to break and could become public knowledge at any moment, Harel felt that it was vital to put forward Israel's case, or rather Mossad's case, as soon as possible. In his eyes, efficient news management meant sending out a powerful, simple, and effective message to create the right first impression. Unless he succeeded in doing this, he knew that Israel's reputation would be at serious risk and its name would become synonymous with acts of state-sponsored violence that its enemies would portray as naked terrorism. The right approach was simply to portray the high level of danger that he felt sure confronted his country, while emphasizing that Israel's actions were wholly justified because there was no other option to deal with such a major threat. Harel now worked out a media strategy to deal with the growing diplomatic crisis and wasted no time in implementing it.

But there was at least one missing link in the Mossad chief's plan. Whether it was because he was accustomed to working independently, or because he was unsure about the reaction he would get, he had failed to outline his plan to the prime minister first, discussing his ideas and winning approval before proceeding. Ben-Gurion had authorized Harel to mobilize domestic and international opinion to support the two captured agents and to try to win their release, but he had also asked him to tone down the significance of the Egyptian rocket program.[243] Without the premier's express approval, Harel must or should have known that his approach, on such a hugely important theme, was an immensely risky one.

The Mossad chief's first move was to host a secret meeting with the chief editors of the main Israeli newspapers. All were highly trusted confidants, and all had close links with Mossad, which used established journalists to plant stories in the media as well as to obtain information on its behalf.

Getting to Mossad's headquarters was easy enough, situated as it was in a building in central Tel Aviv, just off King Saul Boulevard, where it had been based since the end of the Suez War. It had an unimposing entrance. At one side of its main door was a branch of a national bank, a number of business offices, and a simple café. Visitors generally made their way to a rather run-down lobby, located right next to the café, and then waited until, in the far corner of the lobby, an unmarked door was opened and they were invited into the eight-floor building. On the lower floor was the highly secretive listening and communication center, which only a very small number of carefully screened visitors were given access to, while on the next floor were the offices where the junior staff sat. Another floor was devoted solely to research and development, while analysts, planners, and operations personnel were based on the higher floors. The top floor was home to the senior directors and their staff, and it was there that the newspaper editors would have been taken.[244]

At the conference, held there on March 16, Harel informed them of the Joklik spy case, which the Swiss authorities had not yet made public, and briefed them on the Egyptian missile program, Joklik's work in Cairo, and what the Austrian defector had told them about Egypt's plans to develop

WMD. Then, having given all the main papers a broad overview of the situation, Harel personally met with three specially chosen journalists— Naftali Lavi of *Haaretz*, Samuel Segev of *Maariv*, and Yehoshua Ben-Porat of *Yedioth Aharonoth*—and supplied them with details of the people, organizations, and places involved in the European operations that were supplying the Egyptian rocket program.[245] Within hours the reporters had left Israel for West Germany, vying with each other to get the best stories they could about what was happening inside the offices of INTRA and the Jet Propulsion Study Institute.

The logic behind Harel's move was simple. By supplying so much information to the media, he could guarantee the creation of a massive wave of publicity that would rally Israeli public opinion. Mossad's campaign of assassination and intimidation against the scientists would then have mainstream support within Israel and that, in turn, would influence opinion in Europe too. At the very least, he figured, it would make it much harder for the German, Austrian, and Swiss authorities to condemn the Jewish state without risking a full-scale diplomatic crisis.

The next stage in these carefully choreographed media proceedings was an announcement on a government radio station. A number of German scientists in Egypt, stated the commentator, were busy "producing" and "perfecting" weapons that were banned under international law. The experts were helping the Nasser regime to build a "cobalt warhead" for a surface-to-surface missile that had been test-fired and put on public display the previous summer. The missile, continued the announcer, would be able to "scatter radioactive particles over large areas."

This unexpected announcement on national radio, and Harel's detailed briefing to leading editors, now fueled an overwhelming sense of anger and outrage in the Israeli press, just as the Mossad chief had hoped. The headlines of every leading newspaper proclaimed the sensational news that the Egyptians had hired German scientists, many of whom were former Nazis, to produce not just long-range rockets that were capable of striking Israel but warheads with the potential to unleash atomic, chemical, and radioactive fallout. Right from the word go, this media coverage was mixed with hyperbole, even hysteria. The Egyptians, ran the headlines, were developing and manufacturing poison gases, "microbes," "death rays," and, in all likelihood, atomic bombs. The same message was even reiterated abroad, with the *New York Times* giving ample coverage to the supposed Egyptian attempt to develop nuclear warheads for its missiles, as well as mentioning Otto Joklik by name and briefly mentioning his alleged work for the Egyptians.[246]

It was the involvement of specifically German scientists, rather than those of any other nationality, that helped to whip up the sense of hysteria that now gripped Israel. Newspapers, politicians, and members of the public all accused West Germany of following in Hitler's footsteps, claiming that by failing to stop the scientists, when its government allegedly had the power to do so, it was in effect instigating or tacitly approving of the project. Headlines, reports, editorials, cartoons, conversations, and even poems argued that, eighteen years after the fall of the Third Reich, the new Germany was still pursuing the same agenda by different means.

Then, just hours after the Swiss authorities announced that they had arrested the two agents and charged them with "attempted coercion," the Israel government issued another press release. This stated simply that it "would make disclosures of the most horrible nature about the participation of foreign experts in the development of most dangerous arms" if the two captured men were convicted.[247] Yigal Allon, a veteran commander of the 1948–9 War of Independence and now Ben-Gurion's minister of labor, did not mince words, threatening that "the survivors of the death camps will not look on passively while German neo-Nazis in the services of the Cairo dictator prepare the destruction of Israel."[248]

But the most outspoken senior politician in this governmental furor was the foreign minister, Golda Meir. The next day, on March 20, she stood before the Knesset to make an official announcement about the situation, using highly uncompromising and deeply emotional rhetoric to do so. "An evil crew" of "German scientists and hundreds of technicians," she claimed, were helping the United Arab Republic develop "offensive weapons" and "armaments banned by international law" for use against Israel. Then came the more specific revelation that echoed Joklik's claims. The Nasser regime, she went on, was preparing atomic, biological, and chemical warfare to wipe out the Jewish state, "endeavouring to obtain these types of weapons which other powers are not prepared to supply through a group of scientists without conscience." In her view, the motives were clear, being "on the one hand, lust for gold and on the other, a Nazi inclination to hatred of Israel and the destruction of Jews."[249] Above all, the Bonn government now had to act decisively and clamp down on the overseas activities of its citizens. "If legislative or other measures are required for the purpose," she went on, "we demand that such measures be taken at once."[250]

Influenced, as Harel hoped they would be, by the headlines of the preceding few days as well as by Meir's speech, other members of Parliament now weighed in. In the course of a frenzied parliamentary debate, some proposed a "settling of accounts" with the West German government, another referred in apocalyptic terms to the "German death ray," while the leader of one of the religious parties claimed that "we have been led astray and gravely deceived by Germany's statements and promises." Then a resolution was put forward denouncing the activities of the scientists in Egypt. Winning almost unanimous support, it ran: [T]he German people cannot deny its responsibility for this continued criminal activity. It is the duty of the German government to put a stop to these activities at once . . . and to take steps necessary to prevent the cooperation between these people and the Egyptian government.

Harel welcomed this emotionally charged debate because it allowed him to justify Operation Damocles. What was the point in trying to reason with the West German authorities when they knew full well what their scientists were doing and when the risk to Israel was so great? Sure enough, the Israeli media adopted the same argument. "The Germans must recognise that Israel cannot stand idly by while Germans build rockets for Nasser which are intended to destroy Israel," proclaimed the *Jerusalem Post*, while *Haaretz* argued that Germany should be deemed responsible if Israel took "unconventional measures in order to defend itself against the threat of unconventional and cruel weapons." Another newspaper, *Maariv*, stated that the Germans weren't doing enough to stop their scientists and hadn't as yet even condemned them. The Swiss authorities, it continued, were being irresponsible and deeply unhelpful by imprisoning the two agents.

By failing to clear his media strategy with Ben-Gurion in advance, however, Harel had chosen to play with political dynamite. The reason was simple: the prime minister was trying to build closer relations with West

Germany, regarding its support—diplomatic, military, and commercial—as vital to Israel's future. But Harel's press campaign would make that policy much harder to follow, or even impossible to do so, and this meant that Ben-Gurion would have to hold his intelligence chief to account. And if Ben-Gurion lost his political following in Parliament and among the general public, then he would have good reason to pin the blame on Harel for that as well.

Yet it was just such a high political price that the prime minister was already starting to pay. During the parliamentary debate of March 20, not a single member of Ben-Gurion's Mapai party defended him against charges of failing to stand up to a national enemy. A good many press commentators scorned his reference to "another Germany" that he claimed was emerging under Konrad Adenauer. At the same time, West German officials were starting to blame the prime minister for the tense climate of opinion. A few days after the parliamentary debate, the German chancellor sent a private message to Ben-Gurion, explaining that the anti-German campaign in Israel was seriously endangering the secret weapons deal between the two countries that had been brokered after so much painstaking diplomacy.[251]

The uproar in Israel also provoked an immediate and indignant response in Egypt. The minister of information, Dr. Abdel Kader Hatem, categorically denied that any Germans were involved in the manufacture of nuclear weapons, a statement that was backed up by the German embassy in Cairo. Soon afterward came a more vitriolic statement, condemning "Zionist agents [who] have undertaken criminal actions against families of German experts who cooperate with the [United Arab Republic]." The spokesman added that the Israelis were probably motivated not by fear of any supposed threat but rather by "displeasure" with Egypt's "scientific and technological progress."[252]

Two days later, on March 22, a government official in Bonn issued a statement implying that Israel had grossly exaggerated the danger. According to Bonn's own information, continued the official, only eleven German experts were working in Egypt and the rest were all Austrian, Swiss, and Spanish nationals. He added that while the Bonn government disapproved of their involvement in Egypt it had no legal means of stopping them. The scientists were entitled to move around as they wished because the German constitution guaranteed their basic freedom of movement. So the government could only step in, he emphasized, if there was a clear violation either of German law or of the country's obligations under international law. In other words, the affair had nothing to do with them.

There was, however, another reason the German authorities were reluctant to crack down on the scientists, even if some compelling evidence of Israel's claims had been put forward. At a time of so much Cold War tension, the West Germans were desperate to keep Egypt away from Soviet influence. In particular, they feared that if the German experts left the country, then their counterparts from Eastern Europe would simply step in, helping to forge a strategic and political alliance between Cairo and the communist world. One West German official stated simply that for this reason "the West would be the loser" if the scientists departed, and added that Bonn would merely gather information on their activities and find out if any of them were interested in pursuing career opportunities back home.[253]

Then, on March 27, the German government followed this up with a further statement, pointing out—quite correctly—that there was no evidence of any Germans being involved in the production of WMD. The spokesmen went on to say that they would be looking further into the scientists' activities and would put a stop to them if the scientists were in any way aggravating political tensions in the Middle East. If so, then the scientists would be guilty of committing a breach of the German constitution, Article 26 of which prohibited "activities tending to disturb the peaceful relations between nations, and especially preparing for aggressive war."

By now, the Israeli argument had started to win slightly more support within the Bundestag, the West German Parliament. This was mainly because Israel was now being increasingly viewed as an important new friend in the Cold War, at a time of growing tensions with the Soviet Union and its Eastern European allies, as well as an important market for German exporters. On April 2, members of all three main political parties in the Bundestag demanded the recall of the scientists and vowed to introduce new legislation that would aim to outlaw their activities. Furthermore, as one of the leaders of the mainstream Social Democratic Party, Dr. Carlo Schmid, argued, they were in any case already violating Article 26 of the constitution because Egypt and the other Arab states had not formally accepted the existence of Israel. In his view, this meant that the rockets, if they were ever developed, would be deeply destabilizing. Dr. Schmid was undoubtedly a heavyweight regarding such matters because he had been one of the leading authors of the German constitution.

Behind the scenes, German government officials were working furiously to answer their critics, gathering as much information as they could about what was actually happening in Egypt. But when, in the final week of March, the German Foreign Ministry asked the Israeli embassy in Bonn to provide some convincing evidence of the existence of an Egyptian WMD program, they were met with only a hazy response. All the relevant documents, replied the Israelis, had been passed to the German Defense Ministry. Officials in the Foreign Ministry immediately contacted their counterparts in the Defense Ministry but were told that the documents could not be released. To do so, came the reply, might give some clue to the sources of information and put them in danger. Without any information confirming Israeli claims, the Foreign Ministry concluded with sound logic that the Egyptian WMD program simply didn't exist. There could therefore be no question of German citizens being involved in anything disreputable, and Israel's vision, terrifying though it was, was therefore ultimately just a chimera. But in a conversation with an American diplomat in Bonn, an official from the ministry did admit that four German citizens were working on Nasser's rockets, assisted by two Austrians and six East Germans of "unknown allegiance."[254]

Almost two thousand miles away, in Egypt, the German scientists were astonished by the sudden level of international interest in their projects and now busily prepared their own media campaign, one that they hoped would clear their names. We "have nothing whatever to do with the construction of military rockets, as can easily be proven," Goercke and Pilz told the media, emphasizing that the allegations about the development of WMD were a "blatant lie" that was designed only "to justify these criminal acts" perpetrated by the Jewish state.[255] Instead, they continued, their work was restricted to training Egyptian engineers in rocketry and it was thanks to these efforts that the Egyptians would soon be able to carry out space research that could be of enormous industrial benefit to the country. Their claims were backed up by Dr. Sänger, who spoke out from his home in West Berlin to deny ever having had any involvement in "arms development" during his own time in Cairo, which "had nothing to do with the construction of weapons of any kind."[256] Such claims were, of course, fallacious: all of the scientists must have known that they were working on a missile that could be used for military ends just as easily as for space or meteorological research.

In Israel, meanwhile, Harel may have been surprised by just how successful his media plans had been in whipping up the public outrage he had hoped for. But if he was pleasantly surprised, his prime minister was deeply concerned. He may well have remembered the warnings of his former political rival, Moshe Sharett, who had watched a comparable media frenzy and public hysteria in the run-up to the Suez War in 1956. Genuinely alarmed, Sharett had noted how "the press is covered with screaming headlines about Egyptian troop concentrations 'on the border' . . . the impression left is that we are actually on the brink of war, but the sceptical reader can understand that we have artificially exaggerated [this impression] to buttress our demand for arms."[257]

This exactly mirrored Ben-Gurion's own concerns. In speeches and letters he now started to denounce the campaign against the German scientists as "noise . . . in part exaggerated, in part the fruit of demagogy" that was harmful to Israel. Unless the hysteria died down and there was at least some semblance of rational judgment, he feared that either his own political career, or his much valued relations with West Germany, would be in serious danger. He spoke in Parliament of "our grave concern over the designs of the Egyptian dictator to destroy Israel and the assistance he is receiving from German and other scientists" but cautioned that this "should not throw us off our balance." He added that, "to my great regret[,] a large number of falsehoods and distortions have been published in recent weeks in the local press, some of them, I assume, in error, but in several cases on purpose and without a sense of responsibility."

Fortunately for the prime minister, the hysteria started to die down after a few days and at this point a few commentators in the Israeli press started to voice their own apprehensions. One journalist wrote in *Haaretz* that "the mobilisation of public opinion has gone hand in hand with disgraceful manifestations. The worst of all is the panic that has seized Israel and which now appears ridiculous. The description given in the Knesset of the Egyptian death ray, hissing and devouring everything in its path, seems borrowed from the adventures of Flash Gordon."[258]

The prime minister's serious reservations, even anger, about the wave of anti-German hysteria within Israel were deepened by the sudden arrival of Shimon Peres, who had flown back to Tel Aviv from Paris when he heard about the ensuing uproar. Peres, more than anyone else, was desperate not to imperil an arms deal with West Germany that he had spent months negotiating. The deputy defense minister criticized Harel "for his unconsidered action based on speculative reports" and ordered Amit's Military Intelligence to undertake a complete and thorough reassessment of Egyptian capabilities and weigh any risk that they really posed to the Jewish state. Amit's research department, under the command of Aharon Yariv, had already done this the previous summer, just after the missile launches, but in the light of the serious media revelations and the highly charged climate of opinion needed to further revise and update this initial assessment now.

Amit took less than two days to come back with a full summary that painted a very different picture from Harel's. Closely questioned by Ben-Gurion throughout his presentation, Amit stuck to his earlier view that there was absolutely no evidence that the Egyptians were trying to develop chemical, bacteriological, or nuclear weapons. Nor, even if such a Egyptian program did exist, was there any evidence that the German scientists were involved in it. In any case, Amit added, the men at work in Egypt were a group of mediocre scientists who had developed only antiquated missiles, and this meant that the panic that had overtaken Israel's leadership—including a number of experts at the Defense Ministry and the General Staff—was not only unjustified but even dangerous. After years of effort, in other words, the German scientists had nothing particularly important to show. Amit felt sure that Joklik was a "crook" or "charlatan," as the Lakam team had argued all along, and that the so-called Ibis and Cleopatra programs were basically "unworkable."[259]

Peres urged his prime minister to quickly stifle the anti-German campaign in the press. It had already created serious tension between the two countries that could rupture at any minute, he argued, and might easily torpedo the hugely valuable arms deals. Peres's concerns seemed all the more powerful when a West German defense official, Volkmar Hopf, visited Ben-Gurion at his vacation home at Lake Tiberias and reiterated Bonn's concern at the rising tide of anti-German sentiments in Israel.

On March 24, acting without delay, Ben-Gurion summoned Isser Harel to his home in Tel Aviv to discuss the issue. The prime minister strongly criticized his reports, saying that he "was not convinced of the evidence" and that the reports were harmful to Israel's interests. But Harel hotly retorted that Ben-Gurion was sacrificing the country's security to an alliance with Germany. The two men parted late at night in what Harel called a "correct atmosphere" that was underwritten with "a certain tension."

The next day the two men met once again, and almost at once the atmosphere became heated. The discussion followed the same line as the previous day, but this time the prime minister demanded that the Mossad chief give a full explanation and admission of his role in stirring up the media frenzy over the scientists. He added that he would soon be calling a meeting of the parliamentary Defense and Foreign Affairs Committee and that Harel would be asked to testify before its members. Voices were raised in the course of the meeting, and although Golda Meir stepped in to support him, Harel submitted his resignation a few hours later, standing up and leaving his office for the last time as his three secretaries, overwhelmed at this supremely emotional moment, burst into tears. After twelve years of wielding astonishing power and influence over Israel's intelligence community, his reign was over.

Operation Damocles had claimed another victim.

CHAPTER NINETEEN
Mossad Fights On

The circumstances under which Mossad's new chief, Meir Amit, took up his posting did not augur well for his efforts to end the German involvement in the Egyptian rocket program. Right from the word go, the incoming spy chief was confronted by the overt hostility of some of his chief operatives on the ground who had been leading Operation Damocles.

At the start of his very first day in his new job, on March 27, Amit received a coded telex message that expressed regret at Harel's resignation and stated that "every effort must be made to bring him back." One of the signatories, among several other very senior Mossad agents in Western Europe, was Yitzhak Shamir, who had long been fanatically loyal to the outgoing spy chief. Amit, a military man nurtured in a tradition in which orders and authority were followed instead of openly challenged, gave an immediate retort: "I do not accept your behaviour," he telexed back. "I am not accustomed to collective protests." But there was more to come. Within two days of Amit's arrival, Harel's deputy and three of Mossad's most experienced officers had also resigned.

This hostile reaction did not just reflect the loyalty of the field agents to their former boss but also revealed the high degree of interdepartmental jealousy and rivalry between Mossad and Aman, the organization in which Amit had been nurtured. The two organizations had followed different traditions and been led by men of different personalities who had different styles and approaches, and who had a tendency to mock each other's methods and track records. Aman's personnel specialized in military analysis and they openly scoffed at Mossad's inability to assess the armed forces of the Arab countries. Meanwhile, Harel and his senior officers acknowledged that Aman was adept at processing raw data but argued that this was not what ultimately mattered in the world of espionage. For them, it was human intelligence—the work of agents on the ground—that was most important.[260]

Healing this internal rift was an urgent priority if both organizations were to operate successfully and continue with the campaign against the German scientists. Within two weeks, Amit had flown to Paris to meet and clear the air with Shamir and other operatives, well aware that there was no room for such bitter disagreements.

At the same time Mossad was torn by internal feuding, so was the world of Israeli politics. Again, it was Harel's resignation that triggered the dissent, as opposition parties called for a special parliamentary session and a full debate to discuss the German-Egyptian question, and as some of Ben-Gurion's allies, who were a vital link in his parliamentary coalition, threatened to pull their support. All across the political spectrum, members of Parliament—from the Liberal, Communist, Herut, and Mapam parties—accused the prime minister of ignoring and violating the resolution that had been passed on March 20. They also demanded to know more about what lay behind Harel's departure.

This was an immensely difficult conundrum for Ben-Gurion to resolve. On the one hand, he had to keep his coalition intact and could not afford to look complacent at a time when passions were running so dangerously high. On the other, he had to curb the anti-German campaign, whipped up to such hysterical proportions by Harel, if he was to avoid sacrificing his growing ties with Bonn. He tried his best to strike a note of compromise, pointing out that "the Egyptian dictator" wanted to destroy Israel, but emphasizing that the contribution of the German scientists "should not throw us off our balance." Urging the Knesset members to act in a responsible way and remember that much of the most sensitive information could not be made public, he managed to defeat an attempt by his political opponents to force a full parliamentary debate on the issue. As a result, he had, for the moment, narrowly survived the political storm.

Outside Parliament, the prime minister was doing his best to restore relations with West Germany. Using information that had undoubtedly been carefully leaked, an American newspaper reported on March 29 that, according to an "informed source," Ben-Gurion was "highly displeased" and "angered" by the media campaign against West Germany in general, rather than the scientists in particular, and had "decided on dismissals" as a result. The anti-German sentiments, continued the report, "went further than was warranted by the public charges made ten days ago by Foreign Minister Golda Meir and the Knesset" and, as a result, the prime minister was working hard to "undo the damage" and "play down" the propaganda campaign. Government officials in Tel Aviv, added the *New York Times* journalist, were now openly admitting that "hard proof" of the Egyptian WMD program was simply not available and were instead admitting that the government should always have backed up such important allegations with convincing evidence.[261]

At a time when Israeli claims about the rocket program were under so much scrutiny—within Israel as well as in West Germany and in Switzerland, where Joklik and Ben-Gal were still awaiting trial—it was of course more crucial than ever for Israel's single most important agent in Egypt, Wolfgang Lotz, to produce some compelling new evidence about the rocket program. As the political crisis suddenly reached a crescendo, Lotz received detailed instructions to provide as much fresh information as he could about the program. These orders were now issued not by Military Intelligence, which had originally commanded Unit 131, but by Mossad, which, after the resignation of Isser Harel, had taken responsibility for this department.

It was late at night, as usual, when Lotz finished sending his own message, using the transmitter that was carefully hidden in his bathroom scale, and at the same time receiving his new orders from Tel Aviv.

"Is it anything important?" asked his wife sleepily.

"Yes, I'm afraid it is. Very important and most urgent. Top priority, in fact. It's about that rocket base in Shaloufa again."[262]

Mossad knew about the rocket base at Shaloufa, near Great Bitter Lake between Suez and Ismaïlia, from a number of aerial photographs. But its reconnaissance experts wondered if the site might in fact be a dummy, and it was therefore vital that Lotz somehow find a way into the base to verify its existence.

Using a detailed map of the region, Lotz and his wife, Waltraud, carefully scanned the area. Knowing that the base was situated somewhere between a railway line and the main road that ran through the desert, they identified its likely location. Their best chance, they estimated, was to drive along the road that led to the base and then find some way—impossible though it must have seemed—of getting through the armed checkpoints that would inevitably block their way. If they posed as tourists, out for a swim in the nearby Bitter Lakes, then they might just have a chance. Dressed in casual trousers, a bright yellow sports shirt, and a vivid red peaked cap on top, Wolfgang Lotz left his ranch, with his wife in the passenger seat, and headed northeastward toward Suez.

To avoid detection, Lotz had originally hoped to drive off the road a long way ahead of the checkpoint. But it quickly became obvious that this plan was not going to work, for driving even just a few yards into the deep sand would have been impossible. Although they drove mile after mile looking for a stretch of the desert that might be more accessible, they eventually lost hope and gave up. In other words, they now had no option other than to get past the checkpoint, even though they had no papers and no convincing story.

As the checkpoint loomed into view, Lotz urged his wife, now at the wheel, to approach carefully, saying, "Change into low gear and drive on slowly. I want to see what kind of guard they have and if there is more than one."

Seeing just one solitary guard, who was leaning idly against the sentry box, the two decided their best chance would be to pretend that their car had broken down and then wander off for help, or ask the guard to fetch help for them. But as they drove, very slowly, toward the sentry, they realized that they were having the most extraordinary luck.

"Wait, don't get out," Lotz exclaimed, scarcely believing what he could see. "This is too beautiful to be true!"

Barely moments before, it turned out, the guard had disappeared just over the horizon, twenty or thirty yards away, to relieve himself.

"In, quickly!" Lotz shouted. "Drive as fast as you can!" Waltraud slammed into gear and shot off past the sentry box and a large black-and-red sign that clearly marked, in both English and Arabic, a "Prohibited Area." Lotz glanced in the rearview mirror after they went past and saw the unfortunate sentry shouting and waving at them but he calmly urged Waltraud to simply keep driving.

"Don't turn your head, and keep going. Somebody may try and stop us at any minute and I want to get a look at that base first."

With breathtaking audacity and astonishing luck, the Israeli agent was breaking into a top-secret base in broad daylight.

But just a few hundred yards further up the road, their luck seemed to run out. Seeing a jeep carrying armed soldiers approaching them from the opposite direction, Lotz and his wife expected to be stopped and arrested, but, to their amazement, it simply drove past them, with the five guards merely staring inquisitively at them. A short distance farther up the road, however, Lotz looked in the rearview mirror and saw the jeep turning around and starting to follow them. Thinking quickly under pressure, he knew he would now have nothing to lose by taking a drastic course of action.

"Drive the car straight into the sand!" he told his wife. "If you can get us really stuck, we may have to stay there for hours. Quick, off the road—and make it convincing!"

Ignoring a bend in the road a short distance away, Waltraud did as he had told her and drove straight into the deep sand, where the car came to a rapid standstill with a bump.

"Keep the wheels turning," barked Lotz, "it will dig us in deeper."

By now the jeep had caught up with them and the five guards, all armed with automatic weapons, jumped out and surrounded them. Lotz was a very accomplished speaker of the Arabic language, but he feigned total ignorance as the soldiers beckoned them to get into the jeep. Within minutes, they were being driven to the commanding officer for questioning.

This was exactly what the two spies had wanted. They needed to verify that the rocket base was genuine, instead of just an Egyptian decoy, and as they were driven into the compound they took careful mental note of everything they saw, while at the same time trying their best to pretend they had no interest in their surroundings. They were well aware that by taking their prisoners through a top-secret site, the soldiers were acting with a shocking degree of negligence. Standard security procedure in such a situation would be to blindfold prisoners, or take them somewhere on the periphery of the base, but the Egyptian soldiers had instead fallen right into the trap.

Before long, Lotz and Waltraud had the information they wanted and the confirmation they needed. After being driven through several road-blocks and up a steep hill, they saw rocket-launching sites arranged in a wide circle, together with storage bunkers and a number of office build-ings. The Shaloufa rocket site was not a hoax or a false alarm but really did exist after all.

Now they still had to find a way out of the dire situation they had gotten themselves into. They had brazenly strayed into a top-secret military site, ignoring unmissable signs that clearly stated that entry was prohibited and driving straight past a checkpoint. As they waited at the base headquarters, they did their utmost to remain calm and to work out their best line of defense.

After a short wait, they were taken into an office, comfortably fur-nished with leather armchairs, two settees, and thick carpets, where a senior officer, a colonel about forty, slim, dark-haired, and with a black mustache, gestured to them to sit down. Another officer, who appeared to be a lieutenant colonel, was also present, listening intently to every word.

Then the questioning began. The colonel asked them their names and occupations, and for an explanation as to how they had ventured onto the base, before he closed in.

"Why was your wife driving? Isn't it more natural for the man to drive?"

"Perhaps. I hurt my knee last week and I wanted to rest it. Besides, my wife enjoys driving."

"How did you hurt your knee, Mr. Lotz?"

"Falling off a horse, getting out of the bath, does it matter?"

"The sentry at the intersection where our road branches off says he tried to stop you and you went through, ignoring his order to stop."

"I saw no sentry. I'm telling you I was asleep."

"Your wife was not asleep. Why didn't she stop? There is also a written notice prohibiting entrance to unauthorized persons."

"My wife saw nothing of the kind. Certainly no one tried to stop her. If your sentry, who was probably sleeping, is telling the truth, why didn't he telephone your office and report the matter?"

"The line to the first roadblock is out of order, but that is none of your concern. . . . I shall inform the authorities and a full investigation will be made."

Lotz had produced a plausible story but needed more than that if he was to get off the hook. He now wanted to use his contacts, high in the ranks of the Egyptian military, to do so.

"Are you familiar with Col. Mohsen Sabri of the state security?" he asked sharply. "Let me speak to him and speak to him yourself, and if you are not satisfied he'll refer you to an authority you consider competent. Is that fair enough? This is the number."

The colonel was taken aback both by the audacity of his unwelcome visitor and by the name Lotz had dropped. He paused and then nodded his approval.

After some difficulty, the telephone operator was finally able to reach Colonel Sabri, who was astonished to be contacted, out of the blue, by the colonel of a top-secret military base, and just as amazed to hear about the suspicious behavior of a good and trusted friend. The two senior officers spoke at length to each other before the base commander handed Lotz the phone.

"Colonel Sabri wishes to speak to you," he said, his face noticeably paler than before. "What's this trouble you've gotten yourself into? What are you doing in a secret installation of the armed forces?" Lotz noticed that Sabri's voice suddenly had a slight edge to it, as if he was suspicious.

The Israeli agent stuck to his story and gave a long explanation of how he had managed to enter a forbidden area, driving straight past warning signs. He did not have to try hard to win Sabri's sympathy.

"I shall see that you are cleared at once. Now please give me that colonel again. My regards to Mrs. Lotz and apologies for the inconvenience. I'll see both of you in Cairo."

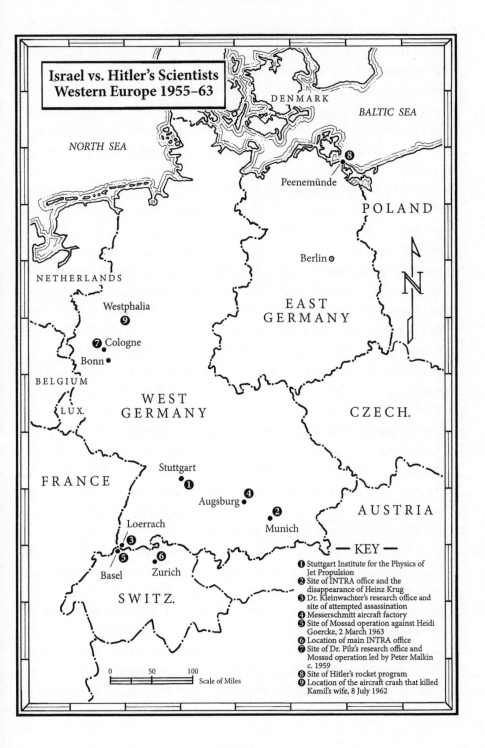

Israel vs. Hitler's Scientists
Western Europe 1955–63

DENMARK

BALTIC SEA

NORTH SEA

POLAND

Peenemünde

Berlin

NETHERLANDS

Westphalia

EAST
GERMANY

Cologne

Bonn

BELGIUM

LUX.

WEST
GERMANY

CZECH.

Stuttgart

FRANCE

Augsburg

Munich

AUSTRIA

Loerrach

Basel

Zurich

SWITZ.

— KEY —

❶ Stuttgart Institute for the Physics of
   Jet Propulsion
❷ Site of INTRA office and the
   disappearance of Heinz Krug
❸ Dr. Kleinwachter's research office and
   site of attempted assassination
❹ Messerschmitt aircraft factory
❺ Site of Mossad operation against Heidi
   Goercke, 2 March 1963
❻ Location of main INTRA office
❼ Site of Dr. Pilz's research office and
   Mossad operation led by Peter Malkin
   c. 1959
❽ Site of Hitler's rocket program
❾ Location of the aircraft crash that killed
   Kamil's wife, 8 July 1962

0   50   100
                    Scale of Miles

Lotz then passed the phone back to the colonel, who was standing right in front of him. The colonel's expression changed dramatically as he heard what Sabri had to say. The two officers were of equal rank but because Sabri was a senior member of Egypt's much-feared security services, he had the authority to arrest, or demote, whomever he pleased. "The commandant's face was a study in discomfort and embarrassment," noted Lotz, and he was reduced to giving monosyllabic replies such as "yes" and "of course."

Lotz had bluffed his way out of a very dire situation and returned home the next day after dining with the commanding officer, who was feeling somewhat red-faced because of the arrest of a man who was so well connected and so highly respected by senior people in Cairo. But Lotz's information about the rocket base did not come to light in time for the trial of the two captured Israeli spies, Otto Joklik and Joseph Ben-Gal, who were still being held by the Swiss authorities. However, while awaiting trial, they had had some good news: the Swiss Justice Ministry would not be handing them over to the West Germans after all, they were informed, because its officials did not have enough evidence linking them to the attempted murder of Hans Kleinwachter. But trying to defend themselves against claims of harassment, which the Swiss police had now charged them with, nonetheless still promised to be a very tough proposition.

The two men were due to appear in court in June, just three months after they were arrested. It would only be a very brief trial, lasting just a few days, they were assured, since the offense they were charged with was a relatively minor matter. In addition, the facts of the case were fairly straightforward and the witnesses were all readily available.

As Joklik and Ben-Gal waited for the hearing to get under way, the Israeli cabinet discussed how best to support the two captured men. Besides speaking out loudly to voice the strength of their feelings, they thought they had another card to play in their battle to win favor in the court of international opinion. Above all, the cabinet members agreed, the two captured agents in Switzerland had to be formidably well briefed about Israel's case and superbly backed up with convincing documentation. Provided they went on the offensive against the prosecutors, there was a good chance they would win a lot of public sympathy and perhaps even be reprieved, or win a light sentence. Amit knew exactly what documentation the spies needed and arranged for a copy of his prized possession—the letter that Professor Pilz had written to the director of Factory 333 in March of the previous year—to be sent to the two men as they awaited trial and prepared their defense.[263]

To many of those in the cabinet, it seemed more important now than at any previous time over the past few years to win this propaganda battle. For on April 17 the Egyptian government had signed an agreement with other leaders to create an Arab federation, whose provisional constitution spoke boldly of "the question of Palestine and the national duty to liberate it." Israel's permanent representative to the United Nations had then written to the Security Council arguing that "the liberation of Palestine" was in fact an unmistakable reference to the destruction of the Jewish state, while David Ben-Gurion feared that the Arabs were moving inexorably toward fulfilling his worst nightmare—the encirclement of Israel that would leave it deeply vulnerable to a coordinated attack. There could be no worse moment to lose out in Basel.

At the same time that Mossad was working so hard to win a favorable hearing in the Joklik trial, another voice added considerable support to its cause. Ever since the Suez campaign, six and a half years before, Gen. Moshe Dayan had been a well-known figure in the West and his opinions as a military commander were highly respected. With his distinctive black eye patch and distinguished war record in the wars of 1948 and 1956, he was well qualified to lend his heavyweight opinions to the controversy that surrounded Egypt's missile program.

The article that caused the stir was published in the Israeli newspaper *Maariv* on April 12. Its basic argument was simple although highly controversial. Mindful of how the two superpowers, Russia and America, were vying with each other to develop long-range ballistic missiles, Dayan asserted that "no army has ever produced [missiles] only to carry conventional warheads." Instead, he claimed that there was an undeniable link between missiles and nuclear bombs. The basic conclusion was obvious: "[E]ven if there has not been tangible evidence that the Egyptians were working on the production of nuclear weapons with the connivance of German scientists and technicians," he argued, "we may suppose without too much risk of error that they are intending to do so." It would not be insurmountably hard for the Egyptians to build a very basic nuclear device, he continued, and even a "primitive" bomb—a reference to a radiological warhead—would allow Cairo to become a member of what he termed "the anteroom of the nuclear club." Maintaining that it made perfect sense for Nasser to want to develop a nuclear missile—it would allow him, he said, to claim leadership over the entire Arab world and destroy the Jewish state, which lacked its own nuclear deterrent—Dayan concluded by emphasizing that Israel would have to confront the emergent threat itself, instead of relying upon anyone else to do so.

Dayan's article showed all the hallmarks of being written on behalf of his political mentor, David Ben-Gurion. Carefully timed to coincide with both the Joklik trial and the aftershocks of the anti-German campaign in Israel, it clearly pointed out the seriousness of the dangers confronting Israel but at the same time strongly emphasized that "the German people and their government" should not be "confused" by the work of the fellow nationals in Egypt. "It is a false identification," Dayan pointed out, "that can only do us harm." There was scarcely any clearer exposition of the Ben-Gurion line.

The debate that Dayan's article provoked in high-level circles provided a good context for Joklik and Ben-Gal to begin their defense in front of the Swiss court. The court proceedings began on Monday, June 10, and right from the start attracted considerable public interest. The courtroom was packed with journalists and members of the public, all of whom were intrigued by the stories, rumors, and revelations of espionage that surrounded the trial. Ben-Gal aroused their curiosity even more when he kept his face averted from the gaze of the public, prompting his onlookers to call him "the man without a face."

Armed with all the information Mossad had passed to them and briefed them carefully about, the two defendants testified under oath that the German scientists were working hard to develop "capsules" of cobalt and strontium that could be used in the warheads of ballistic missiles. Employing highly charged terms, comparable to those used in the Israeli parliamentary and media debates a few weeks beforehand, Joklik did his best to persuade the jury of six judges that these warheads could be used to "poison Israel's atmosphere." He had firsthand experience and knowledge of Egyptian plans, he stressed, because he had personally worked to develop them before fleeing Cairo when he discovered the Nasser regime's "de facto intention" to "exterminate the Jews."

The Swiss prosecutors immediately challenged all these claims but Joklik was well prepared. He produced what he said was $100 million worth of receipts, invoices, and bills of lading for the Egyptian arms program. Furthermore, he went on, he had personally purchased a quantity of cobalt-60 and arranged for it to be shipped to the sister of the program's director, General Khalil. Then came another letter, also of very dubious validity, that he claimed Khalil had written to Wolfgang Pilz, revealing a plan to equip the Egyptian missiles with cobalt warheads. Finally he played his master card, as he showed the court Pilz's letter detailing his plans for Factory 333.

The prosecution case, led by Hans Wieland, had some nasty surprises in store for the two defendants, emphasizing their "grave threats" to Dr. Goercke and his daughter and highlighting clear inconsistencies and question marks that were hanging over the academic record that Joklik boasted of. Wieland also argued that Joklik had violated Swiss export laws by supplying the Egyptians with a "radiation-measuring instrument" several years before. But the two men had mounted an unapologetic and strongly worded defense and refused to back down.

Before long, their approach started to produce the results they wanted. One member of the prosecution team summed up his case by admitting that he was "understanding of Israel's deep anxiety" on the grounds that the German expatriates were developing a missile and warhead that "should disturb not only Israel but the whole world, especially since the weapon being discussed had already appeared in public in a Cairo military parade." The prosecution team recommended that Ben-Gal had acted with "justified concern for his country" and "with honorable intent," and therefore merited no more than a three-month suspended sentence, while Joklik deserved a fine and a hundred-day suspended sentence.

At the end of the proceedings, on Thursday June 13, the jury took ten hours to reach its verdict, which was then announced by the presiding judge, Emil Heberli. He concurred with the prosecution team's suggestions and accepted that Egypt's missile program was sufficiently "offensive" to have justified an Israeli reaction that was not "necessarily lawful." The agents had acted out of "ardent patriotism," he judged, and were merely trying to defend their country. He summarized by saying that: "[I]t is found that between Israel and Egypt reigns an underground war; it is found that Israel is in a position where it is vital to defend itself; it is found that important Egyptian statesmen and politicians have not concealed their views that Israel must be destroyed; it is found that Egypt plans rocket warfare against Israel and that the German scientists play a leading role in these plans aimed at Israel's annihilation."[264]

But this political background, continued the judge, did not let the two men off the hook, because it did not justify them breaking Swiss law. Above all, Switzerland, as a neutral country, could not get involved in the disputes between other states. "It is [the court's] duty," he summed up, "to see to it that these actions are not committed on Swiss territory." In particular, he was concerned that Ben-Gal, "if he was given the order, would return to Switzerland or to another country and repeat the same sort of incidents." The two men were then sentenced to two months' imprisonment but immediately released because they had already served that length of time behind bars since their arrest.

Because the court case attracted huge international publicity, Joklik's claims about Egypt's missile program, and the documents he produced, enormously helped Israel to justify its actions and to repair some of the damage to its reputation that Damocles had inflicted. There was, however, one rather awkward question that had arisen in the course of the proceedings. Under Isser Harel, Mossad had placed considerable faith in the claims, and in the actions, of Otto Joklik. But during the trial the prosecution team had seriously dented his credibility. As one Egyptian official noted at the time, "[T]he only thing he was an expert on was science fiction."

So by the end of the four-day trial, both the Egyptians and the Israelis were united in asking the same question. If Otto Joklik, the man who had made such serious allegations about the supposed Egyptian WMD program, was not the scientific expert he had always claimed to be, then who on earth was he?

CHAPTER TWENTY
The Egyptians Fight Back

E xactly one year after its missiles had first been displayed to the outside world, the Egyptian regime once again made clear its unwavering determination to defy Israeli threats and growing West German disapproval and continue with its rocket program. On July 23, 1963, it marked the anniversary of the Free Officers' coup by staging another military parade in the center of Cairo, one that followed a format similar to that of the previous year.

As usual, the top brass were full of impressive boasts. Marshal Amer proudly proclaimed that Egypt had now developed the Arab world's first submarine, which was ready to be "tested" over the next two weeks. This was economical with the truth, however, because he failed to mention that he had been appealing for Soviet assistance and had asked Moscow to export some of its Whiskey-class submarines.[265]

Public bravado was, of course, a familiar part of the routine, but this year there was a new addition to the regime's armory that was put on proud display. Now, alongside the al Kahir and al Zafar rockets, came a new missile that hadn't been seen before. Painted a uniform gray and covered with black, white, and red cloth, the al Ared—"the Pioneer"—was designed to be a two-stage ballistic missile that was far more impressive than its two counterparts. One commentator announced on the loudspeakers that it could carry a four-ton payload over nearly four hundred miles, while others claimed that its true range was nearly double that figure. All insisted that it had been "successfully" test-fired several times. "We have gone a long way since last year upon the road of technical progress and achieved sure success in the manufacture of missiles and Arab jet planes," proclaimed a triumphant Marshal Amer, even if the missile was officially decreed to be merely a "space research rocket."[266]

Although al Ared had not been test-launched in public or before independent witnesses, word started to go around Cairo that it was just a single part of a much more ambitious program to build a small space satellite, one that would supposedly be called al Negma, "the Star." If this satellite was ever built, then it could conceivably be projected by the al Ared rocket into outer space, where it could be used, according to one highly influential and very respected international journal, to examine the earth's electromagnetic field.[267] Such a project, continued the article, was the fruition of the work of a special research and development team that was predominantly composed of German scientists. The leader of any such enterprise was likely to have been Wolfgang Pilz, who had made his ambitions to build a satellite known to the West German government but whose advances had quickly been spurned.

The Egyptians, in short, were unfazed by international pressure to halt their rocket program, and all the more so when the Israelis failed to win the support they wanted from the United States. Tel Aviv's diplomatic drive in New York was initiated by the foreign minister, Golda Meir, who had met with senior figures in the Kennedy administration in September and October to highlight the work of the German scientists "in the field of poison gases, missiles, etc." and to reiterate claims that the Egyptians had used mustard gas in Yemen. She estimated that within eighteen months Cairo would have "accurate missiles in quantity" and asserted that it had already resolved many of the technical obstacles that were impeding its drive to develop a guidance and control system. She did not produce any new evidence to back up these assertions, however, but merely referred to the claims that had been made in the Joklik trial. After several meetings, Dean Rusk, the secretary of state, refused to declare his support for her position or to make any commitment.[268]

Meir then went on to speak before the United Nations General Assembly in New York. Maintaining that the Arab countries were given a "constant stream" of arms from their various supporters and were helped by "mercenary German scientists," she urged the members not to be "indifferent" to Arab preparations for war against her homeland and to help prevent the risk of another Middle Eastern conflict. She was disappointed, however, when her pleas once again went unanswered.[269]

Perhaps part of the problem was that by this stage the Israelis had started to lose a certain amount of credibility. When, on November 12, senior officials from Israeli Military Intelligence met with their American counterparts in Washington to exchange information, they were forced to take a sizable step backward. The Israeli delegation admitted that the Cairo regime "appears to have shelved its plans for radiological warfare," even if it still had a "continuing interest" in such weapons, and had made no "concrete advances" in its biological program. This was a significant retreat from the earlier Israeli position, although the officials stuck to their view that the Egyptians were producing chemical weapons.[270] In Washington, Robert Komer of the National Security Council seized on Israel's sudden reversal of position on the radiological threat. In particular, he criticized Israeli intelligence for "overselling" Egypt's unconventional weapons capabilities not just abroad but even to its very own government. Arguing that the Egyptian rockets were "far less menacing" than the Israelis alleged, he also pointed out that Golda Meir and Levi Eshkol had talked about alleged Egyptian advances in WMD without providing any evidence to back up their claims.[271]

By this time, however, Israeli action had continued to inflict some heavy blows against the Egyptians, severely disrupting their European procurement network and prompting some scientists to pack their bags and go. The first to leave had been Dr. Karl-Heinz Gronau, who had started work in fuel research for the rocket program three years before. Though he claimed simply that his contract had expired, the real reason may have been concern for his own safety. He appears to have asked the German embassy in Cairo for advice, saying that he did not want to risk being charged with assisting an Egyptian arms program that could ostensibly be used to wage an aggressive war against Israel.[272]

Such losses did not prevent the Egyptians from trying to replace and replenish their scientific stock. By late 1963, however, their main priority had probably changed. It is likely that by this time the Egyptian missile program had entered its production phase and the need for research and development staff, like Sänger and Pilz, had started to diminish. Instead, there was a more pressing need for skilled and semiskilled technicians to start "punching out product"—the trade expression for operating the new, and sometimes quite complex, machine tools that had been installed at Factory 333.[273] But by the summer of 1963 there was still the same huge, glaring weakness right at the very heart of the missile program—the lack of a reliable guidance and control system. This meant that the al Kahir and al Zafar rockets would now have gone into production without any such system already being in place. In other words, they were, for all intents and purposes, completely useless as weapons.

By this time, the HA-300 jet program had also been severely delayed by a number of technical obstacles, and four years after it had begun, the project was heavily over budget and years behind schedule. Many of the German scientists had continued to be very frustrated by the relatively poor quality of their Egyptian staff and by the slow progress of their efforts to build a suitable engine. Repeated static tests of the engine failed, although the director of the engineering department insisted that the problems lay solely with the airframe. But although Ferdinand Brandner was by this time still engaged in the project, he lacked the specialist skills and infrastructure to make much headway. Willy Messerschmitt, for example, had initially shown much enthusiasm for the project but over the past two years had been based at his main factory and research center in Augsburg, and had not made any real contribution. True, the HA-200 program had been much more successful—around forty had been built at Helwan by this time—but of course it had very limited uses in battle, and was designed essentially as a training aircraft.

One of the foreign technicians now contacted by Egyptian agents was Dr. Karl Knupfer, a German engineer who was well qualified to take part in the rocket program and who had good contacts in the German scientific world. In the course of 1963 it seems that Knupfer began working for the Egyptians and became the new head of the guidance program, alongside

Paul Goercke. In addition, he started to recruit new talent in Europe, causing serious alarm within the ranks of Mossad.[274]

Lotz and his wife went to Europe in spring 1964. He needed to head back, he told his Egyptian friends, partly because he wanted to sell some horses to some wealthy buyers but also because his wife needed special medical treatment. The real purpose of the trip, however, was to make contact with his new handler from Mossad. After two days of intensive debriefings, the Mossad operative declared himself satisfied with Lotz's work and proceeded to give him urgent instructions: as a matter of priority, emphasized the spy chief, Lotz had to obtain more information about Knupfer's activities.

Over the next few months, Lotz succeeded in striking up a good rapport with the new recruit as well as introducing himself to a handful of Knupfer's various associates. Before long, the Israeli spy was in a position to report back to his handlers. Knupfer, he said, had "first-class" technical qualifications and while he was "an excellent engineer[,] he showed no interest whatsoever in politics." He also had "a well-paid position, lived in luxury[,] and was able to save money into the bargain." Lotz was also able to obtain a certain amount of information about the man's character, in case it might help the Mossad psychologists who were tasked with finding strengths and weaknesses in the personalities of state enemies. "He's a rather shy and withdrawn man," he wrote back, "strict with his subordinates and has hardly any social contact with them. And he never speaks about his work to outsiders."[275]

Lotz also managed to get a certain amount of information about some members of Knupfer's team, which was made up largely of new recruits. On board the Trieste-Alexandria ferry, on his way back from Europe, he happened to come across a number of Germans who were making their way to Egypt, and, never one to miss an opportunity, he approached one of the men as he stood at the bar.

"I suppose you're a tourist?"

"Oh no. I'll be working in Egypt for the next six years . . . it's a government job, so I really won't know the exact details until I get there."

The man handed Lotz his card, on which was printed simply "Erich Traum, Electronic Engineer."[276]

Several days later, in Cairo, Lotz got the confirmation he needed from Knupfer's wife. Traum and his other colleagues, she told him, were working alongside her husband as senior assistants.

Over the next few months, the Israeli agent continued to do his best to continue building close contacts within the expatriate community, even using his wife's birthday as an excuse to invite several leading engineers to visit his house. But by now the Egyptians were readying themselves not only to step up their rocket research program but also to strike back at the Israelis' espionage operations. True, the Egyptian intelligence service paled by comparison with those of its illustrious adversary, but by 1964 it was starting to sharpen its act.

The Egyptian secret services had always had some strong points. On paper, if not in practice, the services were well organized, consisting of two major departments, each of which was subdivided into a number of bureaus and sections. Of the two, the most important single department was the Mukhabarat al-Amma or General Intelligence Agency, which was vastly bigger and more powerful than the Mabahes al-Amma or Secret Police. Because the Mabahes dealt mainly with internal political dissent, it was the GIA that was responsible for counterespionage, detecting, monitoring, and eliminating the activities of foreign intelligence services. Reporting directly to President Nasser, it also had virtually unlimited, and highly indistinct, powers that gave its agents almost total freedom inside the country to carry out their central task. In practice, however, there was a great deal of rivalry and jealousy between the two departments, on a par with those between other spying organizations elsewhere in the world.[277]

Both bodies had a good number of active agents as well as casual informers who were well paid for any information they provided. However, the information they received was not always willingly volunteered. If anyone under surveillance or suspicion came into contact with almost any servant, doorman, taxi driver, hotel employee, shopkeeper, or even just a passerby, the GIA could easily order the witness to disclose any information he or she had picked up or else face dire consequences.

The sheer size of this informer network was the main reason Wolfgang Lotz rated the services to be "among the most active," as well as the most ruthless, in the world.[278] As a result, he and his wife worked on the assumption that, unless they had good reason to suppose otherwise, their every conversation was always being overheard. It was only in the privacy of their own home, and when no one else was present, that they felt at relative liberty to speak freely. Even then, they still made only veiled, coded references to their espionage work. As a British ambassador, Sir Anthony Parsons, noted at the time, "the ubiquity of the intelligence apparatus on which Nasser had come to depend had disseminated an atmosphere of fear. Telephones were liberally tapped, conversations eavesdropped [upon,] and the Citadel [central prison] was full of people who had allegedly offended against the state."[279]

By the time Lotz arrived in Egypt at the end of 1961, espionage had reached endemic, almost absurd, proportions. Hidden microphones and phone-tapping devices were habitually installed in the homes of most Europeans, and Lotz recalled an occasion when his first home was visited by a former occupant who showed him where the secret transmitters had been hidden. "He explained that he had been the previous tenant," recalled the Israeli spy, "and then proceeded to show me a microphone concealed in the mouthpiece of my phone. I disconnected it and the following day a telephone engineer appeared to check on the connection and put things right."[280] On another occasion, he was invited to the home of a Dutch businessman, who was representing a Western oil group, and was taken aback when his host made a sudden gesture as they walked into the lounge together. "Don't say anything for a minute," warned the Dutchman, pushing aside a large mirror in the wall to reveal a hidden microphone. "Now we can talk freely[;] somebody will probably be along tomorrow to repair it."[281]

Using sources of information like these, the GIA had by 1964 won a number of counterespionage successes against Mossad. The two intelligence services had clashed over Operation Susannah in 1954, but there had also been several previous occasions when they had crossed swords, notably over the cases of an Israeli spy, Jack Thomas, and an Egyptian defector called Captain Abbas Hilmi.

Thomas was an Egyptian citizen of Armenian descent who had grown up in Cairo but had become deeply disillusioned with President Nasser after the Suez War. He moved first to Lebanon, then went on to live in West

Germany, and it was there that he met a Lebanese expatriate, and a Mossad agent, by the name of Emil. It remains unclear whether this meeting took place by chance, or because the Mossad man had been assigned to keep a close watch on the Arab circles in Germany that Thomas moved in. But whatever the reason, the two men soon became good friends.

When, after a few months, Thomas made clear his strong dislike for Nasser, Emil suggested that he should return to Egypt and try to topple the dictator. He could offer Thomas a very substantial amount of money and support, he added, because he was working on behalf of one of the Western European countries that wanted Nasser out of the way. Thomas suspected that the Israelis were involved but, despite some misgivings, agreed to press ahead with the mission. After traveling to Cologne to take part in an intensive training course in the arts of espionage, he returned to Egypt in July 1958.

Within a few months, Thomas and his wife, a West German, had succeeded in building up a small but highly committed spy ring, composed of two fellow Armenians, a Jewish nightclub performer, and a childhood friend who had joined the Egyptian army. He had also acquired some very elaborate spying equipment, and used a novel, Pearl S. Buck's *The Good Earth*, as a codebook to send regular updates and news to Tel Aviv. In addition, Thomas and his wife had a suitcase with a false bottom, an electric shaver with a secret compartment for hiding documents, and a hollow cigarette lighter for storing film negatives.[282]

But in May 1960, less than two years after starting out, Thomas made a serious error of judgment when he approached Adiv Hanna Karolos, an Egyptian army officer of Coptic Christian descent who he felt sure would be sympathetic to his cause. Karolos immediately informed his senior officer about the proposition, and in almost no time the Egyptian intelligence service had set up a trap. The Egyptians provided Karolos with false information that Thomas, wholly unaware that he had been discovered, transmitted back to Israel. After several months, Thomas began to sense something was wrong and prepared to flee the country, providing his spy ring with forged passports to help them along their way. But they moved too late: he and the rest of his team were arrested on January 6, and some of them were hanged the following year. Only his wife and the nightclub dancer escaped, fleeing the country just hours before the police swooped in and made their arrests.

The Egyptians had also struck back at Israel over the case of Captain Hilmi. The captain was an Egyptian pilot who knew that the Israelis were desperate for information about Egypt's latest warplanes, all of which had been obtained from the Soviets. At the time of the Cold War, the engineering designs of these MiG planes were a closely guarded secret and Israeli defense chiefs, as well as their NATO counterparts, were prepared to go to any lengths to get the information they needed. All manner of proposals were put forward to deal with the challenge, at least one of which—intercepting a plane in midflight and forcing it to land in Israel— was so risky that it could easily have sparked a superpower confrontation. Mossad's preferred tactic was much simpler: its officers planned to bribe an Egyptian pilot into defecting and bringing his plane along with him.

But when, in 1964, Abbas Hilmi did defect in his Soviet-built plane, the Israeli authorities were disappointed because he flew not one of Moscow's highly sophisticated attack aircraft, designed to breach NATO air defenses, but a tiny trainer aircraft, a Yak, which was quite useless on the battlefield. But the Israelis nonetheless gave Hilmi a warm welcome, all the more so because he offered them important new information about the workings of Egypt's air force, superbly informed though Mossad already was. To add insult and injury to his homeland, Hilmi publicly condemned Nasser's intervention in the civil war in Yemen and claimed that the Egyptian army was using poison gas there against local tribesmen.[283]

True to their word, the Israeli spy masters offered him a new life in Israel, guaranteeing him a house, a job, and financial support. But Hilmi was unhappy in his adoptive country and, against all advice from Israel, wanted to live in Argentina, using a new identity that Mossad forged on his behalf and a sizable sum of Israeli cash. Yet almost as soon as he arrived in Buenos Aires, he began to commit a series of cardinal errors, which the spymasters had strongly cautioned him against. The first mistake he made was to contact his mother in Egypt, sending her a postcard that was immediately intercepted by the Mukhabarat. The GIA wasted little time in setting a trap, and within just weeks Hilmi had become friendly with one of its agents, a glamorous Egyptian woman whose allure he found too hard to resist. When he went to her apartment in Buenos Aires, he was seized by Egyptian agents, sedated, transported in a crate to the Egyptian embassy, and then smuggled back to his homeland by cargo ship. Within a short space of time, he had been court-martialed, convicted of treason, and shot by a firing squad.

The GIA was less successful at doing what Mossad did so formidably well—the supremely difficult task of infiltrating its own agents and sympathizers into enemy ranks. But in the course of 1962 it did make limited inroads into the Israeli armed forces, using an Armenian recruit, Kobruk Yaakovian, to do so. He had been recruited into Egyptian intelligence almost by chance when he was serving time in a Cairo jail for a minor offense and Mukhabarat officers offered him early release and a generous payment in return for undertaking an undercover assignment in Israel. His swarthy appearance meant that he was already Jewish-looking, they pointed out, and provided he was willing to have himself circumcised beforehand, he would have a good chance of evading capture.

In the summer of 1961, Yaakovian turned up at the Israeli consulate in Brazil with forged documentation, claiming to be a South American Jew by the name of Yitzhak Koshuk. He wanted to start a new life in Israel, he continued, and was seeking full citizenship. After arriving in Israel in December, he worked on a kibbutz before joining the army and serving in one of its transportation units. Yaakovian managed to obtain a certain amount of useful information, which he transmitted back to Cairo, before he was caught by the internal security service Shin Bet in December 1963.[284]

Back home, the Egyptian spy service was continuing to operate much more successfully, uncovering yet more Israeli attempts at infiltration. In particular, the Mukhabarat closed in on a very active spy cell that was based in Cairo and run by two Greek nationals, George Stymatio and Nicola Kois. Both men had easy access to senior regime officials because they worked, respectively, as a caterer for government officials and a high-level exhibition organizer. But though they were given the protection of Mossad's wider underground network inside the country, the Egyptian secret police moved in and the two men were arrested.[285]

Another cell was run by Dr. Katz, a German-born doctor who, by 1961, had become one of the most successful and renowned surgeons in Egypt, having treated the royal family, before the revolution, as well as President Nasser's brother. He was loosely affiliated with a Mossad cell that was based in Alexandria and whose members were led by a native Egyptian who was employed at the giant car manufacturing plant set up outside Cairo by Ford. After the cell was rounded up, the Egyptian was sentenced to death while Dr. Katz was given ten years' imprisonment. His sentence was later commuted and he was granted permission to leave the country.[286]

Nasser's spies also came within a whisker of seizing an Israeli agent who appears to have been sent to Egypt as a result of some mysterious oversight on the part of her handlers in Tel Aviv. If Lotz's account is to be believed, at some point in 1965 a German archaeologist appeared in Cairo alongside his wife "Caroline," who claimed to be half Dutch and half Hungarian. Frequently invited to dinner parties and to day trips along with many other German expatriates, Lotz was alarmed to overhear her frequently trying to steer conversations toward the subject of the Egyptian rockets, "asking very directly where they were located, how many and how powerful they were and so on."[287] She also started trying hard to befriend the wife of Karl Knupfer, even joining the Heliopolis Sports Club, of which Mrs. Knupfer was an enthusiastic member, in a bid to get to know her. And when she had had too much to drink, Lotz was horrified to notice, she started talking away not in Dutch or Hungarian but in Yiddish.

When, late one night, a visibly shaken Karl Knupfer unexpectedly turned up at Lotz's house, in a highly nervous state, the Israeli spy realized it was time to act against "Caroline Boulter." The story Lotz heard was almost too much to believe. Knupfer's wife had invited Boulter back to her home for coffee one afternoon after spending several hours at the gym, but been alarmed when her guest had disappeared from the living room almost as soon as her back was turned. Not knowing where her guest had gone, Mrs. Knupfer went upstairs to look for her. She found Boulter in her husband's study, where he kept many of the blueprints of the missile program, and confronted her. Caroline Boulter turned scarlet red and mumbled some wholly implausible excuse about looking for her child's lost ball, which, for some reason, she thought had found its way into the bedroom upstairs.[288]

At this time, Cairo was awash with rumors about Mossad agents operating in the Egyptian capital. This was not just because of Operation

Damocles but also because Nasser had infuriated both Israel and West Germany by refusing to extradite a Nazi war criminal, Hans Walter Zech-Nenntwich, who was wanted for the mass murder of Russian Jews. Nenntwich had been sentenced to a long jail sentence in West Germany but escaped after just two days' captivity, fleeing first to Switzerland and then to Egypt, using a visa that had been given to him by the Egyptian embassy in Bonn. Knowing that Egypt was not bound by any extradition treaty to deport him, and that there were so many other German expatriates there, it seemed to be a natural haven. By early 1965, West Germany had lost hope that Nasser would bow to their demands, and this prompted speculation that Mossad agents might take the matter into their own hands.

Given the real threat to the German scientists posed by Israeli actions, Dr. Knupfer had felt seriously alarmed by what had happened and wanted to ask a trusted friend like Lotz for advice before going to the Egyptian authorities. The next morning Lotz sent an urgent message to Tel Aviv, pressing his handlers to withdraw "Caroline Boulter" from the country before she was arrested. Within just hours she was ordered to leave immediately. The most likely explanation for her presence in Cairo is that the Israeli authorities had been so desperate to obtain more information about developments in Egypt that they had rushed to send out another agent well before she was ready to undertake such a dangerous mission.

But Lotz himself was also coming under pressure from the Egyptian secret service, even though he had by this time been in the country for more than three years and was highly familiar with the methods that its agents used.

On the evening of February 22, 1965, Lotz and his wife returned to their home in Cairo after spending a few days sightseeing in and around the northwestern town of Mersa Matruh in the Egyptian desert. As he pulled up outside, he was surprised to see four cars, each packed full of men, parked on the opposite side of the street. He got out of the car but barely had time to react before he felt a powerful blow on the side of his head. Although he was concussed, he was aware of several men knocking him to the ground, being handcuffed, and then being pulled roughly to his feet.

Once taken inside his villa, Lotz regained his consciousness and found himself in his living room surrounded by around a dozen plainclothed GIA agents.

"I am Samir Nagy," said a short, overweight man who stood a few feet away, "prosecutor-general for State Security. You are under arrest."

"Under arrest for what?"

"You don't know? I think you have a pretty good idea why we've arrested you, Mr. Lotz."

Always quick thinking under pressure, Lotz tried dropping the names of his best contacts, a tactic that had worked so well when he had been arrested at Shaloufa. This time, however, it did not do the trick: General Ghorab, General Osman, and Colonel Sabri had all also been placed under arrest while the GIA tried to figure out what involvement they had, if any, in Lotz's operations. His best efforts to plead innocence fell on deaf ears. With a single gesture, Nagy instead ordered his men to start searching the house, from top to bottom.

Lotz had mixed feelings as the search got under way and the agents started to pull at the drawers and cupboards, pushing over chairs and ripping down pictures. On the one hand, he knew that the radio transmitter would be very hard to find, hidden as it was inside a bathroom scale, and he quickly noticed that the agents were not being particularly thorough in their approach. But on the other hand, he was unnerved by just how confident they appeared: "[T]hey seemed too sure of themselves for comfort. They were bound to be on to something."[289] He knew that the GIA must have had an extremely compelling reason to arrest and physically assault any wealthy foreigner, particularly one who was so well connected with the top brass and other leading officials. "I was racking my brains, trying to think of what might have gone wrong—a leakage somewhere, something incriminating they could have come across."[290] But try as he did, he was unable to pin down the reason.

As the agents made their ways upstairs and began to search the bathroom, he held his breath. And when they prized open the bathroom scale, prompting Nagy to give a glowing, triumphant look, Lotz simply said nothing, knowing that he would only make things worse for himself. As a photographer moved in to record the scene, Nagy read out a prepared statement formally charging Lotz with espionage, and Lotz was led away, blindfolded, and put into the back of a waiting car. The agents had known all along that he was guilty and must have already known where the transmitter was. And Lotz knew that he would soon be on trial for his life.

Quite how the GIA had succeeded in trapping Wolfgang Lotz, a highly experienced and skilled intelligence operative, remains unclear. It is likely that his regular transmissions to Israel had been intercepted by what he later termed simply as the "agents of another power," which could only have been the KGB, the foreign intelligence service of the Soviet Union. It was significant that just a short while before his own arrest, another Israeli operative, Eli Cohen, had been detected and arrested in Damascus probably because Soviet agents had succeeded in intercepting his transmissions. By this time the Soviets had certainly developed new and highly effective ways of tracking radio messages and pinpointing where they were being sent from, and Lotz was unaware that the KGB had passed their expertise on to their Egyptian counterparts.[291] He had made matters worse by spending more time on air, almost every night, than his procedures probably allowed. It is also possible that some officials within the GIA had started to have their doubts about Lotz after his arrest at Shaloufa—even if he had talked his way out of the situation at the time—and had marked him as a potential suspect.

Israel's watchful eye on the Egyptian rocket program had been blinded. Wolfgang Lotz now faced the same fate as Eli Cohen, who had been hanged shortly earlier.

CHAPTER TWENTY-ONE
The Scientists Pull Out

The interrogation began within hours of Lotz's arrest. Almost as soon as he was charged with espionage, Lotz was blindfolded, handcuffed, and driven off to a prison some distance away.

When his hood and blindfold were removed, the Israeli spy found himself in a small, bare room, facing a large desk. One of the guards gestured at him to sit on a stool and face a team of three interrogators, two of whom had been at his house at the time of his arrest. A switch was then flicked and two powerful spotlights were beamed onto his face, almost blinding him.

Before the questioning began, the man who seemed to be the head of the interrogating team, and who gave his name as Hassan Aleesh, reached into a drawer. "I will convince you it's pointless to tell us any lies. We know all about you." He then produced two large paper files and placed them in front of Lotz. "Do these look familiar to you? Read them, take your time."[292]

Inside the two files were precise transcripts of hundreds of wireless messages that Lotz had transmitted back to Tel Aviv, as well as the incoming messages he had received. He did not have enough time to see exactly how far back this record went, but judging by the sheer quantity of information he thought it could easily stretch back a few years.

So although the GIA had known for some considerable time about the existence of a high-level spy, it had clearly taken them a while to pinpoint the exact source of the leak.

"Makes you think, doesn't it, Mr. Lotz?" purred Aleesh, reading his prisoner's mind. "We have been monitoring your wireless communications for almost three years. This dossier here contains the incoming[;] the other one[,] the outgoing messages." There was no conclusive evidence that linked Lotz to Israel but the interrogators were sure enough about whom he had been in touch with. "The range of your transmitter and direction of your aerial," he added darkly, "prove conclusively that you were transmitting to Israel."

Thinking quickly under pressure, the prisoner realized that it was hopeless trying to deny any of the allegations being made against him. To avoid being tortured, it was better simply to cooperate, telling his captors everything they were likely to find out, confirming everything they already knew, but plausibly denying everything else. "I had my acting abilities," he remembered, "and if I wanted to stay alive and in one piece it was now up to me to give the performance of a lifetime. It was a slim chance but the only one I had."[293]

As the questioning began, though, it became clear that there were still large missing links in the picture that the interrogators had built up of Lotz's operations. For example, they were still not entirely sure who the man they knew as Wolfgang Lotz really was, or why he should be spying on behalf of Israel.

"Isn't it true that you held the rank of colonel in the SS?" they asked, airing a quite unfounded rumor that had been widely heard in German expatriate circles ever since Lotz first arrived in Egypt.[294] "How did you come to work for Israel? What makes a former SS colonel turn into a spy for Israel? Money? Threats? Blackmail?"

Lotz's initial response was to allege bribery, claiming that he had initially been hard up, sorely tempted by an Israeli offer of a free horse farm in Cairo and a generous monthly salary in exchange for sending back a certain amount of information. The interrogators looked unconvinced and emphasized that they would be pressing him for much more information at a later stage. "Someone will sit with you and get the exact details," said one of the team, "how you were recruited, who trained you, what kind of training you underwent and where, what orders you received, who your contacts were, everything. Right now I only want a general outline."

Then the interrogators came forward with a startling suggestion. Did the Israelis know about Lotz's past as an SS officer and had they threatened to expose his past and his whereabouts unless he cooperated? Lotz was amazed by the suggestion and made no effort to deny it, well aware that such a plausible story could save his life.

For the next few hours, he endured a relentless barrage of questions from a rotating panel of security officials who used a classic "good cop, bad cop" approach to try and break his spirit. For short periods, he was treated courteously, even politely, by the panel, while at other times a thuggish henchman would take over and make explicit threats of violence. In each case, the interrogators wanted to know more about the complicity of Lotz's wife in his spying work and pressed him hard for details. How had he first met his wife, and what had their first conversation been about? On whose orders had he taken that particular train on which he claimed he had first met her? What had she been doing in the United States, where she claimed to have been before returning to Germany, and did he know any of her friends? The questions were initially put to him quietly but when there was no firm answer one of the henchmen stepped forward to intervene.

"How would you like it if I went to get the truth out of her?" he jeered. "Perhaps beat a little on the soles of her feet or put her into ice-cold water for a while, say twenty-four hours? Or gave her a few mild electric shocks? Now let's start again."

But suddenly, nine hours after the session had first begun, the interrogation broke off. "I am relieving you," murmured one of the members of the panel; "go rest up for a while." The bright spotlights were switched off and the prisoner was led away to the notorious Turi Prison, just outside Cairo. For the next few months, he would be imprisoned here, alongside other high-profile prisoners such as Hassan Ismail Hodeiby, the leader of the outlawed Muslim Brotherhood; a number of senior officials who had been charged with or convicted of espionage; and others who had been found guilty of treason. But all was not lost, because Lotz enjoyed the company of Victor Levy, a veteran of Operation Susannah, who had been sentenced to long-term imprisonment a decade before.

Yet at the same time the GIA had delivered such a powerful blow to Mossad's secret operations inside Egypt, Nasser's rocket program suffered a huge setback of its own. For in October 1964, without giving any prior warning of their change of heart, two of Nasser's top German recruits, Dr. Paul Goercke and Walter Schuran, suddenly and quietly ended their work on the missile project and returned home to West Germany. They were to lead a wider exodus that now got under way, for, over the next six months, around thirty other scientists, engineers, and technicians followed them and headed for home. The Egyptian military programs were now looking more vulnerable than ever before.

Whatever it was that had prompted them to change course, it was not the threat of any punitive legislation being imposed by the West German government, one that could perhaps have threatened them with imprisonment or withdrawn their rights of citizenship. True, officials and ministers in Bonn had paid lip service to the way in which the government was "exploring" various courses of action against the "uncontrollable and irresponsible activities" of the expatriates. But they privately knew that the difficulties of doing so, when every German citizen had a basic constitutional right to enjoy freedom of movement, would be formidable.[295]

Such obstacles became unmistakably clear in May when a parliamentary working group, the Cross-Party Bundestag Committee, was commissioned to examine the issue and to draft new legislation. If enforced, these laws would have banned West German citizens from contributing to any overseas work on a foreign WMD scheme without the prior permission of the Bonn government. But the proposal, which would have been applied retrospectively to affect the scientists who were already in Egypt, immediately ran into objections from the ruling Christian Democratic Union and never got beyond the committee stage: the legislation was not extensive enough to address the particular issue of the Germans in Egypt, argued the CDU, but more fundamentally it violated the freedom of movement enshrined under German Basic Law. While the constitution forbade activities that "disturb[ed] the peaceful relations between nations," the critics asked how the government could differentiate between scientific pursuits that could contribute to civilian programs and those that served as military ones. In such situations shouldn't the government give the benefit of the doubt to the fundamental right to freedom of movement?

The West Germans tried to find other ways of deflecting political pressure by the Israeli government, which wanted Bonn to take far more drastic action, including strong governmental restrictions on the scientists' travel and even the repudiation of their German citizenship if they failed to leave Egypt by a certain deadline. In the course of 1963, West German government officials distributed letters and circulars to the scientists, warning them that they were "playing with [their] lives" by continuing with their work in Egypt, thereby implying that other countries—an obvious reference to Israel—would use lethal force against them even if the West German government itself was clearly not going to do so. Bonn also struck a blow against them by threatening to withhold funds from any research institutes that in any way supported the scientists' efforts, a threat that immediately prompted one research group to cut its ties with Dr. Kleinwachter's laboratory at Loerrach. The West German government also canceled contracts with a number of German firms that were found to have been supplying the Egyptian missile project.[296]

But even this would not have been enough to dissuade so many of the expatriates from ending their work in Egypt. Goercke, for example, was thought to have been sufficiently interested in his work on behalf of Nasser to be applying for full Egyptian citizenship. And the raw materials needed for the project could conceivably have been found in places other than Western Europe.

What may have happened is that an impassioned plea by Israel's new prime minister, Levi Eshkol, struck a powerful chord among the West German people and their leaders. For on the evening of August 16, 1963, Eshkol was interviewed on West German television and seemed to make a direct plea to his audience. "If sons of the German people who are burdened with the murder of six million Jews," he argued, should now help others realize their plans to destroy Israel, "then the crime is infinitely greater." Aiding and abetting the Egyptian rocket program, in other words, made the West German people guilty by association, and the country risked being classified by Israel as an "enemy" of the Jewish state.[297] Such a message was bound to be particularly heartfelt coming less than two decades after the end of the war.

It is possible that such powerful rhetoric helped to persuade Bonn to step up its efforts to lure the scientists back home. The government had recently established its own space program, setting up its European Space Research Organization in June 1962 with a large injection of public cash to support it. As a result, programs were now commissioned to develop fully recoverable research rockets, high-energy propulsion systems for the European Launcher Development Organization, a satellite, and a space transporter. All of the associated jobs came with generous salaries and the working conditions were highly attractive. This meant that they were all of huge interest to the top experts in the respective fields, including the German scientists in Egypt. Dr. Eugen Sänger was even tempted out of semiretirement to take up a professorship of aeronautics at Berlin Technical University.

As unrelenting Israeli pressure continued to bear down, it is likely that the West German government raised these salaries even more to tempt the expatriates with offers they could not easily refuse. Offers of well-paid work in West German or other European aerospace projects enticed nearly all of those who now left Egypt, including Goercke, Schuran, and five other technicians, who reportedly took jobs at the Messerschmitt-Bölkow-Blohm company. Whereas the scientists' work in Egypt had once been relatively lucrative and promising, by 1964 it seemed that better money and professional prospects were to be found elsewhere. Nor were the European projects likely to be bedeviled by the technical obstacles that had dogged Nasser's missile and jet engine programs from the start.

This exodus of foreign talent affected the aircraft as well as the missile program, for around a hundred of the original team of experts, once numbering around 450 in total, left Egypt in the course of early 1964. The relationship between Cairo and the remaining scientists became even more strained when the regime was unable to pay their salaries and then briefly stopped two hundred of them from leaving the country, even though they had already packed their bags and were ready to leave. Ferdinand Brandner then submitted his resignation when the Egyptians refused to reinstate some of his team members.[298]

The HA-300 fighter project was in any case estimated by American intelligence analysts to be desperately short of raw materials, with just three months of supplies left, and to be in a "state of anarchy" and on the "verge of collapse."[299] Nasser's desire to produce the Arab world's first jet fighter was destined to remain just a dream. And the aircraft and rocket programs were also hampered by a breakdown of the vital link between the Egyptian government and its European middleman, Hassan Kamil. Disputes over money now broke out between them, with Cairo claiming that the Swiss businessman was withholding reserves of $1.4 million, earmarked for paying the expatriate scientists, as well as an additional fund of $350,000 intended to buy spare parts from European suppliers. Cairo then effectively ended Kamil's contract, prompting him to retaliate by instructing the German scientists to return home. Suddenly both the Egyptian military programs seemed ready to collapse.

The Egyptians were not beaten yet, however, and initiated a new campaign to replace the rapidly shrinking pool of overseas talent. In early 1965, Cairo's main English daily, *The Egyptian Gazette*, listed numerous "wanted" advertisements placed by German families who were looking for apartments and houses in and around the city. Most of the house hunters were interested in Maadi, a highly desirable suburb of the capital that was also close to both Helwan and Heliopolis.[300] At the same time, reports began to emerge of an Egyptian effort to hire a number of highly skilled West German technicians who had allegedly been trained by a leading American company, Litton Industries, in anticipation of a contract that had never been implemented.[301]

Once again, the Israeli secret service moved fast and worked hard to prevent the Egyptians from gaining ground. One delegation of West German scientists was about to leave for Egypt when its members received a series of anonymous letters pointing out the privations and low standard of living they would have to endure. This was not an explicit threat to the lives of the scientists, but they knew that the letters had probably been sent by the Israelis, who were clearly watching their every move. If they went ahead, they feared the same fate that Dr. Kleinwachter had so nearly suffered.[302]

Israeli intelligence operations also targeted a number of American companies that were deemed—it seems quite without justification—to have been supporting the Egyptian project. When, in the course of 1965, a series of press reports claimed that Litton Industries and the U.S. Cubic Corporation were aiding the rocket program, officials in the U.S. State Department suspected that Mossad was the culprit, having fed false reports to sections of the media. In January 1966 a senior American official met an Israeli counterpart in Washington to discuss the newspaper reports and tried to settle the matter: examining the export licenses, he pointed out that Cubic had sold electronic equipment to Cairo but emphasized that the exports were readily available from numerous other market sources. Stopping Cubic or any other American company from exporting the equipment would therefore serve no purpose except to "adversely affect U.S. commercial interests."[303] Soon afterward, George Ball, the undersecretary of state, wrote to the Israeli embassy in Washington informing its officials of American displeasure at the media reports about Cubic, which he claimed had the "tacit approval" of Tel Aviv and were further "stimulated by Israeli leaks." It was important, he went on, that the Israeli government now move to end "further sterile and misleading publicity."[304]

Yet no amount of headhunting was likely to fill the void that was now about to be opened. For several months, rumors had abounded that even Wolfgang Pilz, highly committed to the Egyptian program though he professed to be, was considering joining the exodus of scientific talent, provided certain conditions were met.[305] Then, in January 1965, he was interviewed by a journalist and gave further hints of his wish to leave. Admitting that he had been working there on a military program—"we're obviously not making sticks of barley sugar," he said, and claimed he had "nothing against the Jews . . . I am merely a scientist and I have nothing to do with politics"—he affirmed that, like many of his colleagues, he was now hoping to leave for West Germany. The combination of West German political pressure and Israeli threats was causing him considerable personal stress. There had long been stories that he had started to become depressed, and they were perhaps not unfounded after all.

But before he made any move, he wanted an assurance from the Israeli government that he and his family would be safe from retribution: "I do not want to go home and then be murdered in the streets of Bonn," he said. In addition, he wanted the Israeli government to admit "on some official level" to its involvement in the campaign against the expatriate scientists. Even more implausibly, he wanted the Israelis to pay "appropriate compensation" to those they had previously injured during such operations, such as the secretary blinded by the letter-bomb explosion.[306] Not surprisingly, a spokesman for the Israeli Foreign Ministry dismissed such comments and denied any responsibility for any actions against the Egyptian scientists.

There was another reason Pilz had now started to become disillusioned with the Egyptian government. This concerned Nasser's growing links with the Soviet Union and, more particularly, with communist East Germany, a regime that Pilz detested and wanted nothing to do with. In February 1965, the East German leader, Walter Ulbricht, accepted Nasser's invitation and visited Cairo, where he was given a full state welcome by the president. When Pilz's bosses in Cairo suggested that he cooperate with a number of East German scientists who had been recruited to work on the missile program, he was infuriated and regarded the suggestion as intolerable. Within just weeks, at some point in the summer of 1965, Pilz left Egypt and flew home. His lawyer later confirmed that Pilz had not renewed his contract with the Egyptians and was now living "somewhere" in West Germany, while also spending some of his time in Austria.[307]

Without Pilz and Goercke, the Egyptians had no real prospect of resolving the fundamental problem that had dogged their missile program right from the word go—the absence of a reliable and effective guidance and control system. After five years of research and development, the program still had a very basic wire-guidance system that was virtually identical to the one used on the French Veronique rocket, built more than a decade before. But this was just not sufficient to make the Egyptian missiles even remotely as accurate and effective as they would need to be if they were to have any military value. The Egyptians tried their best to hide this very basic deficiency, and in July 1966 a state-controlled Cairo newspaper proudly proclaimed that the scientists working on the program "now have the ability to guide and control missiles on a par with their American and Soviet counterparts" and that Egypt was now the world's sixth major producer of missiles.[308] But such boasts were entirely hollow, and in reality the Egyptians totally lacked the expertise to make any real progress. At the July 23 military parade that year, for the first time since 1962, the missiles were not put on display, suggesting that the leadership wanted them to quietly disappear from public discussion.

Over the coming months, there were further indications that the rocket and jet aircraft program had ground to a halt. In a detailed report sent to President Johnson, Undersecretary of State Nicholas Katzenbach argued that the missile project had "reached a virtual standstill," having lost all of its key staff and having failed to recruit any new members to replace them. It would be at least a decade, continued the memorandum, before the rocket program would be completed.[309]

Israel's own assessments had been enough to reassure Prime Minister Eshkol, who in May 1965 exchanged letters with his West German counterpart confirming their intention of entering into full diplomatic relations. The German chancellor promised Eshkol that he would support legal sanctions against anyone seeking to "encourage" Germans to take up any "underground" activities abroad, but in fact the matter between the two countries had already been closed.

Meanwhile, back in central Cairo, Egyptian interrogators were still pressing Lotz hard to reveal more details about his work. For hour after hour, with a bright spotlight fixed relentlessly on him, he was pressed to reveal the names of his contacts, how much he had paid them, who had trained him, and whom he had met when he traveled abroad. Under such intense pressure, Lotz did his best to stick carefully to his initial story, hoping that the interrogators would believe their own suggestion about his supposed past in the SS. At the same time Lotz was careful not to be taken in by tempting promises: when the head of the Mukhabarat, Salah Nasr, personally assured him that he would be spared the death penalty in exchange for revealing the full truth about his espionage work, Lotz immediately saw the trap. He agreed to cooperate fully but knew that any such assurance was really just the oldest trick in the book.

The prisoner found a number of other ways of increasing his chances of surviving, which seemed to be stacked so heavily against him. At one point, he rose to his feet and slammed his fist down on the desk, shouting at his interrogator that he was still a German civilian and that, when his trial began, he would still be entitled to have full access to the German ambassador. "You'll find descriptions of your interrogation methods on the front pages of newspaper throughout the world," he shouted to the unnerved Egyptians. Such an audacious and aggressive approach helped Lotz survive thirty-three days of interrogation with his story intact. He could now stand trial, still claiming to be a German citizen and a veteran of Hitler's army, who, for some unknown reason, had been working as an agent for Israel's secret service.

During the trial, which began on July 27, 1965, security was extremely heavy. Fifteen officers and eighty heavily armed policemen accompanied Lotz and his wife to the courtroom, which was surrounded by roadblocks, encircled by armed soldiers, and overlooked by machine-gun nests. In the light of Mossad's operations inside the country and the high value of the agent in their custody, the Egyptian authorities were taking no chances.

Right from the start, Lotz was under huge pressure. The press was full of reports about his true identity—claiming, quite rightly, that he was an Israeli citizen and not, as he had always maintained, a native German. Most alarmingly, however, the prosecution had been informed of his Israeli citizenship, having received a letter from an unnamed West German source confirming the truth about the defendant's past. Lotz's defense counsel immediately appealed to the judge to stop any of this coming before the jury. The letter, they said, was simply uncorroborated hearsay and therefore inadmissible, while the newspaper reports were merely biased claims, lacking any substance, that could seriously prejudice a fair hearing. In Europe, Mossad agents had also been working hard to keep such reports from coming to light. An Israeli diplomat had visited the editor of *Der Stern* and persuaded him not to publish a report by its ace reporter, Wolfgang Löhde, that exposed the full truth about Lotz's real identity, even if previous efforts had not been enough to stop reports from emerging.[310]

Lotz was astonished when he found out that the judge concurred with his defense counsel's request. But he thought he knew the real reason the court was willing to overlook allegations of his Israeli citizenship: "[I]t might have been too shameful for the Egyptian authorities to admit that an Israeli intelligence officer had hoodwinked them . . . over a period of five years," he wrote. "It was possible that the Egyptians, who have a very delicate sense of prestige . . . simply could not admit, even to themselves, that the facts about my Israeli identity were indeed true."[311] Instead, the Egyptian authorities preferred to accept the story Lotz stuck rigidly to—that he was a German citizen and a veteran of the Wehrmacht who had fallen on hard times after the war and then been tempted by promises of large payments to pass information back to Israel, a country that he had no loyalty toward and had only visited once, very briefly. This gave him a glimmer of hope, and his spirits were raised even more when he saw that the hearing was being conducted with an admirable impartiality. "We thought the trial was being conducted in a fair manner," wrote the prisoner later on.[312]

But on August 21, in front of the world's press and its camera crews, the verdict was announced and it was as bad as he had feared: Wolfgang Lotz, announced the president of the court, was guilty as charged of espionage and sabotage on behalf of Israel. Lotz was then amazed by what followed. Instead of the death penalty, as he and his legal team had expected, he was sentenced only to life imprisonment, hard labor, and a large fine. "A loud murmur went through the courtroom," Lotz wrote, because "the spectators felt cheated." Within minutes, he was taken down some stairs at the back of the court, put into a prison van, and driven off to start his sentence. Wolfgang Lotz had survived.

Lotz was still in prison when events bore the most unmistakable testament to the failure of President Nasser's rocket program. When, in the early hours of June 5, 1967, conflict broke out between Israel and its Arab neighbors, Egypt and its allies suffered a military defeat of virtually cataclysmic proportions. Egypt's air force was eliminated within the space of just minutes and its army was overwhelmed in a series of lightning movements by the Israeli army, which sustained largely insignificant losses by comparison. Within just six days, the Arab armies had been humiliated.

In other words, eight years after its inception, the rocket program had entirely failed to help defend Egypt. The CIA had estimated that on the eve of the conflict the Egyptians had around twenty such missiles, while the Israelis thought the number was nearer one hundred, but this arsenal was of no military significance either because the rockets were not fit to be fired or because they landed way off target. Although it is unclear if any of the missiles were ever launched—one expert thought that nine al Kahirs or al Zafars were launched in a "panic" in the early hours of the war but then "went awry"—it is certain that none ever hit Israel or its military forces. Nor did the Israeli military ever target Factory 333 because, as a defense analyst wrote at the time, "it was felt that the missiles in their present stage of development posed no threat."[313] The missiles had been militarily useless after all, just as the HA-300, had it ever been developed, would have been no match for the French-supplied Israeli fighter jets. Instead, the balance of power had decisively swung in Israel's favor in 1964, when the Kennedy administration lifted the embargo on weapons sales to the Middle East and authorized the sale of Hawk antiaircraft missiles. From that moment on, Israel had had the upper hand.

As a senior Egyptian officer noted: The non-appearance of Egypt's much-heralded secret weapon, the [al Kahir] missile, is a sordid tale, I regret to say. Al Kahir had been part of Egyptian folklore since word first leaked in the early 1960s that Egypt had its own short-range ballistic missile made in Egypt. . . . When we lost in 1967, of course, the questions started: "[W]here was [al Kahir]?" No answers came.[314]

Nasser's bid to build long-range rockets, and to develop a jet fighter, had been an expensive failure after all.

Conclusion

The truth about President Nasser's ambitious military projects has been clear ever since the Six-Day War in 1967. Far from turning out to be vastly impressive accomplishments that would have resulted in the ability to defend Egypt and its Arab allies or to attack Israel, they remained merely the stuff of dreams. On the eve of conflict, Nasser's scientists were no closer to surmounting the formidable technical obstacles that lay in their way than they had been when the project first started, eight years before, and as a result the rockets and the jet aircraft had no value on the battlefield.

Lying at the very heart of Nasser's plans was a huge fundamental flaw, one that condemned his plans to failure right from the beginning. This was simply that Egypt did not have the means to realize the hugely expensive goals its president had chosen to pursue. Nasser managed to fund the programs from the export of cotton and from the high transit fees drawn from freight that moved down the Suez Canal, but that was not enough to sustain such an ambitious program for long. Years before, the Spanish government had reached essentially the same conclusion over its own HA-300 jet fighter program, prompting it to sell the design to Egypt: it made much more sense, reasoned General Franco and his chiefs, just to admit such limitations and instead appeal to the Americans for military supplies.

Unlike Saudi Arabia and other Arab states, Egypt was not an oil exporter and did not earn enough to purchase the raw materials or hire the top talent that were essential if Nasser's vision was to be realized. Unlike Israel, which became a nuclear power in the sixties, and Pakistan, which followed decades later, it did not enjoy large financial subsidies bestowed by the United States or any other generous and wealthy donor. For Nasser had wanted Egypt to have a "positive neutrality" that was virtually incompatible with pursuing such hugely expensive and ambitious projects. If he had wanted to defend his country, as he claimed, then the president would have done better to have struck a deal with one of the two superpowers, and the events of 1989—when the people of Eastern Europe rose up in revolt and threw aside the communist regimes that had subjugated them since 1945—showed conclusively which one would have been the better choice.

American analysts noted this basic, fundamental weakness in the Egyptian projects. When Israeli representatives claimed that Nasser was committed to building nine hundred missiles, the Special National Intelligence Estimate in Washington was dubious, pointing out that such a program would require an investment of between $400 and $600 million, most of which would have to be drawn from foreign currency reserves that Egypt desperately needed. "Such expenditures, on top of [other] large requirements," said its report, "would be an extremely heavy burden on the foreign exchange resources of a country which is likely to be in difficult economic straits for the foreseeable future."[315] In other words, the letter written by Dr. Pilz, which Mossad had leaned on so heavily to justify Operation Damocles, was in fact more of a dream and a flight of fancy than any serious statement of policy.

So even if the HA-300 jet aircraft had been developed, it would have quickly been outdated and surpassed on the battlefield by one of the French, or later American, warplanes that Israel deployed. Egypt would not have been able to compete with the technical accomplishments of vastly wealthier Western countries that were aiming to keep ahead of Soviet prowess at a time of considerable Cold War tension. The HA-300 would never have rivaled its Russian contemporary, the MiG-21, and aviation experts strongly doubted that it would ever have gotten close to the considerable speed—two and a half times the speed of sound—that the Egyptians always claimed.[316]

Analysts in Washington were also deeply skeptical that the rockets would have had any military importance even if they had been developed: without WMD warheads, they emphasized, the rockets were of "doubtful value."[317] In a worst-case scenario, the Egyptians "might" manage to deploy a "few" missiles, argued the CIA in 1964, but the number was too small to be significant except in terms of "psychological warfare." As for the claims about WMD, the Americans were wholly dismissive: "[W]hile Egypt does have a research reactor and an associated research program," went one report, "both are so small as to preclude their having any potential for nuclear weapons development."[318]

American experts also reached the same conclusion about various other items on Nasser's military "shopping list." The al Ared rocket, for example, which was unveiled in July 1963, was regarded in Washington as a publicity stunt, designed "largely for propaganda purposes." Given that the Egyptians never revealed any footage of the rocket being fired, some experts concluded that the missile was really just a hoax: a leading British journal, for example, was highly skeptical of Egyptian claims of a "successful" al Ared test launch, given the considerable technical challenges of firing a two-stage ballistic missile.[319] Equally, the "Egyptian submarine" that Field Marshal Amer boasted of was really just a Soviet export.[320] This was equally true of another hugely ambitious Egyptian program—the development of the al Negma satellite. This was a project that does not appear to have gotten very far because the Egyptians completely lacked all the vital infrastructure—including several highly sophisticated ground stations for satellite tracking, monitoring, and data readout—that were essential to make it work.[321]

If Nasser was pursuing the projects not for military purposes but to build up his own reputation, then such an effort was also condemned to failure. In the immediate and short term, the development of the missiles and their successful test firing in the summer of 1962 gave the Cairo regime a popular lift, enhancing Nasser's personal prestige as well as Egypt's in the eyes of the Arab masses. But any such lift was not likely to last very long, just as similar programs and technical breakthroughs elsewhere in the world have only bestowed short-term political benefits on other regimes.[322] It could even have proved counterproductive if popular expectations were raised and then dashed as they were when the high hopes for the United Arab Republic, the political union between Syria and Egypt, started to fall apart and then disintegrate in the course of 1961.[323] When the missiles largely disappeared from public view after July 1963, Nasser and his chiefs could easily have lost their credibility and been open to charges of making empty boasts about what the programs had achieved. And even if he had succeeded in developing the HA-300 plane after all, it would have been a very hollow "Arab achievement" when it was designed by Western experts and composed of Western spare parts: "all the parts," as Brandner pointed out in February 1963, came from "Western countries."[324]

For Nasser and the Egyptians, this meant that the military programs were ultimately an illusion they were pursuing but had no true chance of ever making a reality. Not only were the programs improbable but, from the Egyptians' own viewpoint, a dangerous pipe dream. This was because they diverted and wasted an enormous expenditure of resources and effort that could have been better deployed elsewhere: for example, the same funds and effort could perhaps have been channeled into building Egypt's economy or its infrastructure. Equally, if Nasser had recognized from the onset how futile the programs were, then he might have considered taking a more flexible diplomatic approach toward Washington, striking up a rapport with the U.S. administration of President Eisenhower that would have deeply alarmed Israel. In narrowly military terms, he could also have spent the money much more effectively in other ways: as the *Jerusalem Post* argued in 1962, Cairo's new Russian fighter and bombers were "a far greater threat to Israel than any ballistic rocket in an experimental stage."[325]

If, in this respect, the programs were, for the Egyptians, a dangerous fantasy, the pursuit of which was inimical to Egypt's national interest, the same charge can equally be leveled against Israel's response. Isser Harel, Golda Meir, and their supporters can be fairly accused of overreacting and using excessive force against an Egyptian arms program that did not really present any substantial threat to the security of the Jewish state at all. As Meir Amit and Shimon Peres had argued, Israel simply did not know enough about the Egyptian program to justify unleashing lethal force against the key personnel who were involved in it. Until there was clear, compelling evidence that certain technical obstacles had been overcome, there was simply no point in making assumptions about the level of threat the missiles posed.

The essential criticism that can be made of Operation Damocles and other violent Israeli intelligence operations against the German scientists in Egypt, such as Operation Susannah, is that they were extreme measures that should have been used only as a last resort. The circumstances of the time were not desperate enough to justify their adoption. In the summer of 1962, when Harel initiated Damocles, there was no convincing reason to suppose that the Egyptian missiles presented any threat to Israel, and his response was based upon a hypothetical worst-case scenario that was in reality many steps from being realized.

An obvious counterargument in Harel's defense might be that, in the circumstances of the time, Israel simply could not afford to take risks. Given the magnitude of the potential threat and the hostility of Nasser's and Amer's rhetoric, was he not wise to take such determined action? Equally, is there not evidence that the attacks on Krug and Kleinwachter, and the risk of assassination or injury from parcel bombs, helped to dissuade some of the scientists from continuing with their work? Dr. Karl-Heinz Gronau provides one example.

The question of whether and when one country or individual can take the life of another in self-defense is of course a profoundly difficult one, but what is certain is that Israel could initially have tried other methods of steering the scientists away from continuing with their work. Diplomatic pressure on West Germany eventually reaped dividends and could have been tried before, not concurrently with, or after, the use of lethal force. If the Israelis had started off with such a moderate and measured approach, they would also have avoided antagonizing the scientists and making some of them dig their heels in even deeper: the use of force can often be counterproductive, and after the various attacks, Pilz, Kleinwachter, and Goercke all reiterated their determination not to surrender to bullying and instead to continue doing the work they enjoyed.

When there was no compelling evidence of an imminent Egyptian threat to Israel, the campaign of violence also risked unnecessarily denigrating Israel's reputation, associating its name with brutality in a way that played into the hands of its enemies, who were quick to portray it as a "terrorist state." Yet it was just such a reputation that Israel came close to acquiring as a result of its attack on Hans Kleinwachter in West Germany and the harassment of Heidi Goercke in Switzerland. Caught red-handed in the case of Heidi Goercke, Israeli leaders had to work hard to find ways of winning back public sympathy in Western Europe, where the trial of the two captured Israeli agents attracted so much publicity. To risk sacrificing Israel's reputation was surely worthwhile only when it was absolutely necessary, and in the summer of 1962 there was no evidence of any such strategic necessity.

In other words, it is dangerous to conjure worst-case scenarios and then act on them. This is just one of the lessons that the story of Operation Damocles teaches. Decades on, it is certainly tempting to look back at the stories of the scientists and of Israel's response and ask what other lessons they teach to a contemporary world whose stability is also threatened by arms proliferation, weapons of mass destruction, and enmity in the Middle East.

The story is a reminder, for example, of how easily rivalry and mistrust between different countries can degenerate into an arms race that is volatile, inflammable, and never-ending. Nasser and his generals blamed Israel for acting so aggressively, claiming that their rocket program was simply a sensible way of defending both Egypt and its allies, especially when, by 1962, they were aware of Tel Aviv's nuclear ambitions. The Israelis argued that Nasser's plans threatened to dramatically destabilize the entire region and gave them no option except to accelerate their own military programs, including the purchase of sophisticated missiles from the United States that altered the whole balance of power in the Middle East.[326] In the period leading up to Nasser's decision to initiate the rocket and jet aircraft programs, each country blamed the other for committing acts of provocation: Israel blamed Egypt for sponsoring fedayeen attacks, while Egypt blamed the Israelis for launching unprovoked attacks on Qibya and Gaza while aggressively seizing territory along their other borders. But whoever one pins the blame upon, the fact is that the use of violence and force and the threat of their use easily spiral and become self-perpetuating, thereby fueling mistrust and prompting rivals and enemies to tread along the same destructive path. At the very least, this leads to the unnecessary squandering of vast resources that could otherwise be spent much more fruitfully on other projects that are of much greater value to the country in question and its people.

The story is also a reminder of how dangerous it can be when fact gets so mixed up with speculation and raw emotions that rational argument becomes extremely difficult, or even impossible. This is exactly what happened in Israel in the summer of 1963, when, for a brief period, the cooler, calmer heads of Peres, Amit, and Ben-Gurion were drowned out by a chorus of hysterical voices in the media, among the general public, and within Parliament. In a different environment, the deficiencies of the Egyptian missile program would have become apparent, as well as the emptiness of the claims about nuclear, biological, and chemical warheads.

The people of any country, like any individual, can of course fall victim to such a sense of hysteria. Even modern-day democracies, whose people are blessed with a high standard of education, are susceptible, just as, for example, the United States was susceptible to exaggerated fears of communism in the Cold War or, to take a more particular instance, to revelations about "the Missile Gap" in the 1960s.[327] Harel's propaganda campaign in the media provoked such a highly emotional reaction within Israel because of its exposure of the German connection to the Egyptian program, even though the nationality of the scientists would not have altered the threat posed by the missiles.

Equally, it is a story of how every nation's collective fears can also be cynically distorted for political or strategic ends. Sometime after the crisis of 1963, Meir Amit realized that the debate over how to deal with the rockets was also one that concerned Israel's domestic politics and the political struggle to succeed Ben-Gurion after his retirement from politics.[328] At the same time, some U.S. officials thought that Israeli diplomats were deliberately exploiting stories about Egypt's rocket program in order to influence high-level opinion in Washington: "[W]e simply didn't see Nasser's missiles as posing the kind of threat that would require a major Israeli investment in anyone's missiles in return," one leading official, McGeorge Bundy, said.[329] As one leading author on Israel has written, "[T]he imagery of the Holocaust has become part of Israel's political language, not just in its conflict with Arabs but as a rhetorical means of abusing opponents in internal political squabbles . . . it can stretch to the absurd limit of a Tel Aviv pirate radio station calling itself 'Holocaust Survivors' Radio' in the vain hope that its popular Greek music would not be shut down by police."[330]

The story also raises questions about how much importance one country should attach to the hostile rhetoric, rather than hostile actions, of another. One reason Egypt's missile program provoked so much concern, and such an overreaction, in certain quarters in Tel Aviv was that it was accompanied by the bellicose claims of both Field Marshal Amer and the Egyptian president.[331] In the words of one British newspaper, "[T]he most disturbing factor of the development [of rockets] was Nasser's intention to destroy Israel."[332] But to conflate words and actions is, at best, very controversial and could even be quite dangerous. There is no necessary connection between threats and behavior, and there are numerous examples of just how disassociated they can often be. So there have been times when individuals and nations have given no warning of their aggressive intentions or even flatly denied them beforehand, the most obvious example being Hitler's disregard for the Munich Agreement in 1938. Conversely, there are many examples of leaders who have indulged in noisy bouts of saber rattling but never seriously entertained any idea of putting them into practice, even if that might risk some loss of face.[333] During the Iran-Iraq War of the 1980s, for example, the Iranian leadership made numerous references to the annihilation of Israel but at the same time accepted military assistance from Tel Aviv, which wanted to stop the Iraqis from becoming too powerful.[334] And in the Middle East, more so than anywhere else in the world, there is more reason to be skeptical about the value of "threats": analyzing the mind-set of his fellow people, King Hussein of Jordan told Israeli leaders after the Six-Day War in 1967, "[W]ith the Arabs, words don't have the same value as they do for other people. Threats mean nothing."[335]

There are other aspects of this chapter of Middle Eastern history that raise other important issues, all of which have a strong contemporary relevance. For example, it illustrates the vulnerability and susceptibility of even the most efficient and experienced spy chiefs to the most dubious sources, such as "walk-in" figures. Otto Joklik was essentially a fraud and a charlatan, yet his revelations were given an astonishing credence by the chief of Mossad. The parallels with events four decades later, when the U.S. government was lured into a Middle Eastern war by the false testimony of highly dubious "defectors," are clear.[336]

So many decades on, as weapons of mass destruction continue to proliferate and the Middle East remains torn by destructive violence, the story of Operation Damocles continues to resonate.

ENDNOTES

1. "West Germany" was the democratic republic that had been established in 1945, and in 1989 merged with its communist counterpart in the east.
2. Ian Black and Benny Morris, *Israel's Secret Wars: The Untold Story of Israeli Intelligence* (London: Warner Books, 1992), 196–7.
3. "Isser Harel—An Obituary," *The Daily Telegraph*, February 19, 2002.
4. "German Defends His Aid to Cairo," *New York Times*, May 26, 1963, 24.
5. Inge Deutschkron, *Bonn and Jerusalem: The Strange Coalition* (Radnor, PA: Chilton Book Co., 1970), 230.
6. The phrase "lost its soul" is taken from various writings and speeches of Dr. Jonathan Sacks, Britain's chief rabbi.
7. Avri El-Ad, *Decline of Honor* (Chicago: Henry Regnery Company, 1976), 126.
8. Black and Morris, op. cit., 193–4.
9. Stewart Steven, *The Spymasters of Israel* (New York: Ballantine Books, 1980), 148–9.
10. Ibid., 165.
11. Dan Raviv and Yossi Melman, *Every Spy a Prince* (Boston: Houghton Mifflin), 136.
12. See Chapter 7.
13. "German Defends His Aid to Cairo," *New York Times*, May 26, 1963, 24.
14. Mohamed Heikal, *The Cairo Documents* (New York: Doubleday, 1973), 207.
15. Israel had initiated a nuclear arms program in the mid-1950s, and by 1962 was close to crossing the nuclear threshold. See Avner Cohen, *Israel and the Bomb* (New York: Columbia University Press, 1988).
16. Shimon Peres, *David's Sling* (Littlehampton: Littlehampton Books, 1970), 95–6; see Owen L. Sirrs, *Nasser and the Missile Age in the Middle East* (London and New York: Routledge, 2006), 110.

17. Memorandum for McGeorge Bundy, "Summary of Transcript of November 12–13 U.S.-Israeli Talks," in *FRUS Supplement*, Document 154, 3. See Sirrs, op. cit., 125.

18. Memorandum from Robert W. Komer of the National Security Council to Sec. of State Dean Rusk, April 18, 1963, in *FRUS Supplement*, Document 275, 2.

19. Memorandum from Robert W. Komer of the National Security Council to the president's special assistant for National Security Affairs, April 30, 1963, in *FRUS 1961–63*, Vol. XVIII, 625.

20. Avi Shlaim, *The Iron Wall: Israel and the Arab World* (London and New York: Penguin, 2001), 36–7.

21. Protocol of cabinet meetings, May 29 and July 14, 1949.

22. Black and Morris, op. cit., 62.

23. Ibid., 65–6.

24. Ibid., 108–9.

25. Ibid., 95.

26. "Aman" was an abbreviation of *Agaf ha-Modi'in* or "Intelligence Wing."

27. Samuel M. Katz, *Soldier Spies: Israeli Military Intelligence* (Novato, CA: Presidio Press, 1992), 75.

28. "We are suffering increasingly from lack of suitable people for intelligence work abroad," as Reuven Shiloah, a senior official in Israeli intelligence, pointed out in July 1950. Quoted in Black and Morris, op. cit., 79.

29. El-Ad, op. cit., 26.

30. Steven, op. cit., 75.

31. El-Ad, op. cit., 29.

32. Shlaim, op. cit., 77.

33. Ibid., 78–9.

34. El-Ad, op. cit., 116.

35. Ibid., 73.

36. Ibid., 83.

37. Charles Whiting, *Skorzeny* (London: Pen and Sword Books, 2010), 118.

38. Michael J. Neufeld, "Rolf Engel vs. the German Army: A Nazi Career in Rocketry and Repression," *History and Technology*, Vol. 13, 1996, 53–72.

39. El-Ad, op. cit., 109.

40. Ibid., 81.

41. Ibid., 82.

42. Ibid., 95.

43. Ibid., 96.

44. Ibid., 102.

45. Ibid., 85–87.

46. Ibid., 105.

47. Ibid., 113.
48. Ibid., 127.
49. Ibid., 125.
50. Ibid., 126.
51. Ibid., 126.
52. Ibid., 126.
53. Ibid., 135.
54. Shlaim, op. cit., 111.
55. Sharett's diary, January 10, 1955. See Shlaim, op. cit., 123.
56. Sharett's diary, January 27, 1955. See Shlaim, op. cit., 120.
57. Naguib was reinstated as president but his role was largely ceremonial.
58. Said K. Abdurish, *Nasser: The Last Arab* (London: Duckworth, 2004), 101.
59. *New Statesman*, October 10, 1970.
60. Jean Lacouture, *Nasser: A Biography of Gamal Abdel Nasser* (London: Secker & Warburg, 1973), 268.
61. Lacouture, op. cit., 290. These Syrian denunciations were made in 1959.
62. Shlaim, op. cit., 80–81.
63. Jack Nicholls to Evelyn Shuckburgh, December 14, 1954, Foreign Office, Document Number 371/111107, Public Records Office; see Shlaim, op. cit., 118.
64. Lacouture, op. cit., 265.
65. Ibid., 365.
66. Ibid., 27.
67. UN Security Council Resolution No. 95, September 1, 1951.
68. Shlaim, op. cit., 135.
69. Michael Bar-Zohar, *Ben Gurion: A Political Biography, Vol. 3* (Jerusalem: Shabtai Tevet, 1980), 1364.
70. Benny Morris, *Israel's Border Wars 1949–56: Arab Infiltration, Israeli Retaliation and the Countdown to the Suez War* (Oxford and New York: Clarendon Press, 1993), 49, 412: Shlaim, op. cit., 82.
71. Shlaim, op. cit., 82–3.
72. Ariel Sharon, *Warrior: An Autobiography* (London and New York: Simon & Schuster, 1989), 86–91.
73. Commander E. H. Hutchison, *Violent Truce: A Military Observer Looks at the Arab-Israeli Conflict 1951–55* (London: John Calder, 1956), 44; Shlaim, op. cit., 91.
74. Shlaim, op. cit., 125.
75. Patrick Seale, *The Struggle For Syria* (London: Yale University Press, 1987); Keith Kyle, *Suez* (Yale and London: I. B. Tauris, 1956), 65.
76. See Chapter 4.
77. Mohamed Heikal, *Cutting the Lion's Tail: Suez Through Egyptian Eyes* (Westminster, MD: Arbor House, 1987), 66.

78. Shlaim, op. cit., 127.
79. Ibid., 129.
80. Communication of Abba Eban to UNSC, September 29, 1954.
81. Lacouture, op. cit., 61–63.
82. Ibid., 271.
83. Ibid., 159.
84. Shlaim, op. cit., 87.
85. Abdurish, op. cit., 128.
86. Quoted in "Licence to Kill: When Governments Choose to Assassinate," Gordon Corera, BBC News Online, March 17, 2012.
87. Heikal, *Cutting the Lion's Tail*, 103–4.
88. Ibid., 154.
89. Stephen Dorrill, *The Silent Conspiracy* (London and Melbourne: Heinemann, 1993), 254–5; Peter Wright and Paul Greengrass, *Spycatcher* (London and Melbourne: Heinemann, 1987), 84–5, 160–1.
90. Heikal, *Cutting the Lion's Tail*, 154.
91. Ibid., 215.
92. Ibid., 104.
93. Also known as the Central Treaty Organization.
94. Anthony Parsons, *They Say the Lion: Britain's Legacy in the Middle East* (London: Jonathan Cape, 1986), 54.
95. Abdurish, op. cit., 188.
96. Parsons, op. cit., 54–5.
97. Ibid., 66.
98. Kyle, op. cit., 112.
99. Shlaim, op. cit., 163.
100. May Oueidah, "An Examination of Some Structural Elements in the Speeches of President Nasser" (unpublished PhD thesis, London, 1981), 26.
101. Ben-Gurion's diary, August 10, 1956; Shlaim, op. cit., 168.
102. This was after the assassination attempt by Mohamed Abdul Latif on October 26, 1954.
103. The Israelis called it Operation Khadesh.
104. For example, Nasser didn't flinch and simply carried on with his speech when, on October 26, 1954, a would-be assassin fired eight shots at him at close range; see page 70.
105. Kyle, op. cit., 475.
106. Ibid., 447, 449.
107. Ibid., 415.
108. Ibid., 382.
109. Abdurish, op. cit., 121.

110. Wolfgang Lotz, *The Champagne Spy* (London: Corgi, 1974), 44.
111. Kyle, op. cit., 447.
112. Ibid., 418.
113. Andrew Tully, *CIA: The Inside Story* (New York: Fawcett, 1962), 108.
114. Abdurish, op. cit., 74–5.
115. Parsons, op. cit., 66.
116. Sirrs, op. cit., 18.
117. Michael Bar-Zohar, *The Hunt for German Scientists* (New York: Avon, 1970), 169.
118. Quoted in *Life* magazine, May 27, 1962, 77–82.
119. *Life*, op. cit. See also Ferdinand Brandner's autobiography, *Life Between Fronts* (Munich: Welsermuhl, 1967).
120. "Veronique" was an abbreviation for Vernon-Electronique. Vernon was the French town where the research laboratory was established in 1946.
121. Quoted in Judith H. Young, *The French Strategic Missile Programme*, Adelphi Papers, No. 38, July 1967, 2.
122. Bar-Zohar, *The Hunt for German Scientists*, 203.
123. Sanche De Gramont, "Nasser's Hired Germans," *Saturday Evening Post*, July 28, 1963, 61.
124. Tom Bower, *The Paperclip Conspiracy* (London and New York: Little, Brown and Company, 1987), 127–129.
125. See Chapter 2.
126. *Chronologie Ariane: Veronique et Compagnie*, www.capcomespace.net/dossiers/ espace_europeen/ariane/espace_francais/veronique. See Sirrs, op. cit., 27.
127. Sanche De Gramont, "Nasser's Hired Germans," *Saturday Evening Post*, July 28, 1963, 61; Bar-Zohar, *The Hunt for German Scientists*, 205.
128. Naher Osten, "Rusting—36, 135 und 333," *Der Spiegel*, May 8, 1963, No. 19, 62, 65.
129. Ibid., 62; Steven, op. cit., 135.
130. Its velocity was 1,000 feet per second, compared with 6,560 feet per second by the V-2, which was produced later.
131. Eugen Sänger, *The Silver Bird Story: A Memoir: History of Rocketry and Astronautics*, ed. R. Cargill Hall, Proceedings of the Third through the Sixth History Symposia of the International Academy of Astronautics, Vol. 1, 213.
132. G. A. Totaky, "Soviet Rocket Technology" in ed. Eugene M. Emme, *The History of Rocket Technology* (Detroit: Wayne State University Press, 1964).
133. Sänger, op. cit., 217.
134. Sirrs, op. cit., 25.
135. Ibid.
136. See Chapter 1 and Conclusion.
137. Peter Malkin and Harry Stein, *Eichmann in My Hands* (London: Random Century, 1990), 71.

138. Ibid., 83.
139. In his memoirs, Malkin does not mention the date of this operation. But 1959 is the most likely date.
140. Malkin, op. cit., 72.
141. Ibid., 81.
142. Ibid.
143. Ibid., 82.
144. Ibid., 89.
145. Ibid., 98.
146. Ibid., 103.
147. Lotz, op. cit., 12.
148. Ibid., 12.
149. See Chapters 2 through 4.
150. On the fate of the Egyptian Jews, see Chapter 2.
151. Bar Zohar, *The Hunt for German Scientists*, 190–1.
152. Lotz, op. cit., 57.
153. Mohamed Heikal, *The Cairo Documents*, op. cit., 140–1.
154. Michael Bar-Zohar, *Spies in the Promised Land* (Boston: Houghton Mifflin, 1972), 259.
155. German electric steel plants AG, Süddeutsche cable stations, Siemens Plania, Kugelfischer, Siemens Schuckert, Hottinger Measurement, and the nationalized Austrian Böhler-works.
156. Terence Prittie, "Bomb Shop in the Nile," *Atlantic Monthly* 214, 1964, No. 2, 38.
157. Osten, op. cit., 62, 65.
158. Parsons, op. cit., 67.
159. De Gramont, op. cit., 60.
160. Raviv and Melman, op. cit., 137.
161. Lotz, op. cit., 23.
162. Ibid.
163. Ibid., 24.
164. Ibid., 34.
165. Osten, op. cit., 62, 65.
166. Ibid.
167. Cecil Brownlow, "Egypt Plans Satellite Launch Within a Year," *Aviation Week and Space Technology*, September 9, 1963, 33.
168. For a detailed description of how the wire guidance system worked, see Frederic Ordway and Ronald Wakeford, *International Missile and Spacecraft Guide* (New York: McGraw-Hill, 1960), 13.
169. Sirrs, op. cit., 42.
170. "Egypt Imports Rockets from America," *The Times*, July 8, 1961, 8.

171. Sirrs, op. cit., 43.
172. Steven, op. cit., 148–9; Dennis Eisenberg, Uri Dan, and Eli Landau, *The Mossad: Israel's Secret Intelligence Service: Inside Stories* (New York: Paddington Press, 1978), 182.
173. "German Emphasis on Space Travel," *The Times*, November 8, 1961, 10.
174. William Beller, "Sanger's Final Interview with M/R," *Missiles and Rockets*, February 24, 2012, 38.
175. "Bonn Inquires on Work of Scientists in Egypt," *The Times*, March 22, 1963.
176. Deutschkron, op. cit., 222.
177. Sirrs, op. cit., 45.
178. "Missile Potential of the United Arab Republic," DIA Report in *FRUS 1961–63*, Vol. XVIII, 318–20.
179. "Egypt Tests with Rockets Reported," *The Times*, November 8, 1961, 10.
180. Eisenberg, Dan, and Landau, op. cit., 185.
181. Sirrs, op. cit., 45.
182. Ibid.
183. "Four Test Rockets Launched by Cairo," *New York Times*, July 22, 1962.
184. The parades and missiles tests are described by Walz, "Four Test Rockets Launched by Cairo," *New York Times*, July 23, 1962.
185. Richard Johns and David Holden, *The House of Saud* (London: Macmillan, 1982).
186. Lacouture, op. cit., 353–54.
187. Abdurish, op. cit., 191.
188. This happened on June 18, 1953, when members of the Revolutionary Command Council declared Egypt a republic.
189. "Nasser Exhibits UAR Military Might," *New York Times*, July 23, 1962.
190. Sirrs, op. cit., 51.
191. Malkin, op. cit., 138.
192. Ibid., 139.
193. Ibid.
194. Raviv and Melman, op. cit., 101.
195. Malkin, op. cit., 70.
196. Ian Black and Benny Morris, op. cit., 97.
197. Yitzhak Shamir, *Summing Up* (London: Weidenfeld and Nicholson, 1994), 80.
198. The case was resolved in August 1962, when the child was discovered hidden in New York.
199. Malkin, op. cit., 124.
200. Ibid.
201. Ibid., 139.

202. Raviv and Melman, op. cit., 120.
203. Kyle, op cit.
204. Sirrs, op. cit., p. 51.
205. CIA "Current Intelligence Memorandum: UAR Rocket Launching'" in *FRUS 1961–63*, Vol. XVIII, 319.
206. Memorandum from William H. Brubeck to McGeorge Bundy in *FRUS 1961–63*, Vol. XVIII, 319.
207. Steven, op. cit., 135–37.
208. Ibid., 133.
209. Black and Morris, op. cit., 193.
210. Ibid.
211. Steven, op. cit., 137.
212. Eisenberg, Dan, and Landau, op. cit., 141.
213. See Chapter 1; Black and Morris, op. cit., 193–94.
214. Bar-Zohar, *Spies in the Promised Land*, op. cit., 258.
215. Matti Golan, *Shimon Peres: A Biography* (London: St. Martin's Press, 1982), 114; Deutschkron, op. cit.
216. Bar-Zohar, *The Hunt for German Scientists*, 200.
217. Black and Morris, op. cit., 193–94.
218. Steven, op. cit., 145.
219. A lieutenant colonel in the SS.
220. Lotz, op. cit., 37.
221. Ibid., 59–60.
222. Ibid., 51–2.
223. Ibid., 65.
224. Steven, op. cit., 172.
225. Black and Morris, op. cit., 196.
226. Raviv and Melman, op. cit., 130–1.
227. Black and Morris, op. cit., 196.
228. See Chapter 7.
229. Joshua Tadmor, *The Silent Warriors* (New York: Macmillan, 1969), 140.
230. Steven, op. cit., 144.
231. Eisenberg, Dan, and Landau, op. cit., 143.
232. See Sirrs, op. cit., p. 29.
233. Cohen, op. cit., 116.
234. On Nasser's knowledge of Israel's nuclear program, see page 8.
235. Bar-Zohar, *Spies in the Promised Land*, 270.
236. Deutschkron, op. cit., 231.
237. Anthony Cordesman, *Weapons of Mass Destruction in the Middle East* (London: Brassey's, 1991), 141.

238. Aaron Karp, *Ballistic Missile Proliferation: The Politics and Technics* (Oxford and New York: Oxford University Press, 1996), 171.

239. T. V. Paul, *Power Versus Prudence* (Montreal: McGill-Queens University Press, 2000), 139; Karp, op. cit., 178.

240. See Chapter 1.

241. "Sameh" was referred to by Presiding Judge Emil Heberli in the course of the June 1963 trial of the two agents.

242. Black and Morris, op. cit., 199.

243. Steven, op. cit., 148–9.

244. Gordon Thomas, *Gideon's Spies* (London and New York: Pan, 2000), 137–8.

245. Bar-Zohar, *Spies in the Promised Land*, op. cit., 276.

246. Deutschkron, op. cit., 229–30.

247. Osten, op. cit., 62, 65; Deutschkron, op. cit., 234.

248. Deutschkron, op. cit., 229.

249. Elinor Burkett, *Golda Meir: The Iron Lady of the Middle East* (London: Gibson Square, 2008), 194.

250. Deutschkron, op. cit., 228.

251. Howard M. Sachar, *Israel and Europe: An Appraisal in History* (London and New York: Alfred A. Knopf, 1999), 138.

252. Jay Walz, "Nuclear Role Denied," *New York Times*, March 23, 1963, 4.

253. Memorandum of Conversation, "German Technicians in the UAR," June 17, 1963, in *FRUS Supplement*, Document 278, 1.

254. Ibid.

255. Osten, op. cit., 62, 65.

256. "German Scientist Denies Cairo Role," *New York Times*, March 27, 1963.

257. Moshe Sharett, *YoMan Ishi*, Vol. 5, Tel Aviv, 1372, entry for March 12, 1956. Sharett was referring to Israel's search for arms after the Czech arms lift to Egypt in 1955.

258. Bar-Zohar, *Spies in the Promised Land*, op. cit., 281.

259. Steven, op. cit., 148–9.

260. Raviv and Melman, op. cit., 128.

261. W. Granger Blair, "Israelis Deplore Furor over Arms," *New York Times*, March 30, 1963, 3.

262. Lotz, op. cit., 81.

263. See Chapter 1.

264. "Swiss Court Throws Spotlight on Nasser Threat to Destroy Israel," *Daily News Bulletin*, June 14, 1963.

265. "Cairo Unveils Missiles on Revolution's 11th Birthday," *New York Times*, July 24, 1963.

266. "Egyptians Show New Two-Stage Rocket in Parade," *Aviation Week and Space Technology*, July 29, 1963, 26.

267. Cecil Brownlow, "Egypt Plans Satellite Launch Within Year," *Aviation Week and Space Technology*, September 9, 1963, 32.

268. Memorandum of Conversation, September 30, 1963, in *FRUS 1961–63*, Vol. XVIII, 717–8.

269. Arnold H. Lubasch, "Israel Says Arabs Plan a War, Warns UN About Arms Race," *New York Times*, October 3, 1963, 6.

270. Memorandum for McGeorge Bundy, "Summary of Transcript of November 12–13 U.S.-Israeli Talks," in *FRUS Supplement*, Document 154, 3.

271. Memorandum from Robert W. Komer to President Kennedy, "Israel/UAR Nuclear and Missile Capabilities," March 22, 1963, in *FRUS 1961–63*, Vol. XVIII, 432-33; Memorandum for the Record, November 14, 1963, in *FRUS 1961–63*, Vol. XVIII, 780.

272. Deutschkron, op. cit., 233.

273. G. Harry Stine, *ICBM* (New York: Orion Books), 1991, 69–70.

274. Sirrs, op. cit., 91; Lotz, op. cit., 118.

275. Lotz, op. cit., 109.

276. Ibid., 79.

277. On the rivalry between Aman and Mossad, see in general Steven, op. cit., Chapters 14 through 15.

278. Lotz, op. cit., 18.

279. Parsons, op. cit., 60.

280. Lotz, op. cit., 18.

281. Ibid., 19.

282. Raviv and Melman, op. cit., 138–9.

283. Yemen, see Chapter 17.

284. Tadmor, op. cit., 119–23. Yaakovian spent a few years in an Israel prison and was then deported back to Egypt.

285. Aviezer Golan, *Operation Susannah* (New York and London: Harper & Row Publishers, 1978), 298–9.

286. Golan, op. cit., p. 299.

287. Lotz, op. cit., 106–7.

288. Ibid., 108.

289. Ibid., 121.

290. Ibid.

291. Raviv and Melman, op. cit., 146.

292. Lotz, op. cit., 125.

293. Ibid., 126.

294. See Chapter 16.

295. "Curb Hinted in Bonn on Experts in UAR," *New York Times*, May 3, 1963, 5.

296. "German Defends His Aid to Cairo," *New York Times*, May 26, 1963, 24.

297. Deutschkron, op. cit., 237.

298. "Cairo Bars Exit of German Aides," *New York Times*, July 30, 1965; "Cairo Said to Let German Experts Go," *New York Times*, July 31, 1965.

299. Memorandum from the under secretary of state to President Johnson, "The Arab-Israeli Arms Race and Status of U.S. Arms Control Efforts," May 1, 1964, in *FRUS 1964–68*, Vol. XVIII, 814–7. See Sirrs, op. cit., 155.

300. "German Experts on the Rise in Cairo," *New York Times*, January 19, 1965, 2.

301. Arthur J. Olsen, "Bonn Gives Israeli Modern Weapons," *New York Times*, January 21, 1965, 7.

302. "German Experts on the Rise in Cairo," *New York Times*, January 19, 1965, 2.

303. Memorandum of Conversation, "Cubic Corporation"; see Sirrs, op. cit., 151.

304. Telegram from the Department of State to the embassy in Israel, dated February 1, 1966, *FRUS 1964–68*, Vol. XVIII, 293.

305. Deutschkron, op. cit., 240; Bar-Zohar, *The Hunt for German Scientists*, 217.

306. "German Rocket Expert in UAR Tells of Fear of Israeli Reprisal," *New York Times*, January 9, 1965.

307. "Leader of German Rocket Team Reported to Have Left UAR," *New York Times*, July 9, 1965.

308. Quoted in *Washington Post*, July 14, 1966, A-22.

309. Memorandum from the under secretary of state to President Johnson, "The Arab-Israeli Arms Race and Status of U.S. Arms Control Efforts," May 1, 1964, in *FRUS 1964–68*, Vol. XVIII, 814–7.

310. Lotz, op. cit., 150, 154.

311. Ibid., 157.

312. Ibid., 169.

313. Warren C. Wetmore, "Israelis Air Punch Major Factor in War," *Aviation Week and Space Technology*, July 3, 1967, 22.

314. Saad el-Shazly, *The Crossing of the Suez* (San Francisco: American Mideast Research, 1980), 78–9.

315. "The UAR Missile Programme," report by the Special National Intelligence Estimate, 825–6.

316. "New Arab Steeds," *Flight International,* March 26, 1964.

317. Shimon Peres, op. cit., 95–6.

318. "UAR Delivery Capability for Nuclear, Biological and Chemical Weapons," Assessment prepared for CIA deputy director of Intelligence, January 8, 1963, *FRUS 1961–63*, Vol. XVIII, 320.

319. Central Intelligence Agency, "The UAR Missile Programme"; "New Arab Steeds," *Flight International*, March 26, 1964, 468.

320. See Chapter 20.

321. "Egypt Plans Satellite Launch Within Year," Cecil Brownlow, *Aviation Week and Space Technology*, September 9, 1963, 32.
322. An example is Pakistan, which test-fired a nuclear device in May 1998, giving the government an electoral lift that soon wore off.
323. See Chapter 16.
324. "New Arab Steeds," *Flight International*, March 26, 1964, 468.
325. "UAR Launchings Displease Israel," *New York Times*, July 23, 1962, 4.
326. These were the HAWK missiles, supplied by the United States in 1963. See Sirrs, op. cit., 104–6.
327. Christopher A. Preble, *John F. Kennedy and the Missile Gap* (DeKalb, Illinois: Northern Illinois University Press, 2004).
328. Black and Morris, op. cit., 195.
329. Sirrs, op. cit., 132.
330. Anton La Guardia, *Holy Land, Unholy War: Israel and Palestinians* (London and New York: Penguin, 2007), 182.
331. See Chapter 13.
332. "Israel Minimises Achievement," *The Times*, July 23, 1962.
333. See in general Branislav Slantchev, *Military Threats: The Costs of Coercion and the Price of Peace* (Cambridge: Cambridge University Press, 2011).
334. J. Bullock and H. Morris, *The Gulf War: Its Origins, History and Consequences* (London: Methuen, 1991), 189–91.
335. Tom Segev, *1967: Israel, the War and the Year that Transformed the Middle East* (London: Abacus, 2007), 613.
336. "Defector admits to WMD lies that triggered Iraq war," *The Guardian*, February 15, 2011.

INDEX

INDEX

U.S.S.R., 8, 28, 74, 76–78, 81–82, 121,
137, 151, 158, 162, 182, 195, 209,
221–222, 235, 241, 243
German scientists and, 81–86

V
Veronique rocket, 95, 133, 141, 235
V2 rocket, 85, 98, 133, 141, 154
Voice of Israel, 39–40
von Bechtolsheim, Baron Theodor, 26, 35,
39
von Braun, Wernher, 29, 85, 98, 99
von Leers, Dr Johann, 170
von Weizsacker, Carl Friedrich, 169
von Kubie, Dr. Count Willi, 36–37, 41
von Rundstedt, Field Marshal Gerd, 59
Voss, Dr Wilhelm, 26, 29, 78

W
Wagner, Richard, 108
Weimar Republic, 24
Weizman, Ezer, 177–178
Wende, Hannelore, 175
West Germany, 25, 34, 36, 38, 196
Cold War and, 136–137, 195

Egyptian activities in, 89–110, 231
relations with Israel, 4, 162, 165–169,
192–195, 198–199, 202, 230–231
politics and constitution, 3–4, 24, 169,
194–196, 230
post-war scientific opportunities, 86–88,
93–96, 138, 230. *See also* East Germany; German Expatriates
Wieland, Hans, 211
WMD (Weapons of Mass Destruction), 3,
6, 8, 179–182, 192–193, 195, 196, 211,
212, 215, 230, 241
Wolseley, Sir Garnet, 14
Wright, Peter, 61

Y
Yaakovian, Kobruk, 222
Yedioth Aharonoth, 191
Yemen, 181, 214

Z
Zamalek Island, 123
Zech-Nenntwich, Hans Walter, 224
Zimney Corporation, 134
Zurich, 89, 186, 187

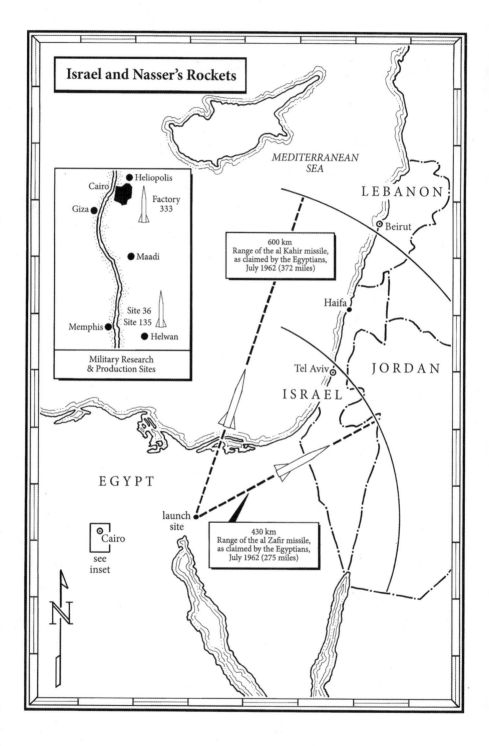

Israel and Nasser's Rockets

MEDITERRANEAN
SEA

LEBANON

Beirut

Cairo
Heliopolis
Giza
Factory
333

Maadi

Memphis
Site 36
Site 135
Helwan

Military Research
& Production Sites

600 km
Range of the al Kahir missile,
as claimed by the Egyptians,
July 1962 (372 miles)

Haifa

Tel Aviv

ISRAEL

JORDAN

EGYPT

Cairo
see
inset

N

launch
site

430 km
Range of the al Zafir missile,
as claimed by the Egyptians,
July 1962 (275 miles)

ML   6-13